About the editors

Carlos Oliva Campos teaches philosophy and history at the University of Havana. He formerly worked as a researcher at the Center for Study of the Americas and the Center for Study of the United States. For many years he served as executive director of the Association for the Unity of Our America, an NGO based in Havana. He is the author, coauthor, or editor of numerous books, including *The Bush Doctrine and Latin America*; *Panamericanism and Neo Panamericanism: The View from Latin America*; *Estados Unidos-América Latina hoy. Alternatives políticas frente a la dominación imperialista*; and *Cuadernos Aportes Teóricos de Nuestra América*.

Gary Prevost is professor in the Department of Political Science, Saint John's University/College of Saint Benedict, Minnesota. He has published widely on Latin America and Spain, including *Politics of Latin America: The Power Game*; *The Bush Doctrine and Latin America; United States–Cuban Relations: A Critical History*; and *From Revolutionary Movements to Political Parties*.

Harry E. Vanden is professor of political science and international studies at the University of South Florida, Tampa. He has lived in several Latin American countries, including Peru, where he was a Fulbright Scholar and later worked in the Peruvian government's National Institute of Public Administration, and in Brazil, where he held a second Fulbright and taught at the State University of São Paulo. His numerous scholarly publications include *Politics of Latin America: The Power Game*; *Latin American Social Movements in the Twenty-first Century*; *Inter-American Relations in an Era of Globalization*; and *The Undermining of the Sandinista Revolution*.

Social movements and leftist governments in Latin America

confrontation or co-optation?

edited by Gary Prevost, Carlos Oliva Campos, and Harry E. Vanden

Zed Books

LONDON | NEW YORK

Social movements and leftist governments in Latin America: confrontation or co-optation was first published in 2012 by Zed Books Ltd, 7 Cynthia Street, London N1 9JF, UK and Room 400, 175 Fifth Avenue, New York, NY 10010, USA

www.zedbooks.co.uk

Set in OurType Arnhem and Futura Bold by Ewan Smith, London

FSC
www.fsc.org
MIX
Paper from
responsible sources
FSC® C013604

Cover designed Rogue Four Design
Printed and bound by CPI (UK) Ltd, Croydon, CR0 4YY

Distributed in the USA exclusively by Palgrave Macmillan, a division of St Martin's Press, LLC, 175 Fifth Avenue, New York, NY 10010, USA

A catalogue record for this book is available from the British Library
Library of Congress Cataloging in Publication Data available

ISBN 978 1 78032 184 4 hb
ISBN 978 1 78032 183 7 pb

Contents

Abbreviations

AD	Acción Democrática (Venezuela)
ALBA	Bolivarian Alliance for the Peoples of Our America
ANDHA	Asociación Nacional de Deudores Habitacionales (National Association of Home Debtors, Chile)
AP	Acuerdo País (Ecuador)
Bolsa/BOVESPA	Bolsa de Valores de São Paulo (stock market, Brazil)
BPN	National Piquetero Bloc (Argentina)
CCC	Classist and Combatant Current (Argentina)
CGT	General Confederation of Labor (Argentina)
CIDOB	Central Indigena de Pueblos del Oriente Boliviano (Confederation of Indigenous Peoples of Bolivia)
CMSP	Consejo de Movimientos Sociales de Peñalolen (Council of Social Movements of Peñalolen, Chile)
COB	Central Obrera Boliviana (Bolivian Workers' Central)
CODENPE	Consejo de Desarrollo de los Pueblos y Nacionalidades del Ecuador (Development Council of the Indigenous Nationalities and Peoples of Ecuador)
CONAIE	Confederación Nacional[idades] Indígena[s] de[l] Ecuador (Confederation of Indigenous Nationalities of Ecuador)
CONALCAM	Coordinadora Nacional para el Cambio (National Coordination for Change, Bolivia)
COPEI	Christian Democratic Party (Venezuela)
CTA	Argentine Workers Central
CTU	Comités de Tierras Urbanas (Venezuela)
CUT	United Workers' Central (Brazil)
DOS	Division of Social Organizations (Chile)
FEI	Federación Ecuatoriana de Indios (Ecuadorian Federation of Indians)
FEINE	Consejo de Pueblos y Organizaciones Indígenas Evangélicas del Ecuador (Council of Evangelical Indigenous Peoples and Organizations of Ecuador)
FENOCIN	Confederación Nacional de Organizaciones Campesinas, Indígenas y Negras (National Confederation of Peasant, Indigenous, and Negro Organizations, Ecuador)
FMLN	Faribundo Martí National Liberation Front (El Salvador)
FrePaSo	Frente País Solidario (left coalition, Argentina)

FTAA	Free Trade Area of the Americas
FTV	Federation of Land and Housing (Argentina)
IFI	international financial institution
IMF	International Monetary Fund
INAMUJER	National Women's Institute (Venezuela)
INTI	National Institute of Lands (Venezuela)
MAS	Movement Toward Socialism (Bolivia)
MBR	Movimiento Bolivariano Revolucionario (Venezuela)
MERCOSUR	Mercado Común del Sur (Southern Common Market)
MPD	Movimiento Popular Democrático (Democratic People's Movement, Ecuador)
MPL	Movimiento de Pobladores en Lucha (Movement of Pobladores in Struggle, Chile)
MST	Movimento dos Trabalhadores Rurais Sem Terra (Landless Workers' Movement, Brazil); Movimiento Sin Tierra (Bolivia)
MTA	Movement of Argentine Workers
MTL	Territorial Liberation Movement (Argentina)
MUA	Movimiento Unitario de Allegados (Unitary Movement of Allegados, Chile)
MVR	Movimiento V Republica (Venezuela)
NAFTA	North America Free Trade Agreement
NGO	non-governmental organization
OTB	Organizaciones Territoriales de Base (Territorial Base Organizations, Bolivia)
PDVSA	Petroleos de Venezuela SA
PJJH	Unemployed Heads of Household Plan (Argentina)
PRIAN	Partido Renovador Institucional Acción (Ecuador)
PSC	Partido Social Cristiano (Social Christian Party, Ecuador)
PSDB	Brazilian Social Democratic Party
PSUV	United Socialist Party of Venezuela
PT	Partido dos Trabalhadores (Workers' Party, Brazil)
UNE	Unión Nacional de Educadores (National Union of Educators, Ecuador)
WTO	World Trade Organization
YFP	Yacimientos Petroliferos Fiscales (state-owned oil company, Argentina)

Preface and acknowledgments

The editors undertook this project to explore the relationship between two important developments of twenty-first-century politics in Latin America – the emergence of a wide range of new social movements and the election of progressive, left-of-center governments in several major countries. The twenty-first-century social movements build on a long tradition of political activity that has challenged the status quo over the last five centuries, but have gained the label of 'new social movements' because they have mobilized certain previously marginalized groups and have also adopted tactics not previously favored. Previously underrepresented sectors like indigenous peoples in Bolivia and Ecuador have emerged as central political players. The movements have adopted non-violent direct action techniques in a region where resort to armed struggle was more common in the past. The election of candidates of the center left is not without precedent but the pattern of leftist victories that began with the triumph of Hugo Chávez in Venezuela in 1998 continued with victories in Brazil, Argentina, Chile, Bolivia, Ecuador, and several other countries.

The editors asked each of the chapter authors to explore the complex interaction that occurs when social movements, previously accustomed only to being an opposition in the face of the governments of the center and right that were in power, must now adjust to having a government in power that they helped bring to office, and to have expectations that such governments will be sympathetic to their long-standing demands. Such a change brings into question whether the often confrontational tactics pursued by the social movements against their opponents in power remain appropriate in the new situation. Similarly, governments in power may face serious restraints in meeting the expectations of the social movements. In some cases the restraints may include conservative legislative opposition that limits the options of a progressive executive branch – a challenge especially faced by President Lula in Brazil in his first term. More commonly, progressive governments often face competing demands from different social movements. An example of this contradiction is in Ecuador, where Rafael Correa faces an indigenous movement that wants to stop further resource extraction from its historic lands in contrast to urban-based supporters of Correa who want significant resource development in order to fund greater government programs of poverty alleviation. Progressive governments often expect that social movements will understand the challenges stated above, and they become harsh toward movements that continue to press their agenda just as forthrightly toward the new governments.

The editors wish to acknowledge their respective institutions that have supported their research: St. John's University/College of St. Benedict (Gary Prevost), University of South Florida (Harry E. Vanden), and University of Havana (Carlos Oliva Campos). The editors are appreciative of the opportunity to present the initial research findings at the meeting of the Latin American Studies Association in Rio de Janeiro in June 2009. All the editors wish to acknowledge the assistance of Suzanne Reinert at St. John's University and College of St. Benedict in the preparation of the manuscript and also are grateful for the insight of our editor at Zed Books, Ken Barlow, and the anonymous reviewers who read the manuscript and provided useful feedback. The chapter authors are all especially grateful to members of the various social movements who shared their time and ideas that have made this a successful project and who continue to make history in Latin America.

Gary Prevost, Collegeville, Minnesota
Harry E. Vanden, Tampa, Florida
Carlos Oliva Campos, Havana, Cuba

Introduction

GARY PREVOST, HARRY E. VANDEN,
CARLOS OLIVA CAMPOS

Social movements in context

The last decade in Latin America has witnessed two important simultaneous and interrelated developments: the rise in prominence of social movements, and the election of a number of left and center-left governments.

The social movements have ranged from the broad, community-organized *piqueteros* of Argentina, which brought down three governments in the space of one month in 2001, to the indigenous-based movements of Ecuador and Bolivia, which have been instrumental in toppling five governments in the two countries within the last decade.

They include the Landless Movement in Brazil (MST), Afro-Colombians resisting displacement in a region coveted by investors, the Cocalaros and the mobilizations against water privatizations and gas pipeline investments in Bolivia, and the Zapatistas in Mexico, who burst onto the scene to challenge the formation of NAFTA and the marginalization of the mostly indigenous peasants in Chiapas. The social movements of Argentina, Brazil, Mexico, Colombia, Ecuador, and Bolivia are complemented across the region by a myriad of organizations that engage on a range of issues from land rights to women's rights to environmental concerns. These groups have been studied in detail under the rubric of 'new social movements,' but they are equally a continuation of a long history of social movements in Latin American history that have resisted the domination of the continent by colonialism, neocolonialism and native elites for centuries and more recently have engaged in vigorous forms of collective action that have reinvigorated the political struggle for economic and social justice in the context of globalized resistance. They have also continued to develop ever wider repertoires of contentious actions and ever stronger and more dynamic forms of participatory democracy. These movements have been the focus of a wide range of academic studies in the past decade. This work will draw most heavily in its analysis on the framework provided by Richard Stahler-Sholk, Harry E. Vanden, and Glen Kuecker, articulated in their 2008 volume *Latin American Social Movements in the 21st Century: Resistance, Power, and Democracy*. The primary argument of the authors is that while the recent social movements are grounded in the centuries-long struggle of Latin Americans against colonialism, neocolonialism, and elite domination, they have brought new forms of struggle into play, often with somewhat different political objectives than their predecessors. Other key works providing a reference point to the analysis of the authors include those of Sonia Álvarez, Evelína Dagino and Arturo Escobar; Joe Foweraker; Sidney Tarrow; Deborah Yashar; James Petras and Henry Veltmeyer; George Reid Andrews; Susan Eckstein; and Margaret Keck and Kathyrn Sikkink.[1]

How can we understand the evolution of social movements during the past two decades in the context of the past? These movements have a rich history which cannot be developed here in great detail but, as is the case today, they arose out of the social condition of the continent – that is, the poverty and inequality that were the legacy of centuries of Spanish and Portuguese colonization followed by British, French, and North American neocolonialism and the ever more intense internationalization of capitalism. Earlier centuries had witnessed primarily rural, peasant-based movements, but the twentieth century also saw the growth of labor-based movements grounded in the region's extractive industries and nascent manufacturing sectors. The twentieth-century movements were often influenced by Marxist and in a few cases anarchist ideas. For the Marxist-influenced movements this meant that the objectives of a workers' or peasants' movement were frequently channeled through the efforts of political parties, both reformist and revolutionary.[2] The movements were grounded in the living conditions of their members but ultimately subordinated to party structures. In all of these cases, the parties of the left did not generally gain state power, so these movements remained outside of government as an oppositional force. However, Latin America did have two unique models of the role of social movements in the political process. In both Mexico and Argentina traditional workers' movements were co-opted by government leaders Lázaro Cárdenas (1934–40) and Juan Perón (1943–55) to play a key role in the maintenance of political power by these leaders in return for an improvement in the standard of living of the working people. This arrangement, dubbed corporatism by political scientists, became deeply embedded in Mexico, providing the party of Cárdenas, the Institutional Revolutionary Party (PRI), unbroken rule until 2000. In the case of Argentina, the party Perón built has sustained itself successfully over almost seventy years to again be the dominant force in Argentine politics.[3]

Before proceeding to an analysis of the relationship between contemporary Latin American social movements and the region's progressive governments it is also necessary to provide some background to the contemporary social movements and the political context in which they have emerged over the last twenty years. The fall of the eastern European socialist camp, which began in 1989 with the political revolutions in eastern Europe and culminated with the collapse of the Soviet Union at the end of 1991, opened a new era of international relationships known as the post-Cold War. President George H. W. Bush declared that there would be a New World Order dominated by democracy and free enterprise (i.e. capitalism), freed from the presence of the socialist countries and their drag on the world economy. It was argued that the mechanisms of the free market, if adhered to by all governments, including those of the less developed world, would lead to a world of greater prosperity for all, including those in the poorer countries who had been marginalized traditionally. These views were operationalized in what became known as the Washington Consensus, which was to be implemented worldwide through the policies of the World Bank and the International Monetary Fund. The key ideas were reduced government spending and downsizing, privatization of state-run utilities and industries, and trade liberalization carried out through regional trade agreements and the launching of the World Trade Organization as the third and final leg of the international financial institutions (IFIs) first envisioned at the Bretton Woods conference in 1944. In the early nineties these ideas resonated well with the political elites in Latin America as well as all of the region's governments, with the exception of Cuba. These even included the traditionally nationalistic government of Argentina, which also embraced the neoliberal Washington Consensus model. The high-water mark of this political consensus occurred at the First Summit of the Americas meeting convened by US president William Clinton in Miami in December 1994. The summit of heads of state, to which Fidel Castro was not invited, enthusiastically endorsed the idea of a Free Trade Area of the Americas (FTAA), a hemispheric-wide customs union that would be fully implemented by 2005 along strongly neoliberal lines.

However, these detailed plans would eventually go off track, and seventeen years later the idea of the Free Trade Area of the Americas is a dead letter. The defeat of the FTAA came about as the result of a variety of factors. Ultimately it was opposition to the pact by several key governments in Latin America – Venezuela, Argentina, and Brazil in particular – that doomed the project. To understand how these governments came to voice the strong negative positions that killed the idea it is necessary to analyze how opposition to the FTAA within Latin American civil society developed, how the opposition was mobilized by an array of social movements, and finally how the anti-FTAA, anti-neoliberal sentiment was reflected in the election of governments of the left and center-left across the region, beginning with the election of Hugo Chávez in Venezuela in December 1998.

The breakdown of the Washington Consensus began when the promises that these policies would lead to better social and economic indicators for the region's poor majority were not realized, especially in the key countries of Venezuela, Argentina, and Brazil. In each of the three, beginning with Venezuela in the late 1980s, aggressively neoliberal government policies were implemented that involved privatization of state-owned companies and a cutting of government services. These policies generally did cut inflation and stimulate macroeconomic growth. The control of runaway inflation that had marked the so-called 'lost decade' of Latin American economies in the 1980s was popular across all classes. However, beyond cutting inflation these policies did little to improve the lives of the majority poor, and the consequent higher unemployment rates and cuts in government subsidies actually worsened the situation of growing numbers of poor Latin Americans. Nor did they improve the horrible disparity in wealth and income that has long been Latin America's nemesis. The macroeconomic gains served to improve the circumstances of the region's better-off citizens and in the process further widened the gap between rich and poor. The objective conditions of the people in Latin America most negatively affected by the neoliberal reforms were reflected first in mobilizations of Latin American civil society that came from a variety of sources, some traditional and others that were new. The 1989 uprising in Caracas and other Venezuelan cities (the Caracazo) is here representative of the growing anger of the masses when confronted with structural adjustment and neoliberal policies.

Against this historical backdrop it is important to analyze the new dimensions that emerged full blown in the last twenty years, the phenomenon that has been called the 'new social movements.' These movements have come to full fruition during the era when Latin American countries have returned to greater political democracy following the era of the 1960s to the 1980s, when key Latin American countries like Brazil, Argentina, Chile, and Uruguay were under the rule of brutal military dictatorships. In reality many of these 'new social movements' – representing women, the indigenous, human rights concerns, Latin Americans of African heritage, and religious

4

reformers – emerged during the era of the military dictators. Some new social movements, such as the Mothers of the Disappeared in Chile and the Mothers of the Plaza de Mayo in Argentina, arose directly in response to the military repression, but most of the others emerged first during the military era as the result of deteriorating economic conditions for wide sectors of the population and wider international factors emanating from different corners of the world. The winds of change in the Roman Catholic Church, embodied in the movements of Liberation Theology, were initiated by the Second Vatican Council (1961–65), and the meeting of the Latin American bishops in Medellín in 1968.[4] The rise of women's movements is part of a second wave of feminism that derived from the push for women's equality in late 1960s in the United States and elsewhere.[5] The consciousness of African heritage was grounded in the civil rights and Black Power movements of the 1960s in the United States and the Caribbean.[6] Greater consciousness of the plight of the first citizens of the hemisphere came in part from United States- and Canadian-based movements, hemispheric gatherings of indigenous peoples, and then gained resonance in the wider world through the awarding of the 1992 Nobel Peace Prize to Guatemalan indigenous leader Rigoberta Menchú on the 500th anniversary of the Columbus voyage.[7]

These international factors, united with the local conditions and new dimensions of globalization on the ground in Latin America, resulted in the emergence of these movements across the continent, beginning in the 1980s but flowering in the 1990s. The 1990s in Latin America was a time when conservative, neoliberal governments pursued a political agenda that ran counter to the needs and issues of masses of Latin Americans and the social movements described above and formed in previous years. The changed situation was such that these new social movements could organize openly with full legal status, freed from the previous likelihood that their political organizing and street demonstrations would be crushed by harsh military repression. Authorities might use the police to break up certain kinds of more militant actions, such as strikes and land occupations, but their organizations were no longer banned, nor were their leaders killed or placed in jail for long periods of time. Indeed, they found that they had an increasing number of spaces in civil society in which they could operate and organize.

The social movements that have arisen in recent years in Latin America have been marked by several key attributes. They have tended to seek autonomy from the traditional political parties, to practice horizontal and participatory processes in decision-making, and to seek social justice based on race/ethnicity, gender, and/or traditional marginalization from the political process or economic benefits. These principles have engendered some rethinking of traditional concepts of revolution in the context of seeking fundamental social change. For decades the concept of social change was linked to armed revolution in Latin America and a commitment to construct socialism with the Cuban experience as the guide. Often connected to the paradigm were political parties of a vanguard nature. The language and tactics of the contemporary movements have gone in a different direction; tactically they have focused on non-violent direct action and programmatically they have stressed broad themes of social and economic justice without an explicit commitment to radical socialism. Emblematic of the approach is the commonly heard declaration 'another world is possible.' This phrase became a popular rallying cry of social movements that came together in the last decade at the World Social Forum in Porto Alegre, Brazil, and Caracas, Venezuela, and at numerous alternative Summits of the Americas (e.g. Mar del Plata, Argentina, in 2005). Scholars of the contemporary social movements also emphasize that these movements arose during the era of the neoliberal free market project that began with the structural adjustment programs of the 1980s and continued with the imposition of the so-called Washington Consensus of the 1990s. Many Latin American governments led by Venezuela, Argentina, and Brazil implemented such reforms in the 1990s, but their general failure to achieve economic and social success led to a questioning of the principles in the new century. However, the power of these programs and the earlier Latin American military regimes of the 1960s and 1970s severely damaged the political capabilities of the traditional parties and social movements. It was that crisis of the traditional working-class-based labor movements and many political parties that created the political space for new social movements to then come to the fore to resist the projects of the Washington Consensus.

Beyond the fact that the movements which emerged full blown in the 1990s faced a different Latin American political climate, more open and more favorable to dissent, one is prone to ask, what about them was 'new'? Clearly part of their 'newness' was that they were raising issues that were recent in the Latin American political scene and often were issues not being raised in a serious way by political parties of either the left, middle, or the right: women's rights, black rights, gay and lesbian rights, environmental issues, indigenous concerns, continued marginalization of the masses. In other cases the issues were not new – for example, unemployment and workers' rights in Argentina. The picketers' movement backing the unemployed of Argentina's cities was a new phenomenon discussed in detail in the Argentina chapter. The focus of Brazil's Landless Movement, the MST, was a time-honored issue, land reform, but using a myriad of tactics including actual provision of services for those engaging in the traditional tactic of land takeover and occupation.

Another area of interest in the new social movements is in the arena of tactics and how they contested power. Many of the tactics and political actions that were employed were not unprecedented but some were quite novel – for example, *cortar ruas* (closing streets) and other actions were employed by the *piqueteros* in Argentina. The indigenous movements and their supporters in Bolivia and Ecuador utilized the tactic of blocking ground access to the capital city and transit on other major thoroughfares by barricading roads with material at hand and in the process stalling much of the transit and commercial activity of their countries. Twice in each country within the last decade this tactic succeeded in forcing the resignation of elected governments. Massive mobilization and occupation of central spaces in the capital and other major cities was also employed. In both countries the dominant issues were that the indigenous majorities were being marginalized economi- cally and politically and that the established government was selling off the country's assets and sovereignty to foreign interests. The issue was not new, but their articulation and the swiftness of the movements' success was startling. In both cases new elections eventually brought to power the progressive governments of Evo Morales and Rafael Correa. The success of the movement's tactics in Bolivia and Ecuador must be credited in part to their creative actions and the changed political climate. In an earlier era of military rule such non-violent acts of political protest would likely have been broken up by the army and the disruptions to the commercial life of the country prevented.

The new social movements have also been seen as adopting a dif- ferent stance toward the political parties, largely refusing to interact with them and remaining in a more independent stance, less available to be co-opted. This observation is reasonably accurate, especially in comparison to movements of the twentieth century that were wedded to traditional parties of the left. Such an independent position was natural, because the movements often arose outside of the political party structures which ignored their issues. This phenomenon is not unique to Latin America. When similar movements arose in Europe and the United States, their issues were not generally championed by the mainstream parties, even those on the left. However, in the North, eventually their issues were adopted and the independence of these movements came to be significantly compromised. This can especially be seen with respect to women's and environmental movements in Europe and the United States, where, following adoption of their ideas by mainstream parties, the goals of these movements were either fully or partly reached, demonstrating that co-optation is not necessarily a negative result for the social movement. That level of co-optation has not fully arrived in Latin America, but with progressive governments in power across the region, the possibilities for co-optation become greater. It is significant that the greatest amount of co-optation in the region occurred in the country with the longest time period of progressive governments, Chile. Another key factor in co-optation may be the ability of the progressive government in power to co-opt social movements and some of their leaders, and it may turn on their ability or willingness to make major gains on behalf of the movement's goals. For example, in the United States the civil rights movement became wedded to the Democratic Party because leaders of that party in the Congress and White House delivered on major reforms of civil rights laws in the United States in the mid-1960s. In contrast, the government of Luiz Inácio da Silva (Lula) in Brazil was unwilling to make any significant concession in the area of land reform. As a result, the Landless Movement does not have much to show for its backing of Lula in the 2002 and 2006 elections and has remained politically independent and critical of government policy in this area.

Electoral victories of the left

The past decade has also witnessed the electoral triumph of a number of political parties and coalitions of the left and center-left. The trend started with the election of populist challenger Hugo Chávez in Venezuela in 1998. Chávez has revised the constitution, created mechanisms of political participation and access to services for hitherto marginalized neighborhood residents, has been reelected twice, and he and his supporters have been able to mobilize popular support to defeat a coup and a referendum designed to remove him from power and stop his reforms. Further, he has moved significantly to the left, committed to what he has labeled 'twenty-first-century socialism,' and launched several region-wide anti-neoliberal projects, most importantly the Bolivarian Alliance for the Peoples of Our America (ALBA). In 2002 the Chávez victory was followed by the election of socialist

Tabaré Vásquez in Uruguay, populist Lúcio Gutiérrez in Ecuador and, most importantly, Workers' Party leader Luiz Inácio da Silva (Lula) in Brazil in his fourth run for the presidency. Lula was reelected for a second term in 2006 and his anointed successor, Dilma Rousseff, extended Workers' Party control of the Brazilian presidency until 2015 with her October 2010 landslide victory. Also, in Uruguay ex-Tupamaro guerrilla and socialist José Mujica triumphed in 2008 to continue the domination of the leftist Frente Amplio. In 2003 Néstor Kirchner was elected president in Argentina on a political platform that returned the Peronist Justice Party to its traditional center-left stance following a long detour to center-right neoliberalism under Carlos Menem; this leftward tilt was validated by the election of Cristina Kirchner in 2007. The momentum of progressive electoral victories was also manifested with the 2005 election of socialist Evo Morales to the presidency of Bolivia as the country's first indigenous leader. He was reelected in 2009 with 64 percent of the vote and has carried out broad constitutional reform that has moved the country in a progressive direction against the wishes of the long-ruling traditional oligarchs. The last five years have also seen the election of center-left candidates Rafael Correa and Fernando Lugo in Ecuador and Paraguay. Lugo's election in Paraguay in 2008 on a left platform ended the long hold of the country's oligarchy on the office of the presidency. Correa was first elected in 2006 following the removal of previous president Lúcio Gutiérrez by massive social-movement-led street demonstrations. Correa was reelected in 2009, validating progressive constitutional reforms enacted during his first term.

Central America was also not immune to the leftward trend. In 2006 Daniel Ortega, long-time leader of the once revolutionary Sandinista National Liberation Front (FSLN), returned to power after a sixteen-year hiatus, and in 2007 center-left candidate Álvaro Colom won a surprising victory in Guatemala, breaking a more than fifty-year hold on power by the right. Mauricio Funes, of the Faribundo Martí National Liberation Front (FMLN), broke two decades of rightist control in El Salvador when he was elected president in 2009. In Honduras President Manuel Zelaya began to drift to the left after his election in 2005. A *coup d'état* ultimately resulted in his removal from power by the traditional elites in June 2009, but it also stimulated the development of new social and political movements in Honduras. In Mexico, the center-left Democratic Revolutionary Party of Mexico nearly won the 2006 presidential election, losing by only a single percentage point in highly disputed results.

The leftward tilt in Latin American politics has been clear. Numerous scholarly studies have zeroed in on this development, most importantly *Leftist Governments in Latin America: Successes and Shortcomings*, edited by Kurt Weyland, Raúl Madrid, and Wendy Hunter.[8] Others have endeavored to categorize the new leftist political movements as, to use Jorge Castañeda's strained categories, a 'good' left that only wants moderate change and can work with the United States, and a 'bad' left that is too closely tied to the populist tradition in Latin America and would not as easily conform to liberal democratic and neoliberal economic policies more similar to those of the United States and western Europe.[9] The idea of two lefts was actually articulated by Teodoro Petkoff in his article 'Las dos izquierdas' in *Nueva Sociedad* in 2005, a year before Castañeda's article was published. Petkoff sees one left that moves away from real socialism, seeking to deepen social equity and democracy, and another radical current that operates through 'personalism, authoritarianism, the steel control of public power,' and at the margin of formal democracy.[10] Another approach is seen in Benjamin Arditi's 2008 article, which proposes a slightly different conceptual framework to discuss the left and left turns in Latin American politics.[11]

It is, then, entirely appropriate to speak of the political trend to the left in Latin America that began with the Chávez victory in Venezuela in 1998, but it is necessary to analyze the variety of progressive politics that are practiced by the various parties of the left that have come to power during the past decade. As a result, scholars of Latin American politics have begun to create typologies to help us define this process and analyze what their progressive governments have accomplished. Some of these, like Castañeda and Petkoff, project the type of leftist parties that gained election as indicators of the type of government and thus carry their categorization of a moderate left and a radical left into their characterization of the leftist governments now in power. With regard to the actual governments in power, the aforementioned volume edited by Kurt Weyland et al. is the most comprehensive to date.[12] Weyland argues that the attempts to categorize the various presidents have met with controversy and disagreement. He asks whether some of them are populists, and if so, based on what definition of populism? Similarly, he wonders whether others are social democratic and, if so, what would that notion mean in contemporary Latin America? Can one even speak of social democracy, he queries, in a setting in which the 'working class' (strictly defined) is small and shrinking, trade unions are weak, and external economic constraints are often tight?[13]

The main differences over categorization revolve around multi-dimensional versus more simplistic, less theoretically sophisticated categorizations.[14] The multidimensional approach is epitomized by Livitsky and Roberts in their book *Changing Course: Parties, Populism, and Political Representation in Latin America's Neoliberal Era*.[15] The authors are more sympathetic to the approach of Weyland, which emphasizes primarily the differences in strategy and tactics of Latin America's left governments, distinguishing a moderate group from a more radical one along a continuum. The approach of Livitsky and Roberts may be especially useful in helping to understand the diverse origins of the leftist parties, but the authors, like Weyland, are more interested in comparing the programs and policies these movements have pursued once they have achieved power. This approach facilitates our fundamental task of understanding the contention between left governments and social movements in the current moment of leftist state power.

The authors adopt the term Contestatory Left to describe the governments at the most progressive end of the continuum. This term avoids the categorization of 'radical,' or good, bad, or *permitido*, to acknowledge that none of the current parties in power is pursuing policies in the manner of the revolutionary governments of the twentieth century, most notably the Cuban communists and the Sandinistas of the 1970s. While virtually all of the left governments under study embrace the concept of socialism, all of them are operating within the framework of a capitalist system in each of their countries. There is general agreement that Hugo Chávez and his Bolivarian revolution in Venezuela are both in rhetoric and action the most radical among the six countries that will be studied in detail in this volume. Chávez first won the presidency without reference to socialism, but over thirteen years in power has definitely moved to the left and for nearly a decade has spoken of constructing 'twenty-first-century socialism' in his country, and does so through the explicitly socialist United Socialist Party of Venezuela (PSUV). His close alliance with the revolutionary government in Cuba and his use of explicitly anti-imperialist language to evaluate the international scene underscore his rhetorical position at the left end of our spectrum. In reality his programs are not as radical because he operates in the framework of the Venezuelan capitalist system, which controls the greater part of the country's economic activity outside of the oil sector. However, Chávez has pursued limited nationalizations of land and factories as a strategy for long-term expansion of the state sector.

The project that tracks closest to that of Venezuela is that of Evo Morales' Bolivia. Since assuming power in 2005, Morales and his Movement Toward Socialism (MAS) party have pursued a policy of radical reform centered around the nationalization of the country's hydrocarbon industry and the empowerment of the majority indigenous population for the first time in the country's history. Another sign of Bolivia's radical stance is its membership in ALBA and its willingness to make close ties with Cuba. Not too far behind Bolivia on the scale would be Ecuador, where Rafael Correa identifies himself as a socialist and pursues policies of wealth redistribution and nationalization of natural resources. Though not initially a member of ALBA, Ecuador has now joined and has moved closer in its ties to Bolivia, Cuba, and Venezuela. However, like his counterparts in Bolivia and Venezuela, Correa operates within the framework of the dominance of the Ecuadorean economy by private interests. At the other end of the political spectrum is the Brazilian model of President Lula and now Dilma Rousseff and the now out-of-power governments of the Chilean socialists, Lagos and Bachelet. While some might see the Chilean case much farther to the right end of the spectrum than Brazil, in reality, both pursued a similar strategy of almost completely accepting the neoliberal frameworks of their predecessors but pursuing government programs aimed squarely at reducing the level of absolute poverty in their countries. For the Workers' Party-led governments this has meant food and income subsidies and expanded educational opportunities. The most difficult government to categorize is that of the revived Peronist Party in Argentina and its late leader Néstor Kirchner and current president Cristina Kirchner. Because of its amorphous and often changing character, many analysts, including Weyland, are reluctant to place the Peronists definitively on the left, but others believe that the policies pursued by the Kirchners are in reality very close to those of Chile and Brazil and place them in that part of the political spectrum for the purposes of this volume. In the views of the authors the Peronists have returned much closer to a progressive orientation, distancing themselves almost completely from the decade-long neoliberal detour under Carlos Menem.

How social movements have brought the left to power

The electoral victories of the progressive governments have often been directly tied to the work of the social movements. In the cases of Argentina, Bolivia, and Ecuador the victories of the left came about after massive street demonstrations had removed a previous government from power and left a caretaker administration responsible for conducting new elections. In Bolivia street demonstrations in 2003 forced the neoliberal Sánchez de Lozada from power, and when his successor and vice-president Carlos Mesa failed to deliver on promised reforms, he was driven from power by a massive mobilization and general strike in 2005. These actions paved the way for elections organized by a caretaker government that were won in a landslide by Evo Morales in December 2005, and again with 64 percent of the vote in a second election in 2010. In Ecuador the social movements first exercised their muscle in 1997 with the removal of Abdala Bucaram, but they were not able to shape the regime of Jamil Mahuad that followed. However, in 2000 they forced Mahuad from office and threw their support behind Lucio Gutiérrez and his anti-neoliberal platform in the elections that followed in 2002. Gutiérrez won the election but once in office moved to the right and carried out a pro-US agenda. As a result, he was driven from office in 2005 by street demonstrators from the same social movements that had supported him in the 2002 elections. The departure of Gutiérrez and establishment of a caretaker government led to the 2006 election of socialist Rafael Correa. Correa was not organically a candidate of the social movements but his victory was facilitated by their defeat of the discredited Gutiérrez.

In many ways the developments in Argentina were the most dramatic. In 1999 the Argentine people had elected a center-left government headed by Fernando de la Rua as a repudiation of the ten-year presidency of neoliberal apostle Carlos Menem. However, once in office de la Rua carried out policies that were essentially a continuation of Menem's. In December 2001, de la Rua tried to carry out a series of currency reforms that were particularly unpopular and resulted in massive strikes and street demonstrations that forced his resignation. De la Rua's chosen successor, and a subsequent appointee, failed to quiet the demonstrations, resulting in four different Argentine presidents in one month. The political crisis ended only when the man whom de la Rua had defeated two years earlier, Peronist Eduardo Duhalde, assumed the presidency, pledging to reverse the neoliberal policies of his Peronist predecessor Menem and call new elections in early 2003. Duhalde carried out his promises and the March 2003 elections brought to power Peronist Néstor Kirchner, who pledged to carry out a progressive agenda.

In the case of Brazil the social movements, such as the powerful Landless Movement, the MST, have not facilitated the removal of a neoliberal government as in the above-described cases, but nonetheless, they were instrumental in helping Luiz Inácio da Silva (Lula) win the presidency in 2002, following twelve years of neoliberal rule in that country. They also supported his reelection in 2006, despite some reservations.

Social movements and progressive governments

The position of the social movements once these progressive governments take power becomes an interesting issue that up until now has received relatively little scholarly attention. It is necessary to close that significant gap and offer insight into one of the most important features of contemporary Latin American politics and its full transition to democratic functioning. The following questions are asked: Once in power, does the progressive government view the country's social movements as partners in government to be consulted or, as is frequently the case, co-opted in support of government policies, or, conversely, to be held at arm's length as continuing opponents? Does the government in power reach out to the social movements and seek to bring key leaders into posts in the new government? If the social movements continue their street mobilizations against the government, how does that government respond to such challenges? Are the police and military used in the same manner as a rightist government would have been likely to use them? From the social movements' side, how do they view the new government that they may have helped to put in power? Do they initially give that government the benefit of the doubt and suspend their street protests or do they continue the pressure? If the incoming government offers positions to social movement leaders, do they accept such posts? If such posts are accepted, how long do social movement leaders remain in government if the demands of the movements are not significantly met? In a general sense, do the social movements act as actors independent of the government or do they become merely cheerleaders for the implementation of government policies? And, ultimately, can the social movements achieve their demands without a political movement or party that can govern and implement their demands? The answers to these questions vary widely from country to country where the left has achieved power.

Bolivia, following the election of Evo Morales in 2005, is one of the most interesting, and probably the country where the social movements, especially those grounded in the indigenous community, have had the greatest success in having their demands articulated by the leftist government in power. In the wake of Morales' initial victory and his subsequent reelection in 2009, hundreds of local, regional, and national social movements have emerged to fill the void created by the collapse of the traditional political party system. In the process they have strengthened civil society and energized and consolidated a more democratic society in Bolivia that speaks to the needs of the country's long-suffering majority poor through government programs financed by the newly nationalized energy sector, a key demand of the social movements that brought Morales to power.

These social movements have also contributed to a reexamination and redefinition of citizenship, the basis and content of Bolivian national identity, and the intimate relationship between culture and power in a multi-ethnic and multicultural state. As the Morales government has faced a hard backlash from the traditional landowning elites of the Bolivian lowlands, the support of the social movements has been central to the implementation of the Morales reforms, especially the wholesale constitutional changes that validated the multi-ethnic character of the state and state control of the country's natural resources. The ongoing challenge for the Bolivian social movements is to provide important tactical support to the MAS-led government in its confrontation with the traditional elites, while maintaining enough independence to criticize the government when it does not move forthrightly to tackle the country's deep-seated poverty and underdevelopment. Sustained demonstrations at the end of 2010 and the beginning of 2011 against perceived unreasonable government-backed price increases indicated a willingness to display such independence.

Argentina bears some resemblance to Bolivia in that the government in power since the beginning of 2002 has worked hard to both meet the needs of the powerful social movements that arose in the years before 2002 and to seek to bring these movements under the control of the dominant Peronist Party after its political transformation from 2002 onward. When Peronist Eduardo Duhalde took power at the start of 2002, after a month of turmoil that saw three governments fall, he began a complex process of reestablishing traditional Peronist control of the social movements that was begun by the founder of the Justice Party, Juan Perón. In classic corporatist style, the Peronists had taken almost full control of the population by granting significant social benefits while keeping a tight lid on any independent political action by unions or other organizations. That control evaporated in the 1980s under Carlos Menem when he moved the Peronist agenda to the neo-liberal right and broke its historic ties to Argentina's popular classes. When Radical Party leader Fernando de la Rua continued Menem's rightist politics and was driven from power by social-movement-led street demonstrations in December 2001, it provided the Peronists with an opportunity to reposition themselves to the left and regain its historic domination of the country's politics. That process began when Duhalde, the defeated Peronist candidate in 1999 who assumed the presidency in the wake of the street demonstrations, acted to meet the protesters' demands and to work systematically to co-opt the *piqueteros* movement that had been at the heart of the demonstrations. The *piqueteros* were primarily unemployed city dwellers, the victims of Menem's neoliberal policies that slashed employment. Duhalde not only created new jobs but also put many *piquetero* leaders in charge of the neighborhood-based job programs. The strategy was successful, and in 2003 the endorsed Peronist candidate, Néstor Kirchner, defeated Carlos Menem's attempted political comeback. Once in office Kirchner continued the populist direction of government policies and the party was rewarded with the election of Cristina Fernández de Kirchner, Néstor's spouse, to the presidency in 2007. Following Néstor's death in 2010 it now appears that Peronist domination of Argentine politics and the relative demobilization of the social movements will continue with Cristina's likely reelection in the fall of 2011.

The case of Venezuela has some parallels with that of Bolivia and Argentina but has its own distinct characteristics. Like Bolivia, the ruling party of Venezuela, the United Socialist Party of Venezuela (PSUV), has its roots in anti-neoliberal social movements that arose in the streets in 1989 and the early 1990s in reaction to the austerity measures of the government of Carlos Andrés Pérez. The symbolic leader of those protests was army officer Hugo Chávez, who led a failed coup attempt and was subsequently jailed. However, in 1998 Chávez reemerged as a populist, anti-liberal presidential candidate. He scored an impressive victory against the country's two traditional parties by mobilizing popular support from the people and organizations that had been in the streets earlier in the decade. However, the Venezuelan case takes on a somewhat different framework during the thirteen years that Chávez has been in power. It can be argued that the large-scale resources available to the Venezuelan state from its oil and gas revenues allow Chávez to create a state whose policies border on corporatism, where key constituencies, primarily poor urban dwellers, are wedded to the state by the provision of government programs in health, education, and food security that were never previously available on such a significant scale. On the other hand, Venezuela is home to numerous social movements, especially in the labor arena, that maintain their distance and independence from the government.

The country with arguably the most contentious relationships between the government and the social movements, especially indigenous ones, is Ecuador. Socialist Rafael Correa came to power in 2006 following the removal of the previous president by street demonstrations, and he has pursued a program of radical reform geared to the country's poor majority. However, the social movements have generally kept at arm's length from the president. When voters in Ecuador approved a new constitution by a wide margin in September 2008, both President Correa and powerful social movements claimed responsibility for the victory. Ecuador's strong and well-organized social movements have long been able to pull down governments they opposed but have been repeatedly frustrated in their attempts to build concrete alternatives. Social movements have not experienced much success in the electoral realm, often being defeated at the hands of populist candidates who steal their leftist rhetoric but act in favor of the oligarchy once in office. Correa's predecessor, Lucio Gutiérrez, was a prime example of that duplicity. Given that history, the social movements approached Correa's government with a good deal of caution. Although Correa shared the social movements' criticism of neoliberal economic policies, he had not risen through their ranks. In particular, indigenous movements resented Correa for occupying political spaces that they had previously used to advance their concerns. At the same time, the new constitution was the most progressive one in Ecuador's history and codified many of the aspirations of the social movements. Ecuador is a dramatic example of how political parties and social movements can be in significant tension even as they embrace similar visions but follow different paths to realize their objectives.

The governments of Brazil, under the Workers' Party, and Chile, under the Socialists, were probably closest in their overall political strategies, and definitely less radical than Venezuela, Ecuador, or Bolivia. Both progressive governments pursued social democratic policies of poverty alleviation aimed at the most vulnerable sectors of their societies while basically accepting the broad neoliberal policies of the more conservative governments that preceded them. Programs of education and food security received priority attention in both countries and both achieved enough success to sustain themselves once in power. In the case of Brazil, that continues into the present with the election of Dilma Rousseff. The Socialists lost power in the 2010 election in Chile after being part of the *concertación* ruling coalition for twenty years. However, these social democratic policies played out differently in each country in terms of their relations with important social movements. The case of Chile is one of classic co-optation of social movements by a ruling progressive party, with significant gains for both sides in the process. During the dictatorship, powerful neighborhood-based movements developed that contributed to the defeat of Pinochet in the 1989 referendum. It might have been expected that these movements would have flourished with the return of democratic civil liberties, but twenty years later, with a few important exceptions, such as the Mothers of the Disappeared, the neighborhood groups were largely demobilized through the integration of the key activists of the movements into positions of local authority, implementing government programs that responded positively to some of the needs of the community long neglected under the dictatorship. When protest movements did emerge during the *concertación* period, they often came from unlikely sources such as high schools.

The Brazilian case is an interesting one from the perspective of the Workers' Party government and the social movements. First of all, the Workers' Party itself emerged from the social movements of the period of the dictatorship, primarily the Christian-based communities and newly formed trade unions, especially in the auto industry. As an electoral party, the Workers' Party has drawn on those bases throughout its twenty-five-year history. In the last fifteen years, the country's most prominent social movement has been the Landless Movement (MST), which has mobilized tens of thousands of rural workers to occupy unused farmland and to pressure the government for land reform. The MST has openly supported the candidates of the Workers' Party in a tactical alliance against the neoliberal right while maintaining its full independence from the government. It has done so out of recognition that President Lula has championed the interests of large-scale commercial farming to bolster Brazil's growing role in the world economy. Such an alliance makes significant progress on land reform unlikely and leaves the two sides in a position of an uneasy truce where both benefit from the arrangement.

Where does this review of case studies leave us twenty years after the triumph of the first leftist government in Chile in 1990? As demonstrated, the relationship between leftist governments and social movements is a complex one with many peculiar national characteristics; generalizations are difficult to make. However, one pattern does generally emerge. The relationship is a symbiotic one. In the face of the traditional elites and their political parties the parties of the left need the enthusiasm and renewing qualities of the mass social movements if they are to achieve state power, either directly by street mobilization or through elections. On the other hand, no matter how powerful they may be, the social movement cannot hope to achieve all or part of their ambitious projects without the mechanisms of the state apparatus that a left party in power can provide. Inevitably their relations will be filled with conflict, but that is the nature of politics.

Notes

1 The key contributions to scholarship in this area in recent years include: Sonia Álvarez, Evelína Dagino and Arturo Escobar, *Culture of Politics, Politics of Culture, Re-visioning Latin American Social Movements* (Boulder, CO: Westview Press, 1998); Richard Stahler-Sholk, Harry E. Vanden, and Glen David Kuecker (eds), *Latin American Social Movements in the 21st Century: Resistance, Power, and Democracy* (Lanham, MD: Rowman & Littlefield, 2008); Susan Eckstein (ed.), *Power and Popular Protest, Latin American Social Movements*, 2nd edn (Berkeley: University of California Press, 2001); Sidney Tarrow, *Power in Movement: Social Movements and Contentious Politics* (Cambridge: Cambridge University Press, 1998); Joe Foweraker, *Theorizing Social Movements* (London: Pluto Press, 1995); Deborah Yashar, *Contesting Citizenship in Latin America: The Rise of Indigenous Movements and the Post Neoliberal Challenge* (New York: Cambridge University Press, 2005); James Petras and Henry Veltmeyer, *Social Movements and State Power: Argentina, Brazil, Bolivia, and Ecuador* (London and Ann Arbor, MI: Pluto Press, 2005); George Reid Andrews, *Afro-Latin America 1800–2000* (New York: Oxford University Press, 2004); Sidney Tarrow, *The New Transnational Activism* (New York: Cambridge University Press, 2005); Margaret Keck and Kathryn Sikkink, *Activists beyond Borders: Transnational Advocacy Networks in International Politics* (Ithaca, NY: Cornell University Press, 1998) and Benjamin

Dangl, *Dancing with Dynamite, Social Movements and States in Latin America* (Oakland, Edinburgh, Baltimore: AK Press, 2010).

2 For an overview of the role of Marxism in Latin American politics, see Sheldon Liss, *Marxist Thought in Latin America* (Berkeley: University of California Press, 1984) and Donald Hodges, *Latin American Revolution: Politics and Strategy from Apro-Marxism to Guevarism* (New York: William Morrow, 1974).

3 See also Harry E. Vanden, *Latin American Marxism: A Bibliography* (New York: Garland, 1991), especially the introduction, and, in regard to peasant mobilization, Harry E. Vanden, 'Marxism and the peasant in Latin America: marginalization or mobilization,' *Latin American Perspectives*, IX(4), Fall 1982, pp. 74–98.

For good overviews of corporatism, see Howard Wiarda, *Corporatism and Comparative Politics: The Other Great Ism* (Armonk, NY: M. E. Sharpe, 1997) and Peter Williamson, *Corporatism in Perspective: An Introductory Guide to Corporatist Theory* (London and Newbury Park, CA: Sage, 1989). Also, for the application of corporatist theory in two newly democratized countries, Georgia and South Africa, see Brian Grodsky, 'From neo-corporatism & delegative corporatism? The empowerment of NGOs during early democratization,' *Democratization*, 16(5), October 2009, pp. 898–921.

4 For an overview of Liberation Theology and the Latin American movements it spawned, see Philip

Berryman, *Stubborn Hope: Religion, Politics and Revolution in Central America* (Mary Knoll, NY: Orbis Books, 1984).

5 For an overview of women's movements in Latin America, see Lynn Stephen, *Women and Social Movements in Latin America* (Austin: University of Texas Press, 1997).

6 For an overview of race and race-based social movements in contemporary Latin America, see George Reid Andrews, *Afro-Latin America 1800–2000* (New York: Oxford University Press, 2004).

7 For an overview of Latin American indigenous movements, see Hector Díaz Polanco, *Indigenous Peoples in Latin America* (Boulder, CO: Westview Press, 1997). See also Donna van Cott, *From Movements to Parties in Latin America: The Evolution of Ethnic Politics* (New York: Cambridge University Press, 2005) and van Cott, *Radical Democracy in the Andes* (New York: Cambridge University Press, 2009).

8 Kurt Weyland, Raúl Madrid, Wendy Hunter (eds), *Leftist Governments in Latin America: Successes and Shortcomings* (New York: Cambridge University Press, 2010).

9 See Jorge Castañeda, 'Latin America's left turn,' *Foreign Affairs*, 85(3), May/June 2006, pp. 28–43, and Jorge Castañeda and Marco A. Morales, *Leftovers: Tales of the Latin American Left* (New York: Routledge, 2008). For a different take on the 'good' and 'bad' left, see Maxwell Cameron, 'Latin America's left turns: beyond good and bad,' *Third World Quarterly*, 30(2), 2009, pp. 331–48.

10 Teodoro Petkoff, 'Las dos izquierdas,' *Nueva Sociedad*, 197, May/June 2005, pp. 114–28.

11 Benjamin Arditi, 'Arguments about the left turns in Latin America:

a post-liberal politics?' *Latin American Research Review*, 43(3), 2008, pp. 59–81.

12 Weyland et al., *Leftist Governments in Latin America*. For related literature, see Petkoff, 'Las dos izquierdas'; Castañeda, 'Latin America's left turn'; Matthew Cleary, 'Explaining the left's resurgence,' *Journal of Democracy*, 17(4), October 2006, pp. 35–49; Cynthia Arnson (ed.), *The 'New Left' and Democratic Governance in Latin America* (Washington, DC: Woodrow Wilson Center Press, 2007); Andreas Boeckh (ed.), 'Die lateinamerikanische Linke und die Globalisierung', *Lateinamerika Analysen*, 17, July 2007, pp. 69–197; Wendy Hunter, 'The normalization of an anomaly: the Workers' Party in Brazil,' *World Politics*, 59(3), April 2007, pp. 440–75; Kenneth Roberts, 'Latin America's populist revival', *SAIS Review*, 27(1), Winter/Spring 2007, pp. 3–15; Castañeda and Morales, *Leftovers*; Carlos de la Torre and Enrique Peruzzotti (eds), *El Retorno del Pueblo: Populismo y Nuevas Democracias en America Latina* (Quito: FLASCO & Ministerio de Cultura, 2008); Raúl Madrid, 'The rise of ethnopopulism in Latin America,' *World Politics*, 60(3), April 2008, pp. 475–508; Maxwell Cameron and Eduardo Silva, *Challenging Neoliberalism in Latin America* (Cambridge: Cambridge University Press, 2009); Kurt Weyland, 'The rise of Latin America's two lefts: insights from rentier state theory,' *Comparative Politics*, 41(2), January 2009, pp. 145–64; Steven Levitsky and Kenneth Roberts (eds), *Latin America's Left Turn* (New York: Cambridge University Press, forthcoming).

13 Kurt Weyland, 'The performance of leftist governments in Latin America,' in Weyland et al., *Leftist Governments in Latin America*.

14 For a slightly different

bifurcated classification of the left as *'permitido'* (permitted by or acceptable to bourgeois democracy and the empire and thus not capable of making the radical structural changes needed) and a left *'no permitido'* (not allowed by Western-style liberal bourgeois democracy or the empire, and thus truly radical and capable of making necessary change), see Jeffrey R. Webber and Barry Carr (eds), *The Resurgence of Latin American Radicalism: Between Cracks in the Empire and an Izquierda Permitido* (Lantham, MD: Roman & Littlefield, forthcoming).

15 Steve Livitsky and Kenneth Roberts, *Changing Course: Parties, Populism, and Political Representation in Latin America's Neoliberal Era* (New York: Cambridge University Press, 2011).

1 | Argentina's social movements: confrontation and co-optation

GARY PREVOST

In December 2001, a popular uprising led to the fall of the constitutional government of Fernando de la Rua. Over the course of the following days more governments fell victim to the mass mobilizations until the appointment of Eduardo Duhalde to the presidency ended the crisis and paved the way for the election of Peronist Néstor Kirchner in March 2003. In what ways does the political crisis help us understand social movements in the Argentine context and their relationship to governmental power? In the previous history of Argentina the fall of governments were episodes characterized by military coups, often in the context of an economic crisis of the capitalist system. In most past instances the overthrow of government was instigated by the military at the behest of powerful economic interests fearing revolutionary insurrection. This had occurred most recently in 1976, followed by the repression of the Dirty War and its 30,000 deaths. However, in 2001 the mobilized people were the main protagonist in government eviction, a relatively rare scenario for Argentine politics. The events of 2001 can only be understood with reference to the cycles of resistance that preceded them and likewise the present conjuncture of Argentine politics. In particular, how are we to assess the current relationship between the social movements that brought down the de la Rua government and the Peronist administration that came to power by election in 2003 and 2007? These movements, particularly the neighborhood-based '*piqueteros*' (picketers), have established a seemingly permanent niche in Argentina's political and social life, and their relationship with governmental authorities is a complex one.

The roots of the overthrow of successive governments in December 2001 are to be found in the era of President Carlos Menem (1989–99). Peronist leader Menem was elected in 1989 in the wake of major economic problems that developed during the previous military regime (1976–83) and the subsequent administration of Radical president Raúl Alfonsín. The Peronists had historically championed protectionist and nationalist economic policies that had improved the lives of Argentina's working class. Menem won the presidency as an apparent traditional Peronist but once in office moved to implement sharply neoliberal policies. He curtailed government social spending, privatized industries, tied the country's currency to the US dollar and liberalized Argentina's foreign trade relations. The Argentine apostle of the Washington Consensus was Domingo Cavallo, whose service to the Argentine political elites lasted from 1976 until 2001. He served as finance minister in the military government and held various policymaking posts in subsequent governments. He was responsible for Argentina's decision in the 1970s and 1980s to take on significant foreign debt as part of its overall economic strategy. But above all Cavallo was known as the creator of the decision to tie the Argentine peso to the US dollar, a significant economic step away from Argentina's traditional wariness of North American domination. That wariness had been reinforced by US support of the British in the war over the Malvinas in 1982.

Not surprisingly, the working-class base of the Peronists responded negatively to these policies with strikes and street demonstrations. Menem responded harshly to his opponents, making no concessions and proceeding with his neoliberal agenda. In the short term, Menem's approach carried the day as the economy stabilized and rampant inflation was checked. These successes allowed Menem and the dominant Peronist Party to engineer constitutional changes that permitted Menem's successful reelection in 1995. However, in the process a significant layer of people among the working class and the newly unemployed fell out of the orbit of the Peronist movement and developed a culture of political mobilization and protest independent of the traditional political elites.

Throughout his second term, Menem faced a decline in economic growth, a dramatic rise in unemployment, and severe socioeconomic crises in the provinces. The midterm elections of 1997 resulted in the triumph of an opposition coalition of the Radicals and a left coalition called FrePaSo (Frente País Solidario). That election victory, backed by many of the alienated political groups in the streets, catapulted the same Radical/FrePaSo alliance to a ten-point electoral victory over the Peronists in the 1999 presidential elections. Radical Party leader Fernando de la Rua was elected with a clear mandate to reverse the neoliberal agenda of Menem and meet the demands of the mobilized groups that had been building support since the early 1990s. The hopes of these forces were tied closely to the FrePaSo leader Carlos Alvarez, de la Rua's vice-president. However, in October 2000 Alvarez resigned, convinced that de la Rua was not at all committed to a reversal of the neoliberal agenda. Symbolic of that lack of commitment to change was the continued linkage of the Argentine peso to the US dollar.

Crisis of 2001

In the second half of 2001, amid a growing recession and unemployment, de la Rua faced a rising tide of withdrawals of dollar-denominated deposits from banks and was forced to suspend these withdrawals to prevent a collapse of the financial system. This dramatic step by the Argentine president, called the *'corralito'* or little pen, set in motion the events that shook the Argentine political system to the core. Middle-class bank depositors whose life savings were now threatened took to the streets, where they joined up with the previously mobilized working-class forces to challenge the legitimacy of the government. There were multiple confrontations with the security forces as the unemployed demonstrators known as *piqueteros* blocked main highways and bridges demanding jobs, food, and subsidies while also organizing alternative institutions like soup kitchens and community health and educational services. The emergence of the *piquetero* movement can be traced to the privatization of the state-owned oil industries in the southern cities of Cultural Co and Plaza Huincul, Neuquen, that began in 1995. These cities had been major centers of oil extraction and refining since the 1930s under the state-owned Yacimientos Petroliferos Fiscales (YFP). The oil workers developed a strong combative tradition and not surprisingly moved into action when the 1995 privatization of YFP resulted in massive layoffs and a dramatic drop in local average incomes. Their protests came to a head in Cultural Co on 21 June 1996 when the laid-off YPF workers and their supporters blocked an interstate highway and in the process their struggle gained national attention. The initial roadblock was followed by numerous others and forced some concessions from the local government authorities. Known as the *Cutralcazo*, the events brought a new actor to the Argentine political scene, the unemployed. Decades of largely full employment in Argentina had made organized labor a primary political actor, but now the unemployed came to the forefront as the labor movement was weakened by Menem's policies. Prior to privatizations and layoffs Argentine unemployment had generally been in the 6 percent area, but by the mid-1990s it was 17 percent.[1] The events in Cultural Co also legitimized their chosen form of protest, the roadblock or picket. By 1997 the tactic had been copied throughout most of the country, including Buenos Aires, where blocking the streets became referred to as *'cortar ruas.'* The *piquetero* movement had been born in the minds of the protesters themselves and was now a permanent national media feature of the Argentine political scene, in some ways replacing the traditional Argentine means of working-class action, the strike.

The *piquetero* movement that arose in Buenos Aires in December 2001 had some important differences with its southern cousin. Unlike those behind the *Cutralcazo*, the Buenos Aires *piqueteros* were independent of the Peronist unions and openly critical of them. The new *piquetero* constituency was composed of younger unemployed workers, many of whom had never held steady jobs or enjoyed worker benefits. Their leaders, however, had deeper roots in political activism, closely connected to local organizing, non-Peronist unions, and left political parties such as the communists. Leaders and the rank and file of the December 2001 movement saw their actions as the potential prelude to revolutionary actions that would overturn the whole Argentine capitalist system. However, even prior to December 2001 the national *piquetero* movement also had less revolutionary aspects. In response to the early wave of protests, the Menem administration had by 1998 dramatically increased payments to the unemployed under Plan Trabajar as a means of undercutting and blunting the appeal of the *piquetero* constituency. In a direct way the appeal of the *piqueteros* was diminished when the government made the payments conditional on non-participation in protest activity.

Another element of the December 2001 protest movement was the *cacerolazos*, which consisted of groups of people banging pots in their houses and in the streets as an expression of their protest over worsening economic conditions and the policies of the government. The first protest occurred on 19 December 2001 with no apparent prior plans or organization and was in direct response to the freezing of bank withdrawals, the so-called *corralito*. The protesters, aided by media attention, formed their own organizations, primarily using the Internet as a means of communication.

The *caceroleros* were mainly middle-class but drawn from a heterogeneous group of people, from unemployed small business managers to working professionals. Their protests were centered in Buenos Aires but quickly spread to many parts of Argentina. Initially it was a virtual movement, but it quickly morphed into something more as the *caceroleros* began to meet regularly in neighborhood assemblies. Like their initial movement, the assemblies or '*asambleas de barrio*' were predominantly in Buenos Aires but with some replication elsewhere. Also, as a reflection of the character of the *cacerolero* movement, the assemblies tended to be concentrated in middle-class neighborhoods rather than the poorer areas. The assemblies operated on a basis of grassroots democracy and tended to be suspicious of organized political tendencies, including the parties of the left, which often participated in the forums. The assemblies were not affiliated with the *piquetero* movements but coordinated with them during broad mobilizations, such as those of late December 2001.

The coalition of middle-class and low-income demonstrators took to the streets of Argentina's major cities in late 2001, demanding the resignation of the national government and a renovation of the political establishment. The rejection of all the major parties was embodied in the demand '*Que se vayan todos!*' (They all must go). The radical character of the protest movement was also characterized by the instigation, independent of the political parties, of neighborhood assemblies that organized the demonstrations and also coordinated local activities such as soup kitchens. The movement was fundamental in its challenge, questioning the authority of all three branches of the Argentine government, executive, legislative, and judicial. No state institution was spared.

The intensity of the demonstrations, together with increasingly violent confrontations with the police, led to a response from President de la Rua. He formed a government of national unity with the Peronists, but that step quite predictably did not quell the demonstrations and de la Rua resigned on 20 December. In the following ten days, three different Peronist politicians were inaugurated as president, only to fail to quell the protesters and resign. However, many economic measures were announced that went to the heart of demonstrators' political demands as the linkage of the peso to the US dollar was ended and a default on Argentina's external debt was announced. The solution to the December crisis demonstrated both the strength of the protest movement and also its limitations. On 1 January 2002, Eduardo Duhalde was inaugurated as Argentina's fifth president in ten days. Duhalde was the former governor of Buenos Aires, vice-president under Menem, and the defeated Peronist presidential candidate in 1999. In one view, his installation and subsequent two-year term in office was an anticlimax. The movement that had demanded a fundamental reorganization of the country's political system achieved only the overturning of the results of the previous election and the return to presidential power of the Peronist Party, which had dominated the country's politics for the previous sixty years. The results were validated when, in March 2003 elections, Peronist Néstor Kirchner, a relatively unknown governor of the southern province of Santa Cruz, won the presidency with

Duhalde's backing. The continued hold of the Peronists on Argentine politics would be validated by the 2007 election of Cristina Fernández de Kirchner, spouse of Néstor, to the presidency.

However tempting it may be to dismiss the 2001 social movement as succeeding only in returning the Peronists to power, a deeper analysis is required. The Argentine example seemed to suggest that even though the new social movements could consistently topple governments and virtually make a state ungovernable, their ability to 'rule from below' was in no way established, and the fact that they did not have a party or political movement that was explicitly based on their interests left them unable to achieve many of their demands. However, in one fundamentally important way the 2002 protest movement succeeded. It brought an end to the decade-long era of neoliberalism in Argentina and moved the country onto a different political course.

Peronist response

It is true that from 1 January 2002 the Peronists regained control of the system from their traditional rival the Radicals and kept their new left opponent, FrePaSo, at bay. However, to do this they were forced to reinvent the Peronist governing philosophy to respond to the demands of the demonstrators, especially the middle-class elements. During his two years in office, Duhalde set the stage for the 2003 Peronist electoral victory by a variety of measures that explicitly rejected the neoliberal policies championed by Menem and continued by de la Rua. The dollar 'convertibility' came to a formal end and the value of the peso stabilized at three pesos for a dollar. Depositors were forced to exchange their dollar-dominated funds at a third of their value in pesos or to accept promises of long-term repayment in dollars at low interest rates. While not a painless solution, it served to placate the concerns of the middle sectors who had feared a total collapse of the economic system and a loss of all of their savings. Negotiations were initiated with the IMF, the World Bank and foreign lenders to restructure the debt and reschedule payments. Later, under Néstor Kirchner, with financial assistance from Venezuela, Argentina largely paid off its IMF and World Bank debts. These actions allowed the Argentine government to reject the neoliberal conditionality of the international financial institutions (IFIs) as had been demanded by the protesters in the streets, who frequently chanted *fuera FMI* (IMF out). Largely freed from these international constraints, the Peronist leaders were able to return to a position closer to their nationalist roots. Simultaneously, Duhalde and subsequent Peronist governments were also able to make some progress in the socioeconomic arena by introducing payments to the unemployed, engaging in some public investment and increasing expenditures on health, education, and housing. These initiatives, begun under Duhalde, deepened under Néstor Kirchner when the overall Argentine economy improved, buoyed by higher commodity prices for Argentina's exports and the reduced debt burden following the cancellation of IMF obligations.

Another element of the social movement challenge to Menem and de la Rua had been their failure to prosecute those responsible for the atrocities of the Dirty War. On this front, Kirchner moved to implement some of the demands of Argentina's human rights movement, symbolized by the Mothers of the Plaza de Mayo. The Kirchner administration supported and implemented a number of legal, judicial, and symbolic initiatives designed to punish human rights violations that had been overlooked by the previous post-military administrations. Amnesty laws were rescinded and, as a result, a number of human rights violators who had escaped prosecution or been freed in previous years were detained, tried, and incarcerated. Museums and memorial sites were created to commemorate the victims of state terror and the role of human rights organizations was officially recognized.

Kirchner also played to the nationalist tendencies of the social movements by distancing himself from the United States on several important policy matters. He refused to support the Bush administration decision to go to war in Iraq and the militarization of the anti-drug efforts. Most importantly, Kirchner was a key player along with Luiz Inácio da Silva (Lula) and Hugo Chávez in blocking the US-inspired Free Trade Area of the Americas (FTAA). In fall 2003, Argentina joined with Brazil and other Third World countries in forming a bloc within the World Trade Organization (WTO) meeting in Cancún that thwarted the neoliberal agenda of the United States and Europe. Soon after, Kirchner hosted a strategy session with President Lula in Buenos Aires that detailed their objections to the FTAA. This subsequently prevented the establishment of the FTAA at the November 2003 meeting in Miami of the hemispheric finance ministers that was to have drafted the final FTAA treaty for implementation two years later. Kirchner was also central in the final defeat of the FTAA in 2005. President Bush came to the November Summit of the Americas in Mar del Plata hosted by Kirchner with a personal plea to the Argentine president to resurrect the FTAA plan, but he was firmly rebuffed. The summit ended with the Argentine social movements surrounding the summit venue with a 50,000-strong demonstration, rejecting the FTAA and denouncing President Bush. These demonstrators generally saw President Kirchner as their ally, not their adversary. Other Kirchner foreign policy initiatives also bonded with the political positions of the Argentine social movements, including closer ties with Cuba and Venezuela, membership in the newly formed Bank of the South, and closer integration with Brazil and other members of MERCOSUR, as well as the integration of new members such as Venezuela.

Argentine social movements today

What is the state today of the Argentine social movements that can be credited, not as in the cases of Bolivia, Ecuador, and Venezuela with the fundamental restructuring of their country's politics, but with reordering the political policies and priorities of the long-dominant Peronist Party? What is their capability to present an actual political alternative that would break the long-term hold of the Peronist Party on Argentine politics? Do the movements need to coalesce into a new political movement or party to achieve their ends? The basic answer to these questions is that they are a work in progress with no clear path to success in spite of the political troubles that have been endured by the administration of Cristina Fernández de Kirchner (2007–11).

As Roberta Villalón argued in her 2009 article, all the new forms of Argentine resistance developed between 1995 and 2002 continue to exist in various forms.[2] The *piqueteros* have evolved into three primary factions based in significant measure on their relationship with the state.[3] Closest to the state is the Federation of Land and Housing (FTV) and the Argentine Workers Central (CTA). Second-closest are the Classist and Combatant Current (CCC) and the more radical organizations such as the Territorial Liberation Movement (MTL), which have joined the National Piquetero Bloc (BPN). The FTV-CTA has the most affiliates and government subsidies. The CCC is intermediate in size while the BPN has the most affiliates, but it manages the fewest state subsidies. Alcañiz and Scheier demonstrate that the ability of the MTL to persist in a more radical stance is based in part on the independent stream of financing that comes to the MTL from the Institute for Mobilization of Cooperative Funds (IMFC), the financial arm of the Communist Party, deeply rooted in Argentina's history of worker cooperatives. In contrast both the FTV and the CCC have been significantly co-opted by the system of government grants. In April 2002, partly in response to a new round of demonstrations against the government, President Duhalde instituted a new social program, the Unemployed Heads of Household Plan (PJJH), by which unemployed workers with children would receive a cash payment of 150 pesos, in return for job training and community service. In a new turn PJJH funds were to be distributed and monitored by local administrative councils made up of political authorities, churches, and NGOs. The inclusion of NGOs in the process encouraged the *piquetero* organizations to directly manage subsidies by formally organizing as NGOs. Simultaneously, it allowed for the expansion of clientalistic networks among municipal leaders. *Piquetero* organizations were forced to compete for funds and to develop management skills to administer the PJJH subsidies. The role of NGOs actually expanded under Néstor Kirchner as the national government rewarded the NGO sector to counter the influence of local political leaders. By 2006, the FTV was controlling 75,000 subsidies and the CCC 40,000.[4] In contrast, even though the BPN has 90,000 members, it manages only 10,000 subsidies. In reality many BPN members receive subsidies, but not through the BPN or MTL, thus allowing the organization to remain more politically independent of the government.

The fundamental point of weakness of the Argentine social movements of December 2001 as a force for radical social change is that they were never united with a clear long-term vision, nor did they have a party or political movement to which they could be linked or which was beholden to them. However, the segment that can be associated with the forces to the left of Peronism does represent a clear alternative and continues to be a factor in Argentine political life. At the end of 2008, in response to a call from the Movement of Argentine Workers (MTA), 25,000 representatives from some seven hundred Argentine social organizations convened in Jujuy province together with an abundance of delegates from different parts of the world, especially the Latin American region. The political attention of the gathering was focused on the success of the social movements in Venezuela, Bolivia, and Ecuador in fundamentally changing their country's politics and asking how such a movement could be constructed in Argentina. This gathering demonstrated that there are organizations in Argentine political life that are seeking an alternative to Peronism and a political mechanism that will allow their effective participation.

Another wing of social movement activity which emerged before and after 2001 is embodied in the *piqueteros* and the recovered factories movement. As mentioned earlier, the *piquetero* movements are made up of unemployed workers who demand jobs and economic support by demonstrations and street blockades. Since 2001, they have evolved into more formalized organizations of the unemployed who have been successful in the Kirchner administrations in obtaining subsidies from the government for some of their social work projects, as well as a measure of political influence. Inevitably this has meant that some divisions have arisen within the *piquetero* movement between those willing to cooperate with government and those holding to a more radical position. This situation accords with a long-standing practice of Peronism to co-opt potential challenge to its domination of Argentina's working classes. The recovered factory movement is made up of workers who have taken control of closed factories and other enterprises such as those in the service industry, transforming them into self-managed units. As of 2008 there were more than 150 of these recovered companies with more than 15,000 workers.[5] Like the *piqueteros*, they have received some support from the Kirchner administrations but face many challenges, including divisions between radical and moderate elements. Like the MST in Brazil, they are a potentially powerful new social movement, but as a force for fundamental political change they are weakened by their overall strategy of seeking immediate gains for their followers. In that regard, these arrangements represent the classic trade-off of co-optation. The movement organization gets tangible, immediate benefits for its members while the government gains a measure of social stability. In other words, by its very nature co-optation is a two-way street.

The Argentine labor movement is another piece of the social movement puzzle. Over the past twenty years the movement has vacillated between a position fully co-opted by the Peronist Party and one of a more clearly independent character allied more closely with the independent social movements. In 1994, a group of Peronist unions led by the transportation workers broke away from the Peronist-dominated General Confederation of Labor (CGT) to form the Movement of Argentine Workers (MTA). In 2000, the MTA confronted de la Rua over his continuation of Menem's neoliberal policies, providing a preview of the December 2001 protests, which they also joined. However, a significant percentage of the Argentine workforce remained allied with the Peronist CGT. As a result, the MTA reunified into a single CGT in 2005 under the leadership of Hugo Moyano of the truck drivers' union. Not surprisingly, the reunified CGT has maintained relatively friendly ties with the Kirchner administrations, given the generally progressive drift of their policies. However, during the second Kirchner administration there have been periodic confrontations with the CGT over attempts by Cristina Fernández de Kirchner to limit wage increases and keep the government out of labor disputes.

Conclusion

To understand the manner in which Argentina's contemporary social movements fit into the pattern of social movements across the region it is necessary to reflect on the profound changes that have occurred in Argentina over the past thirty years. As Aldo Vacs has observed, for most of the twentieth century Argentina's vaunted political instability was based on the inability of the system to balance the populist demands coming from the working class with the desire of the Argentine elites, allied with the military, for political stability.[6] Liberal democratic government felt threatened by populist uprisings against attempts to implement free market policies. On the other hand, populist regimes, beginning with that of Juan Perón, were perceived as incompatible with liberal democracy and neoliberal economic programs because they often engaged in authoritarian practices and favored state interventions in the economy, and economic liberal programs were implemented through authoritarian means by the elites and the military owing to their inability to gain electoral support and popular backing for the free market policies. The events of late 2001 and early 2002, centered on the collapse of the de la Rua administration, challenged the stability of the reestablished democratic system of Argentina, but ultimately may have strengthened the system. The broad social movement that brought down de la Rua and successor governments can be seen as a corrective measure in Argentina's search for stable democratic institutions. Because de la Rua had failed to carry out the political policies for which he was elected, the reversal of neoliberalism, he was extremely vulnerable to widespread public anger. As the chapter has demonstrated, that popular anger, across social classes, was effectively mobilized by creative means to force the removal of an unpopular government.

However, what is equally interesting in the Argentine case is how the political establishment of Argentina responded to the crisis and the role that the protest movements played in ensuing years. Most significantly, Argentina's democratic institutions regained credibility in the years following 2002 because the three Peronist administrations that have governed acted to implement policies that moved in the direction of those advocated by the majority of the social movement organizations, while rejecting the demands of the more marginalized social movements for revolutionary change. For their part, the social movements described in this chapter have taken advantage of the political space provided by the Peronist government to consolidate their role as non-governmental organizations operating within the Argentine system, not outside of it. For the traditional social movements, primarily labor, this phenomenon of social integration was not new, but for the new social movements, such as the *piqueteros*, this process of incorporation into the mainstream, as implementers of government social welfare programs, was a new path that they chose to take. As described, not all of the new social movements chose to integrate into the system, some choosing to remain independent, often at the cost of less organizational capacity. The current result of these developments is that a symbiotic relationship has developed between the Peronist governments and the social movements. The government achieves social stability because the movements limit their volatile street actions while the movements are satisfied by the tangible economic benefits that their constituents receive from government programs. However, the jury is still out on whether or not this represents a stable, long-term relationship. Argentina's long-standing social inequalities leave the country and its democratic system vulnerable to new forms of political protest that may arise if the government is unable to meet the needs of its citizens.

Notes

1 Statistics from the Argentine Ministry of the Economy, www.inded.mencon.gov.ar.

2 Roberta Villalón, 'Neoliberalism, corruption, and levels of contention: Argentina's social movements, 1993–2006,' in Richard Stahler-Sholk, Harry E. Vanden, and Glen Kuecker, *Latin American Social Movements in the 21st Century* (Lanham, MD: Rowman & Littlefield, 2008).

3 Isabella Alcañiz and Melissa Scheier, 'New social movements and old party politics: the MTL piqueteros and the Communist Party in Argentina,' in Stahler-Sholk et al., *Latin American Social Movements*.

4 Ibid., p. 279.

5 Aldo Vacs, 'Argentina,' in Gary Prevost and Harry E. Vanden, *Politics in Latin America: The Power Game*, 3rd edn (New York: Oxford University Press, 2009).

6 Ibid., p. 426.

2 | The Landless Rural Workers' Movement and their waning influence on Brazil's Workers' Party government

HARRY E. VANDEN

The last few decades have seen diverse forms of popular mobilizations that have changed the conduct not only of domestic politics but of foreign policy in many of the Latin American countries. Thus protests and mobilizations against the implementation of structural adjustment policies and neoliberal economic policies created an atmosphere in which it became increasingly difficult to subordinate national economic policy to conditionalities imposed by the International Monetary Fund, the World Bank, the Inter-American Development Bank or the US Agency for International Development. These protests took on varied forms: the Zapatista rebellion against NAFTA in Mexico; the Fifth Republic Movement protest against structural adjustment led by Hugo Chávez in Venezuela; the national indigenous movement led by the Confederación Nacional Indígena de Ecuador (CONAIE) in Ecuador; the popular mobilization for regime change and against IMF policies in Argentina; the mobilizations against Sánchez de Lozada and his ties to US policies and the US Drug Enforcement Administration and then against his successor Mesa and in favor of Evo Morales in Bolivia. In Brazil this is well demonstrated by the continued mobilizations and land occupations of the Landless Workers' Movement (Movimento dos Trabalhadores Rurais Sem Terra or MST) resisting the traditional political and economic elites and the policies they favored. The backlash against economic neoliberalism and the globalization process that they helped to generate is quite interesting.

As has been the case in the United States, the national and international economic elites have used all the mechanisms of intellectual and cultural hegemonic domination at their disposal to convince people in all classes of the virtues of globalized neoliberalism. Despite their best efforts, however, there has been a genuine change in Latin American politics. Indeed, the progression of events suggests that there is a more profound realignment afoot – one that may well represent a political sea change in the region and restructure at least part of the foreign

policymaking process. The leftist regimes in Venezuela, Ecuador, Bolivia, Brazil, Uruguay and Paraguay document this pink tide, as has
the return to office of Sandinista leader Daniel Ortega in Nicaragua
and the election of FMLN presidential candidate Mauricio Funes in
El Salvador. In South America, the role of new social movements has
been key to these successes.

There was, then, a search for new structures and new policies that
could respond to the perceived – and not always clearly articulated
– demands being formulated from below by the popular sectors.
Throughout Latin America a broad segment of the population (from
the lower and middle classes) began to mobilize and seek new and
different political involvement and responses in parties, governmental structures and social movements. They wanted something that
worked for them. Indeed, the increasing promotion of democracy and
democratization told them that their voices should be heard and that
the political system should somehow respond to them. When it was
unclear how, if at all, their votes counted and whether the political
class was responding to their hue and cry, many became disillusioned
and angry. As other chapters in this volume demonstrate, this process
played out differently in a variety of national contexts. In Brazil, the
interplay between a radical social movement and a left party that took
power is unique.

Previous attempts to enfranchise the masses and gain a greater
degree of autonomy from outside economic and political domination
led to various revolutionary activities: Mexico (1910), Cuba (1959) and
shorter-lived experiments in Bolivia (1952), and by the Sandinistas in
Nicaragua (1979). Before a developing radical movement could gain
any momentum in Brazil, conservative forces coalesced to facilitate a
US-tolerated (some might say sanctioned) military coup in 1964. Elections were canceled, the legislature and traditional parties disbanded,
progressive organization and movements attacked, leftists repressed,
tortured, killed and imprisoned, and rule by decree by the military
juntas was enacted. Military rule lasted till 1984, when Brazil began
to democratize anew. During the military years (1964–84), there were
restrictions placed on society, political activity, labor, and social organizing. Yet in the latter days of military rule, three organizations with
ties to the workers' movement and the landless rural workers gained
considerable support from suppressed members of the masses and
other segments of society. The first was a leftist workers' movement
that set the stage for the formation of a new union in 1983, the United
Workers' Central (CUT). The second was also related to the workers'

movement and was premised on the conclusion that the workers needed their own party – one that would serve their interests and was not controlled by the traditional political-economic elites. Thus the Workers' Party (PT) came out of the radical workers' movement among the metalworkers in greater São Paulo in the late 1970s and early 1980s (formed in 1980) and was designed to respond to the workers' needs and aspirations. The Partido dos Trabalhadores (PT) included former members of communist parties and other leftists, and with the return to nominal democracy, it began to contest elections. It was gradually able to win a few municipalities and then take the governors' mansions in a few states such as Rio Grande do Sul and Pará. The third related organization, the Landless Workers' Movement (MST), came out of the struggle for land in the southern states of Rio Grande do Sul and Paraná and was founded in 1984. It eventually became the largest social movement in Brazil and indeed in Latin America, and has been one of the few organizations in Brazil to continue to advocate radical change.

As the nineties progressed, dissatisfaction with traditional political leaders, traditional political parties, and unresponsive administrative institutions became more widespread in Brazil and elsewhere in Latin America, as did a growing trend to doubt the legitimacy of the political system itself. Traditional *personalismo*, *clientelismo*, *coronelismo*, corruption and personal, class and group avarice became subjects of ridicule and anger, if not rage. The effects of neoliberalism and continued racism and classism amid ever stronger calls for racial and economic equality began to be felt. And they were cast against this background of corruption and clientelism and were added to the increasing calls for a return to more effective democracy and honest government.

Indeed, as background, we believe growing abstention rates suggested a general dissatisfaction with the political system. For instance, the 1998 national elections in Brazil saw such a phenomenon, with 40.1 percent of the electorate either abstaining, or casting blank or annulled ballots.[1] Similarly, in the Mexican presidential election of 2000, the abstention rate alone was 36 percent.[2] This strongly suggests that a substantial segment of the population no longer believed that the systems of governance that the electoral processes had produced were adequate. There seemed little point to electoral participation if the elected officials did not respond to the needs of the electorate or the decisions made at the polls. But this was the calm before the raging storm of popular participation that soon swept Latin America, mobilized new social and political movements, caused an upsurge of newer leftist parties, and put a series of leftist governments in power or – as in the case of Mexico – came very close to doing so.

New social movement in Brazil: the MST

In Brazil, the radically different nature of these new social movements and the new politics can perhaps best be seen in the largest of the new social movements in Latin America, the MST or Movement of the Landless Rural Workers. Their ranks exceed one million and on one occasion they were able to mobilize 100,000 people for a march on Brasilia. Their views are well articulated. In a draft document on the 'Fundamental principles for the social and economic transformation of rural Brazil,' they note that 'the political unity of the Brazilian dominant classes under Fernando Henrique Cardoso's administration (1994–2002) has consolidated the implementation of neoliberalism [in Brazil],' and that these neoliberal policies led to the increased concentration of land and wealth in the hands of the few and the impoverishment of Brazilian society. The document goes on to say that 'Popular movements must challenge this neoliberal conceptualization of our economy and society.'[3]

In a pamphlet entitled 'Brazil needs a popular project,' the organization calls for popular mobilizations, noting that 'All the changes in the history of humanity only happened when the people were mobilized.' And that in Brazil, 'all the social and political changes that happened were won when the people mobilized and struggled.'[4] The organization's political culture and decision-making processes break from the authoritarian tradition. It is 'a rural political movement advocating the fundamental transformation of the structures of power via grassroots collective mobilization.'[5] The movement was heavily influenced by Liberation Theology and the participatory democratic culture that is generated by the use and study of Paulo Freire's approach to self-taught, critical education.[6]

The MST itself was formed as a response to long-standing economic, social and political conditions in Brazil. Currently Brazil is one of the ten largest economies in the world. Yet land, wealth and power are allocated in very unequal ways and have been since the conquest in the early 1500s. Land has remained highly concentrated and, as late as 1996, 1 percent of the landowners (who owned farms of over 1,000 hectares) owned 45 percent of the land.[7] Conversely, as of 2001 there were some 4.5 million landless rural workers in Brazil. Wealth has remained equally concentrated as well. In 2001, the Brazilian Institute of Government Statistics reported that the upper 10 percent of the population averaged an income that was nineteen times greater than that of the lowest 40 percent.[8] Even after Lula's PT (Workers' Party) government was put in office, Brazil did not experience a thorough-going land reform. Further, in the last few years of the Workers' Party government, Brazil's fundamental problem with income disparity and the continued existence of extreme poverty for a substantial part of the population have persisted, despite some amelioration through direct subsidies to the poorest citizens.

The plantation agriculture that dominated the colonial period and the early republic became the standard for Brazilian society. The wealthy few owned the land, reaped the profits and decided the political destiny of the many. Slavery was the institution that provided most of the labor on the early plantation system and thus set the nature of the relationship between the wealthy landowning elite and the disenfranchised toiling masses who fueled Brazilian development. Land has stayed in relatively few hands in Brazil, and the agricultural laborers continue to be poorly paid and poorly treated. Further, after the commercialization and mechanization of agriculture that began in the 1970s, much of the existing rural labor force was no longer needed. As this process continued not only were rural laborers let go, sharecroppers were expelled from the land they had farmed and small farmers lost their land to larger family or commercial farms. This resulted in growing rural unemployment and the growth of rural landless families. Many were forced to migrate to the cities, where they swelled the numbers of the urban poor while others opted for the government-sponsored Amazon Colonization program whereby they were transported to the Amazon region to cut down the rainforest and begin to cultivate the land. Few found decent jobs in the city and the poor soil of the former rainforest allowed for little sustained agriculture, nor was income distribution much better in urban areas. In 2005 the poorest 10 percent of urban households got less than 1 percent (.9 percent) of income, while the wealthiest 10 percent got nearly half (49.8 percent).[9]

When the MST was founded in southern Brazil in 1984 as a response to rural poverty and lack of access to land, wealth and power, similar conditions existed in many states in Brazil. Indeed, there were land-less workers and peasants throughout the nation. Thus the MST soon spread from Rio Grande do Sul and Paraná in the south to states like Pernambuco in the northeast and Pará in the Amazon region. It rapidly became a national organization with coordinated policies and strong local participatory organization and decision-making, and frequent state and national meetings based on direct representation.[10] It became known for its forceful land takeovers and militant demonstrations and protests. By 2001 there were active MST organizations in twenty-three of the twenty-six states.[11]

In Brazil, traditional politics and traditional political parties had proved unable and unwilling to address the deteriorating economic conditions of the marginalized groups who were suffering the negative effects of economic globalization. This led not only to the formation of the MST but to the formation of and strong support for the Workers' Party, which had also developed in the eighties as a response to the concentration of wealth and power in the hands of traditional elites. Although radical at its inception, the growing Workers' Party engaged in more traditional party activity while the MST response consisted of grassroots organization and the development of a new repertoire of often radical actions that broke with old forms of political activity. Developing organizational and group actions began to tie individual members together in a strongly forged group identity.[12] They were sometimes assisted in this task by progressive organizations concerned with economic and social justice. In the case of Brazil and the land-less, this assistance came from the Lutheran Church and especially the Pastoral Land Commission of the Catholic and Lutheran churches. Although these organizations helped the landless, as did some seg-ments of the Workers' Party, the organization never lost its autonomy nor its radical agenda. It was decided from the onset that this was to be an organization for the landless workers that would be run by the landless workers for their benefit as they defined it. Options were discussed and decisions taken in popular assemblies at every level. The process led to direct actions such as land takeovers from large estates and public lands, local demonstrations, the construction of black-plastic-covered encampments along the side of the road to call attention to their demands for land, and marches and confrontations when necessary. The MST even occupied the family farm of then president Fernando Henrique Cardoso in 2002 to draw attention to his landowning interests and the consequent bias they attributed to him. They were at times brutally repressed, assassinated and imprisoned, but they persevered, forcing land distribution to their members and others without land. Their ability to mobilize as many as 12,000 people for a single land takeover or 100,000 for a national march on the na-tion's capital suggested just how strong their organizational abilities were, how contentious their actions could be and how well they could communicate and coordinate at the national level. By the late nineties they also garnered a great deal of national support and helped to create a national consensus that there was a national problem with land distribution and that some substantial reform was necessary.[13] Their ties with the Workers' Party remained strong and cordial.

The landless were well attuned to the international globalization struggle and considered themselves part of it, helping to organize and participating in the World Social Forums in Porto Alegre and sending their representatives to demonstrations and protests throughout the world.[14] They were one of the new type of internationally connected social organizations – new social movements – that met together in places like Seattle, Prague and Geneva as well as at the World Social Forums. Further, the MST and similar organizations were part of a developing global backlash against economic globalization.[15] Struggles that were once local and isolated were now international and linked. The news media and growing international communications links, especially electronic mail, greatly facilitated the globalization of struggle, and the globalization of awareness of local struggles, and support and solidarity with them. This and the dramatic actions like massive land takeovers by the MST also generated considerable support at the national level during this time period, and helped to define what might have been considered a local problem as a national problem that required national-level attention and resources to remedy it.

Today, those who are part of the movement number more than a million. Nor does the MST limit its demands to the redistribution of land through land reform. They challenge the neoliberal model of economic growth, the continued concentration of wealth, the lack of adequate urban housing and subsequent homelessness, and lack of educational access and need for educational reform in the state and federal universities. They have continued their land takeovers and occupations. They are, then, clearly on the radical left and are aligned with similar radical movements, parties and governments discussed in the Introduction. They are leftists who are not acceptable to the Brazilian establishment or the Washington Consensus.

Lula and the PT

Meanwhile the Workers' Party (Partido dos Trabalhadores or PT) was growing in influence and numbers as it began to campaign on a national scale. Former metalworker and union leader Luiz Inácio da Silva, affectionately known as Lula, led the party. As suggested above, the party had grown out of the successful union organizing of the metalworkers in São Paulo in the 1970s and early 1980s that also generated the new, linked militant labor organization the CUT. Meanwhile, during the 1980s, workers, former communists, progressives and other leftists as well as labor militants, intellectuals and legions of the MST also joined the party and helped to contribute to its growing successes. By 1989 the party was able to field a presidential candidate in the person of Luiz Inácio da Silva, Lula. Although he spoke to the impoverished masses, leftists and many members of the middle class, he was perceived as too far to the left, especially by the business and commercial elites. Even though the PT continued to enjoy electoral success at the municipal and state levels, its representation in the Brazilian Senate and Chamber of Deputies was growing but never extensive. In the 1998 election the PT took a little less than a third of the Senate and had only 82 out of 187 seats in the lower house. Lula continued to run for president on the PT ticket, but lost in 1994 and 1998, in large part because of the view that he and his party were radical and dangerous to the economic interests of the upper class, if not much of the middle class. That is they, like the MST, were an unacceptable left.[16] Elitist mass media like the Globo network sustained and disseminated these views.

Brazil gains economic strength

In the meantime, Brazil was developing a growing economy that was based on increasing exports, including new crops such as soybeans and sugar-cane-based ethanol, and industrial goods such as the different training and commercial aircraft that the state-supported aircraft company EMBRAER was selling on the international market. This growing economy was open to foreign investment, but was in part based on an import substitution industrialization model that nourished and protected Brazilian industries. This established a pattern whereby imported electronic and manufactured goods (especially if they come from outside of MERCOSUR) were relatively costly, allowing the Brazilian-made goods to compete with them if not undersell them. This helped to solidify and strengthen Brazilian business interests – particularly the São Paulo business-industrial elite – and link Brazilian economic success to them. Brazil's economy grew, exports flowed and by the twenty-first century Brazil was one of the up-and-coming economies in the world, forming part of the newly classified rapidly developing BRIC countries (Brazil, Russia, India, and China). As suggested previously, this type of growth did not distribute wealth well or alleviate the persistent extreme poverty that characterizes Brazil. It did, however, help to develop a vigorous capitalist economy complete with a dynamic stock market (BOVESPA, the Bolsa de Valores de São Paulo), which is the largest stock market in Latin America, and a well-off capitalist class that vigorously protected its interests.[17]

Resisting the strong impetus of the United States for a Free Trade Area of the Americas (FTAA) and/or an expansion of NAFTA, Brazil charted a more nationalist economic course that steered clear of such US-dominated economic integration. Instead, Brazil continued to chart an independent course and increase and strengthen its participation in its own experiment in regional integration, MERCOSUR, which it had founded with Argentina, Uruguay and Paraguay in 1994 (Bolivia, Chile and Peru later became associate members, as did Venezuela, which pressed its case for full membership in 2009). This helped to strengthen growth even more and expanded the market for tariff-protected Brazilian goods. The result internally was not only continued high levels of economic growth, but the strengthening of the Brazilian industrial and commercial bourgeoisie, while maintaining the power of landowners and a newly expanded group of businessmen in commercial agriculture. Indeed, in recent years Brazil has radically increased its production of soy (Brazil now exports more soy than any other nation) and geared up sugar production to produce ethanol (Brazil is now the world leader). In the last few years this wealth spread to the middle class and even segments of the working class. Before the 2008 world economic downturn (which also affected Brazil and its stock market), credit and banking were expanding rapidly, as were sales of consumer goods, including Brazilian-made automobiles. But basic structural inequalities in wealth, income and landownership continued and poverty, unemployment, homelessness and low wages for most of the working class persisted.

The Workers' Party and the MST

And so it was that Lula and his Workers' Party continued to appeal to the impoverished masses while reassuring the economic elite that they would respect their interests as well, while the MST continued their militant policies and confronted the economic elite through their radical actions. After his three previous unsuccessful presidential runs, Lula and the PT mounted a different kind of campaign in 2002, formed an alliance with the more moderate Liberal Party and took on a businessman as their vice-presidential candidate. Lula now dressed in coat and tie and paid his respects to São Paulo state's dynamic capitalists. He even made a point of visiting the São Paulo stock exchange and also paid his respects to Wall Street on a visit to the USA so as to reassure US and other foreign investors. This calmed capitalist nerves and increased his appeal among more conservative Brazilians. This and his strong support from the lower classes enabled him to win the presidency in 2002, and again in 2006, despite blowback from a PT vote-buying scandal. As he consolidated his rule, he defined his administration as being on the moderate left, linking it to the successful Brazilian growth model and the economic elites that were leading it. In doing so, he did, however, alienate progressive sectors of his own party, particularly the MST. It had become apparent that the radical changes initially advocated by the PT would not come to pass under his moderate administrations. Nor did the MST moderate its course. Although they communicated with the PT and Lula's administrations, they continued to engage in land takeovers, occupied public buildings, supported university reform and even took over a Swiss seed company that was disseminating genetically modified seed in southern Brazil. In this latter occupation, a violent confrontation ensued and an MST militant was killed by the hired thugs the seed company sent to try to retake the premises.

Despite such militant actions by the MST and their campaign against commercial agriculture and their efforts to champion the small family farm, the agro-business sector continued to grow. Under Lula the Workers' Party government initiated its 'Fome O' (O Hunger) and 'Bolsa Família' programs, whereby direct cash subsidies of some $35 were sent to the poorest Brazilian families each month so they would not go hungry.[18] This did help to alleviate some of the worst poverty and, along with slightly better wages for some workers, reduce the rate of absolute poverty. It did not, however, alter the existent inequitable class structure, nor give the vast majority of the poor opportunity for well-paid employment or access to land in rural areas. Indeed, the MST argued that such programs did not address the underlying socio-economic problems and only dulled the poor's political consciousness and made them less likely to join those demanding fundamental change.

The interaction between the MST and the PT is also instructive. Although relations between the two organizations were generally excellent at the local level, with overlapping affiliations, the national leaderships remained separate and not always as cordial. The MST has maintained a militant line with regard to the need to take over unused land and assert their more radical agenda, whereas in recent times much of the PT leadership has wanted to be more conciliatory with the large landowners. Thus, the landless backed and supported Lula and the Workers' Party in most local campaigns and the national campaigns for the presidency. In this way they helped to achieve significant regime change in Brazil, where Lula was elected with 61.27 percent of the vote in the second round of voting in 2002. Indeed, recognizing the PT's historic challenge to neoliberal policies and elitist rule, the landless turned out heavily in the election to join some 80 percent of the registered voters who participated in the voting in both rounds.[19] However, once the election was over, the landless did not press to be part of the government. Like many new social movements, they preferred to exert pressure from below and not risk co-optation. They continued to press the government for a comprehensive land reform program and a redistribution of the land and the wealth. But they did so as outsiders who did not seem to have very much to contribute to the dynamic capitalist growth model that the Workers' Party government began to develop and support once in office. They continued to occupy unused large farms and some public land, set up encampments along the side of the road, challenged government at different levels through demonstrations and building occupations and militated for thoroughgoing land reform and the redistribution of wealth. As commercial agricultural exports became an ever increasing element in Brazilian economic success, the Lula Workers' Party administration became increasingly friendly to the agricultural elites that accounted for the preponderance of Brazil's all-important agricultural-based exports. Thus the government that the Landless Movement had championed and supported formed an alliance with their class enemies, the very group that resisted their pressure for land reform and the redistribution of wealth, particularly in rural areas. Politics had made for some new bedfellows, and the MST was once again relegated to the floor. There would be no return to politics as usual. The PT would press its 'O Hunger' and 'Bolsa Família' programs and other social and economic initiatives, and the MST would press the PT government for the structural reforms (e.g. comprehensive agrarian reform) that it considered necessary.

Lula's reelection in 2006 cast MST and PT policies into even sharper relief. The second Workers' Party presidential term proved to be even more receptive to capitalist interests than the first and more resistant to the call for radical reform of land tenure. Agro-business interests in the form of large soy producers and cane producers for the ethanol industry had good access to the government, while the MST did not. The Workers' Party felt obliged to support such big capitalists because their production and exports were fueling Brazilian economic growth. The same was true for the industrial, commercial and growing banking interests as well. Land reform and economic redistribution were pushed by the Landless Movement but the governmental response was not radical reform. Rather, the government redistributed a little land and further evolved the O Hunger program, so that a Bolsa Família, a basic family 'food basket,' would allow the poorest to buy the basic foodstuffs to survive and would also diminish some of their political fervor. This program was even supported by the World Bank.

The PT government was becoming ever more acceptable to the Brazilian capitalists and was rapidly moving to the right on the political spectrum to become a 'good' or 'acceptable' left that could work with and become part of the international capitalist system, albeit with full awareness of Brazil's specific national interests. In Venezuela, Ecuador and Bolivia, the governments depended on the new social movements for support and sometimes to mobilize on behalf of the leftist regimes. In Brazil the PT leadership reasoned that when elections came, they could count on support from most of the poor and most of the MST supporters because of Lula's working-class origins, state subsidies, and Lula's immense popularity, and because the opposition parties such as the powerful Brazilian Social Democratic Party (PSDB) were so much more conservative and allied with the most reactionary segments of Brazilian society, such as the *bancada ruralista*, the rural agricultural bloc in the Brazilian legislature. Indeed, the MST was reticent about backing PSDB or other rightist parties or their candidates because, if elected, they would certainly not accede to MST calls for land reform and restructuring and might well engage in increasing repression and persecution of their movement. On the other hand, Lula's closer alliance with the agro-exporters and industrialists gained significant elite support and the growing economy (which recovered quickly from the 2008 international capitalist crisis) garnered considerable middle-class support and support from better-paid workers.

Indeed, it could be said that in the last few years Lula and the PT government were pursuing a dual tract: working with the Bolsa of São Paulo (stock market) and the interests it represented while distributing the Bolsa Família to the poor. Radical change would not be forthcoming, the capitalist economy would grow and prosperity would hopefully spread, but the hungry would not starve in the meantime. Indeed, this policy and Lula's popularity paved the way for the continuation of the Workers' Party in power as Lula's chief of staff, Dilma Rousseff, was elected to the presidency in 2010. Yet as one recent *Guardian* article warned, 'Despite some advances in poverty by her predecessor, President Lula, Dilma Rousseff inherits leadership in a country where about half of the cultivable land is owned by 1% of the population.'[20] The MST response was the same as it had been to Lula. They orchestrated three large land takeovers and occupied various government buildings on her inauguration on New Year's Day, 2011. They demanded a speed-up in land distribution and an end to the inequality, injustice and the violence that it perpetuated.

Conclusion

New social and political movements were changing politics, if not the political culture, in Bolivia, Ecuador and Venezuela and challenging control by the old economic and political elites. The masses were forcing more progressive if not radical politics that challenged traditional business interests. In Brazil segments of the masses had consistently mobilized through the MST and other popular organizations, had gained some support and a few changes, but had not been able to turn national policy in the more radical direction that they desired. Indeed, at the beginning of 2011 the land reform the Landless Movement had so passionately advocated since the 1980s was not on the horizon. Lula's Workers' Party had become more moderate and had begun to work with key sectors of the Brazilian economic elite. It had become a very acceptable left. As though trapped by the economic growth and exploding consumerism and credit revolution that Brazil has experienced, the social and economic revolution the PT leadership had flirted with in the early days of the party was no longer on the policy agenda. Lula, Dilma Rousseff and the Workers' Party were taking a much more calculated pro-business line to continue recent Brazilian growth and prosperity. Lula was still a popular figure among many of the poor, and his policies had gained wider acceptance among the wealthy classes, but the MST and many in his own party were disillusioned with the apparent turn to the right. Further, the PT government was not challenging the marginalization and vilification of the MST by elements of the economic elite and much of the mainstream press, such as the popular weekly magazine *Veja*. Nor did the government or the PT resist what was a deliberate effort to paint the MST as a violent organization that was disruptive of democracy.[21]

As Brazil weathered the world financial crisis of 2008 and elected a new president, it continued with a policy of growth and prosperity for the upper and middle classes and some workers, but not for the rural poor or marginalized who formed the basis for the social movements. Nor would such a policy direction address the severe and persistent poverty and the misery of the *favelas* or the declining fortunes of the rural poor or small family farmers, nor, in all likelihood, staunch Brazil's phenomenal crime rate. It might feed some of the hungry with the Bolsa Família, but the Bolsa in São Paulo would still get the lion's share of the wealth and the MST and other social movements such as the Sem Teto (homeless or literally roofless) movement would be left out in the cold.

Notes

1 Banco de Dados Políticos das Américas, *Brazil: Eleções Presidenciais de 1998*, georgetown.edu/pdba/Elecdata/Brazil/pres98.html. 2002 (accessed 19 April 2002).

2 Instituto Federal Electoral, *Elección de Presidente de los Estados Unidos Mexicanos*, ife.org.mx (accessed 9 April 2002).

3 The Landless Rural Workers' Movement (MST), 'Fundamental principles for the social and economic transformation of rural Brazil,' trans. Wilder Robles, *Journal of Peasant Studies*, 28(2), 2001, pp. 146–52.

4 Secretariat of Popular Consultation of the MST, *O Brasil Precisa de um Projecto Popular*, São Paulo, 2001, translated by author.

5 Robles, 'Fundamental principles,' p. 147.

6 Paulo Freire, *The Pedagogy of the Oppressed* (New York: Continuum, 2000).

7 James Petras, 'The Rural Landless Workers Movement,' *Z Magazine*, March 2000, pp. 32–6.

8 Brazilian Institute of Statistics, *Statistical Report 2001*, as cited from 'Pais termina anos 90 tão desigual como começou,' *Folha de São Paulo*, 5 April 2001, in Tom Lewis, 'Brazil: the struggle against neoliberalism,' *International Socialist Review*, June/July 2001.

9 Economic Commission for Latin America and the Caribbean (ECLAC), *Statistical Yearbook for Latin America and the Caribbean* (Santiago, Chile: United Nations, 2006/07).

10 Sue Bradford and Jan Rocha, *Cutting the Wire* (London: Latin American Bureau, 2002).

11 Geraldo Fontes (member of collective national leadership of MST), Interview by author, São Paulo, 17 September 2003.

12 These general processes are described in Sidney Tarrow, *Power in Movements, Social Movements and Contentious Politics* (Cambridge: Cambridge University Press, 2nd edn, 1998).

13 It should, however, be noted that much of the press was not always sympathetic and condemned their land takeovers as illegal actions. The rural landowners also did all in their power to stop their actions and discredit them in the public eye.

14 For more on the Social Forums see Tevio Teivainen, 'World Social Forum: what should it be when it grows up? Open democracy, free thinking for the world,' www.Open Democracy.net, 2003 (accessed 31 October 2003).

15 See Robin Broad, *Global Backlash, Citizen Initiatives for a Just World Economy* (Lanham, MD: Rowman & Littlefield, 2002).

16 See Teodoro Petkoff, 'Las dos izquierdas,' *Nueva Sociedad*, 197, May/June 2005, pp. 114–28; Jorge Castañeda, 'Latin America's left turn,' *Foreign Affairs*, 85(3), May/June 2006,

pp. 28–43; Jorge Castañeda and Marco A. Morales, *Leftovers: Tales of the Latin American Left* (New York: Routledge, 2008); and especially Kurt Weyland, Raul Madrid and Wendy Hunter (eds), *Leftist Governments in Latin America: Successes and Shortcomings* (New York: Cambridge University Press, 2010).

For a different take on the 'good' and 'bad' left, see Maxwell Cameron, 'Latin America's left turns: beyond good and bad,' *Third World Quarterly*, 30(2), 2009, pp. 331–48.

17 It should be noted that the Brazilian capitalist class is far from uniform, and includes traditional landowners who continue to make their fortunes from coffee production or the cultivation of sugar cane, agribusiness that raises cattle in land taken from the Amazon rainforest, or soybeans in southern Brazil, to the producers of manufactured goods of all types – electronic goods and even cars, aircraft and computers.

18 The Bolsa Família program, which is supported by the World Bank, is an attempt at poverty alleviation in Brazil. It reaches 11 million families, some 46 million people. This constitutes a significant portion of the country's low-income population. Poor families with children get 70 reales monthly (about US\$35) in direct transfers. They commit to keeping their children in school and taking them for regular health checks. It does not provide further education, technical training, or employment opportunities for the parents or for the children once they finish their basic schooling.

19 International Foundation for Election Surveys (IFES), ifes.org/eguide/turnout2002.htm (accessed 24 March 2003).

20 Benjamin Dangle, 'Why land reform makes sense for Dilma Rousseff,' guardian.co.uk, 27 January 2011 (accessed 18 February 2011).

21 See Miguel Carter, 'The Landless Rural Workers Movement and democracy in Brazil,' *Latin American Research Review*, Special Issue, 2010, pp. 186–217, for a cogent discussion of the forces working against the MST, particularly what he terms concentrated, conservative media power.

3 | Social movements and revolutionary change in Bolivia

WALTRAUD Q. MORALES

Overview

The historic election of Juan Evo Morales Ayma as Bolivia's first indigenous president in December 2005 represented an unexpected victory for the Andean nation's new social movements in many respects. Not only had Evo Morales overcome class, ethnic, and racist barriers to the highest office in the land, but he was also Bolivia's first new social movement president. Over the previous decade, as Bolivia's traditional political party system and elite rule had faltered and fallen into disrepute, militant grassroots social movements emerged to fill the void. Popular participation in hundreds of local, regional, and national associations and movements revived democracy and reenergized civil society. Social movement democracy provided unprecedented opportunities for popular leaders and community representatives – many indigenous and peasant-based like Morales himself – to be elected and to challenge the entrenched centers of power, wealth and governance of the Andean country.

Through diverse social movements, nontraditional political actors drawn from historically marginalized groups, such as the poor, peasants, coca growers, indigenous peoples and women, organized activist networks and protest campaigns to achieve specific and often limited goals. However, soon these movements of Bolivia's common people joined in the wider collective struggles against unpopular and unjust governmental policies encompassing economic neoliberalism, rampant globalization, the militarized Andean drug war, and chronic environmental and human rights abuses. In the process, popular social movements sought to amplify the meaning of citizenship, to redefine the basis and content of national identity, and to restructure the intimate relationship between culture and power in Bolivia's multi-ethnic and multicultural state and society. Consequently, not since the historic 1952 National Revolution has the country's class- and ethnic-based status quo been threatened so fundamentally from below.

These comprise the central issues and themes to be explored further.

Key questions to consider are how and to what extent Bolivia's new social movements, particularly radical 'new left' and indigenous ones, have facilitated, fashioned and at times challenged the constitutional and socioeconomic reforms of the progressive Morales government. As Bolivia's first social movement president, has Evo Morales made a significant difference? Has he been constrained by his popular movement base and responsive to its radical and reformist demands? Or, despite his indigenist, populist and socialist rhetoric and pedigree, has President Morales followed a more moderate and conciliatory agenda in practice at the expense of social movements? And, as some have argued,[1] has the Morales–MAS (Movement toward Socialism, Movimiento al Socialismo) government been ready to accommodate powerful economic interests at home and abroad, compromising authentic socialist revolutionary change?

Typically for Bolivia, the answers to these fundamental questions vary greatly based on whom and when one asks. With the support of his new social movements base, Evo Morales (and his MAS party) was reelected in December 2009 with an even greater margin of political success. However, not even halfway into his second term, the celebratory euphoria of victory had dissipated. Despite a new reform constitution approved by the voters in 2009 and the steady implementation of progressive, pro-indigenous laws by the Morales government, Bolivia was once again disrupted by food and fuel shortages, strident street protests and frustrating road blockages – this time instigated not by Morales' conservative opponents but by powerful and radicalized sectors of the new social movements in confrontation with the government.

Historical and comparative context

'... new political actors are emerging throughout Latin America to challenge the region's peaceful coexistence with intolerable conditions.'[2]

The unprecedented rise, extent, and vibrancy of social movement politics in contemporary Bolivia can best be understood through the prism of history – and not just localized Andean or even regionalized Latin American history. Moreover, from the vantage of comparative politics, social movements represent neither a new phenomenon in Latin America nor, for that matter, in the developing and developed world. In the case of Bolivia, however, what does appear to be new is the explosion of social movements over the last decade and their rapid politicization and formal incorporation into the Andean nation's governing structures. What is also new is the shifting divergence and convergence of indigenous movements with radical left and progressive class-based movements. The premier example of this (partial) melding of agendas and interests is Evo Morales' hybrid socialist-indigenist-populist movement turned political party, the Movement toward Socialism (MAS).

As with social movements historically and comparatively, the rise of Bolivia's new social movements and their expanded role in policy-making have sharply polarized opinion within the country and abroad, and hardened political positions in support of or in opposition to Morales' progressive and social-movement-based government. A number of conservative critics have characterized social movement politics in Bolivia and the region with a bold and indiscriminate brush as 'policy lunacy' or retrogression into authoritarian rule and old failed socialist policies.[3] Critics on the left have the opposite view, faulting the Morales–MAS government for failures to deliver on the promises to social movements and as a pseudo-reformist, neoliberal democracy in disguise.[4] Judging by Morales' stunning 2005 and 2009 electoral victories, however, a majority of Bolivian voters have seized upon the ascendancy of populist and social movement politics as the long-awaited triumph of the dispossessed and disenfranchised over the 'blancoide' elite and moneyed establishment, or *la nueva oligarquia* (the new oligarchy) that has traditionally controlled Bolivia's economy and society, and its centralist and discriminatory state.

Historically, social movements in Latin America have arisen during volatile periods of national transition and crisis when traditional political institutions and political cultures have failed to accommodate the interests and demands of society. Typically, specific conditions created a climate conducive to social movement development and growth: economic collapse, strain or breakdown in democracy, widening social inequality, population movements and pressures, and long-suppressed ethnic tensions and grievances. These critical facilitating conditions developed gradually in Bolivia with the reestablishment of democracy in 1982.

History also demonstrates that social movements can readily become politicized and co-opted as vehicles for mass political parties. Thus Argentine Peronism, which 'mobilized masses of people previously excluded from society' because of the country's 'failure to redistribute income effectively or enhance democratic participation,' equally applies to the rise of 'Evoism' and the Movement toward Socialism in Bolivia.[5] Often historical and contemporary social movements have in common 'the politics of rage, race and revenge,' as well as class.[6] This conflation of class, ethnicity and race, compounded by nationalism and regionalism, is central to the Bolivian case. Moreover, in Bolivia, as in Peronist Argentina, populist and charismatic leadership is instrumental in the social movements' success, particularly the effective political mobilization of the electorate, the ultimate institutionalization of the movements' agendas, and the regimes' legitimacy. Further, in a number of historical cases social movements have become radicalized into revolutionary movements and have precipitated full-blown political or social upheavals. Indeed, in sociological terms, social revolutions are social movements whose purpose is to effect radical change in a country's political, economic and social systems. In the current Bolivian case, the Morales–MAS government has characterized constitutional reforms in revolutionary terms and as the progressive 'refounding' of the nation.

Therefore, classic preconditions and causalities influenced the rise of Bolivia's new social movements. The democratic transition in the 1980s and earlier constitutional reforms in the 1990s that expanded civic expectations and decentralized structures of governance were especially necessary for the development of Bolivia's new social movements. This supportive environment provided the critical opening for the resurgence of political activism and the expansion of civil society after nearly two decades of oppressive military rule. By 2000, key social movements, despite their origins in very specific and often localized goals and grievances over water privatization, gas exports and coca leaf eradication policies, embraced a more comprehensive and radical reform agenda. Employing extensive grassroots organization and mobilization, and aggressive street tactics from demonstrations, hunger strikes, and road blockages, these new social movements basically waged war on three governments.

Out of these targeted struggles an interlinked, nationwide solidarity network of social movements was born that sought to advance democracy and indigenous rights and to reform and restructure the country in fundamental ways. A product of the social movement formation process, the MAS served as the political apparatus and electoral vehicle for Morales and other affiliated movement-based leaders. In the end, the support of Bolivia's new social movements proved indispensable to the solid electoral mandates of Evo Morales both in 2005 and 2009. And for most of Morales' two-term presidency, the conciliatory and contentious interactions among social movements, the government, and the official MAS party, on the one hand, and key economic and regional actors, on the other, have variously radicalized, moderated, and/or stalled the executive's ambitious reform program.

Beginning in 1999, Bolivia experienced increasing instability and civil unrest that the 2005 elections quelled temporarily. Bolivia's popular classes, many of indigenous heritages, had been severely impoverished by neoliberal privatization policies that governments had implemented since 1985. By 2000, citizens' groups were in open rebellion against economic neoliberalism and globalization, and the country's elitist governing system and the corrupt political establishment that had imposed the policy – often forcibly – against their strong opposition. Popular militancy found a ready outlet and vehicle in the new social movements that emerged partly because of important constitutional, administrative and electoral reforms introduced since 1994. New laws attempted to decentralize, open up, and democratize government. Especially significant was the new 1994 Bolivian Constitution, which officially recognized the unique multi-ethnic and pluricultural composition of Bolivia's population and guaranteed and protected the special rights of indigenous peoples.

Other important democratizing reforms included the 1994 Law of Popular Participation (*Ley de Participación Popular*, LPP), the 1995 Law of Administrative Decentralization, the 1996 Electoral Law, the 2001 Law of National Dialogue, and the 2004 Law of Civic Associations and Indigenous Peoples. The decentralization reforms strengthened local and regional government, providing greater funding, and extending direct fiscal administration and self-rule to hundreds of new municipalities and indigenous communities. Electoral reforms created a mixed system that combined the previous straight proportional representation system with the direct election of representatives, weakening the power of the central government and the national party leadership in favor of local and regional actors and interests. Reforms included gender quotas mandating that a percentage of a party's electoral slate be reserved for women candidates (30 percent for party lists – later increased to 50 percent – and 50 percent for citizen associations and indigenous groups).

Greater popular participation was also encouraged and significantly amplified by legislation between 1994 and 2004. The Popular Participation Law extended legal recognition to Territorial Base Organizations (Organizaciones Territoriales de Base, OTB), which represented peasant communities, indigenous peoples' communities, and neighborhood committees and organizations. The National Dialogue Law ultimately established indigenous municipalities and provided them with additional funds to reduce poverty.[7] Municipalities and OTBs were given direct control over elections, policymaking and budgets. This devolution of power and governance was especially important for the OTBs because it allowed indigenous groups to follow their cultural practices and traditions in the selection of their leaders and political representatives. It also allowed civic groups and social movements to play a greater electoral role because potential candidates no longer had to hold official party membership to run for office.

Independence of social groups from party tutelage and spoils steadily increased with each legislative round. Initially, social and civic groups were represented indirectly by forming fronts or coalitions with political parties. However, with the 2004 reform (Law of Civic Associations and Indigenous Peoples), civil society organizations, OTBs, and social movements were allowed to run their own candidates independent of political parties. The law also mandated a gender quota for social movements, so that 50 percent of candidates were women. Consequently, a large number of citizens' associations, social movements, and women's and indigenous groups ran candidates in the 2004 municipal elections for the first time.[8] Moreover, amplifications to the 2004 reform in 2005 provided for the direct selection and election of the nine departmental prefects or regional governors for the first time in December 2005, further opening up the political system to a greater role for local and regional actors and movements. Previously the president had appointed prefects, making these officials more susceptible to pressure from the executive and ruling party or coalition and less attentive to regional interests.

Thus, decentralization and participation reforms proved critical to the development of social movement democracy. By providing funds, and increasing local and indigenous civic participation, organization, and experience in politics and governance, the reforms promoted a more inclusive and engaging political culture that encouraged the growth and effectiveness of social movements. And in short order, these popular movements empowered indigenous and other marginalized citizens to challenge the government on several fronts – in local office, the national legislature, and in the streets. An unprecedented number of nontraditional candidates ran and were elected to local and national office in this period. Over three hundred new municipalities were established with newly elected mayors, many drawn from among community and indigenous leaders. At the same time, civil society actors – indigenous organizations, neighborhood committees, workers' and peasant associations, coca leaf growers' federations, housewives' and women's groups – organized demonstrations independently or in coalitions, and confronted policymakers directly with their demands and grievances. Thanks in large part to decentralizing reforms, these closely interlinked solidarity groups were well positioned to mobilize thousands of supporters and diehard militants behind the fierce nationwide social protest movements that arose almost spontaneously against the official privatization of water and commercialization of natural gas resources.

Social movement wars: water and natural gas

Between 1999 and 2005, popular protests and confrontations steadily escalated into major civil insurrections or 'wars' over resources: the so-called Water War and the Gas War. Overwhelmed by the angry public explosion, desperate governments were forced to hold a series of national referenda to appease the social movements and resolve the crises. However, the protests against water privatization and natural gas and oil policy escalated further, stirring up older grievances over forcible coca leaf eradication and stalled land reform. This chronic climate of discontent and instability ultimately reignited the regional autonomy dispute (which continued to worsen after Morales' election). Thus the country in the five years prior to the 2005 elections had reached a very precarious and revolutionary state, for which social movements were largely responsible and which these movements would exploit fully to achieve social change.

Resource wars have had a long and sad history in Bolivia. Since the Spanish conquest, corrupt governments and foreign capitalists have exploited and squandered the country's wealth. Most Bolivians benefited little from the record profits extracted from gold, silver, guano, nitrates, tin, and oil. More recently the struggle has been over water and natural gas. Water, however, is special; it is essential for life, and a vital resource for everyone, especially the country's poor majority. Typically in rural areas 60 percent of Bolivians lack access to drinking water and 90 percent lack water for crops. In many cities water service has been precarious as well. Consequently, following the World Bank's neoliberal directives, the Bolivian governments signed contracts with transnational corporations to privatize water services in major cities. However, when these corporations raised rates exorbitantly, local residents rebelled and ignited a resource war and nationwide social movement against water privatization, neoliberalism, and globalization known as the 'Water War/s.'

Cochabamba Water War The first water war erupted in the city of Cochabamba. Citizens launched a mass protest against Aguas del

Tunari, a transnational consortium and subsidiary of the US Bechtel corporation, which had privatized the city's water system in 1999. As Bolivia's third-largest city, Cochabamba had more than doubled its population between the 1970s and 1990s. Yet less than half the population had access to drinking water, and for the rest access was sporadic. Privatization was intended to solve the problem, but it was imposed upon residents without consultation and the contract unfairly favored the transnational companies. Aguas del Tunari prohibited private wells and rainwater collection, even charging for these, and imposed a 200–400 percent increase in water rates.

Civic and neighborhood committees immediately organized themselves into a powerful social movement, the Coordinating Committee in Defense of Water and Life (la Coordinadora de Agua y Vida), which was led by Oscar R. Olivera, head of the city's Federation of Factory Workers.[9] Over 15,000 irate citizens kicked off the Cochabamba Water War with protests in December 1999. The next February, a two-day street war left 175 people injured. In April, over 30,000 protesters shut down the city and forced the government to declare martial law as demonstrations spread to the capital, La Paz, and El Alto. After six persons were killed and dozens injured, the government cancelled the contract with Aguas del Tunari. However, the war was not completely over. There were more protests when Olivera was arrested later that year. In 2002, the demonstrations became even more strident and directed against globalization after Aguas del Tunari/Bechtel sought $25 million in damages. And in April, Oscar Olivera and 125 protesters descended on Bechtel's corporate headquarters in San Francisco.

The Cochabamba Water War generated global sympathy and support, to such a degree that a localized Bolivian social movement quickly mushroomed into an international anti-privatization and anti-globalization movement. With a presence on the Internet and solidarity from nongovernmental organizations (NGOs), and the support of a network of like-minded social movements and private citizens (Michael Moore) around the world, one small city's heroic campaign against Bechtel was a movement success. In early 2006, the Bolivian government and the shareholders of Aguas del Tunari announced a settlement that imposed no monetary damages. Consequently, Cochabamba's 'David and Goliath' struggle was heralded as a victory in the global anti-globalization movement.[10]

El Alto Water War Skirmishes in Bolivia's second water war, the El Alto Water War, broke out between late December 2004 and January 2005.

Encouraged by the success of Cochabamba's Water Wars, residents of the primarily indigenous city of El Alto rebelled against Aguas del Illimani. The predominately Aymara citizenry complained that the transnational consortium, which had controlled water services since 1997, had raised rates excessively and denied water to thousands of very poor families. Abel Mamani, who was the Aymara leader of the El Alto Water War, was also the president of the Federation of Neighborhood Councils of El Alto (Federación de Juntas Vecinales, FEJUVE). This meant that, in the struggle, Mamani could count on the backing of an entire, very militant, highland community. In short, he could command a powerful social movement.

The El Alto protests and roadblocks shut down the greater metropolitan area around La Paz, preventing all movement in or out of the capital and leaving the city's million residents effectively stranded. The economic, social and political costs of the shutdown and of the El Alto anti-privatization movement were especially high. The government quickly tried to defuse the explosive situation and initially promised to cancel the water consortium's concession but then failed to work out an acceptable deal. So, protests and roadblocks continued into April and then petered out. Finally, Aguas del Illimani closed shop in 2006.

These water war movements had major repercussions within the country and beyond. In Bolivia the protests and roadblocks effectively shortened four presidencies, and cleared the path for Evo Morales and the MAS party. The anti-water privatization wars also helped mobilize and draw indigenous groups into the anti-globalization movement, creating new social movement linkages. Indigenous peoples throughout Bolivia viewed water as a sacred natural resource and inviolable human right and not a commodity for private, especially foreign, profit. Internationally, the Cochabamba and El Alto water wars popularized and linked Bolivian social movements with progressive movements around the world. The international community extended moral and material support to Bolivia's social movements, which had contributed to the wider debate and struggle over water rights elsewhere in the world.

El Alto Gas War

'The Gas War wasn't the main victory; it was just one battle in a longer war.' Oscar Olivera[11]

Another resource war and national social movement, the Gas War, had equally significant, if not greater, political and economic repercussions. As in the water wars, the protests over various governments' natural gas policies also contributed to the demise of four presidents. Moreover, the nationalization of hydrocarbons became not only central to the program of the MAS party and Morales' electoral bid, but ultimately one of the crowning achievements of his first presidency and an early indicator that his government would break with the past and seriously respond to the demands of Bolivia's social movements and popular classes.

The populist Gas War began in 2003 and overthrew the neoliberal government of Gonzalo Sánchez de Lozada on 17 October. The reason for Sánchez de Lozada's hasty resignation after only fifteen months in office was the wave of civil violence over proposed natural gas exports and other grievances that began with a tax revolt in January/February 2003, and escalated between September and October. In both instances, the government's security forces responded repressively and ruthlessly shot and/or killed demonstrators. These atrocities so horrified the country that they came to be known as 'Black February' and 'Black October.' The protests – the first in a cycle of confrontations known as the Gas War/s that disrupted the country into late 2005 – were over an unpopular commercialization scheme to export natural gas via a pipeline terminating in a Chilean port. Given the still-rancorous memory of Chile's defeat of Bolivia in the nineteenth century War of the Pacific, in which Bolivia lost its access to the sea, the government had expected opposition, but had grossly underestimated its vehemence. By the time the worst of Sánchez de Lozada's rule was over, the body count approximated a hundred dead. The legacy of this repression, however, was greater citizen solidarity and a more forceful and unified social movement.

Vice-President Carlos Mesa Gisbert, who had condemned the violence, took over and restored temporary calm by promising a national referendum on gas and oil policy and early presidential elections. Although initially popular, Mesa also became increasingly vulnerable to social movement politics. While disruptive protests over the privatization of natural resources – the Water Wars and the Gas Wars – continued unabated, the referendum on the future of Bolivia's extensive natural gas reserves took place in July 2004. Despite high abstention, the majority of voters (80 percent) roundly opposed the existing neoliberal Hydrocarbons Law (of Sánchez de Lozada), and supported a new law that would nationalize Bolivia's extensive natural gas and oil resources. However, because the referendum's dense and convoluted language evaded outright nationalization, the Gas War protests refused to die and instead were amplified by the El Alto Water War demonstrations. Mesa now faced the combined force of two militant social movements.

Over 80,000 demonstrators paralyzed La Paz/El Alto with blockades, strikes and street battles in a second-stage Gas War in May 2005. The predominantly indigenous protesters from the Aymara communities of El Alto demanded the nationalization of natural gas and water. At their head were prominent indigenous leaders, among them Evo Morales, president of the coca growers' federations (Six Federations of Coca Growers of the Tropics of Cochabamba); Felipe Quispe, head of the peasants' union (Confederation of Peasant Unions of Bolivia) and indigenous party (Pachakuti Indigenous Movement); and Abel Mamani, leader of El Alto neighborhood committees and El Alto Water War protests. Pressured, the Bolivian Congress enacted a new Hydrocarbon Law on 6 May that failed to nationalize but increased the state's share of oil and gas royalties. Demanding nationalization, the social movements escalated their protests, forcing Mesa to resign in early June, and a caretaker government to schedule elections for December.

These popular uprisings, ostensibly motivated by simple and immediate demands, actually reflected complex and inherent class and ethnic grievances of socioeconomic and cultural inequality, discrimination and injustice. And as Bolivia's marginalized social classes (predominantly of indigenous heritage) embraced this new environment of direct and uncompromising social movement democracy, business as usual by the country's elite (primarily white and mestizo) political and economic governing class and associated foreign interests was over. These massive, social-movement-inspired mobilizations, in which an estimated one in seven citizens actively participated, delivered a major social victory and 'powerful message that even the highest leader of the nation can become directly accountable to the people.'[12]

Social movements and Evo's revolution in governance

'We believe in a democratic revolution, an indigenous revolution, to claim back our land and all of our natural resources.' Evo Morales[13]

The first electoral victory of Evo Morales and MAS was described in the national press in effusive terms as the historic explosion of Aymaras and Quechuas, and as the ascension of the first Amerindian president in 500 years since Tupac Katari. Moreover, the sacred indigenous ceremony held among the ancient ruins of Tiwanaku on 21 January 2006 was a celebration of the glorious heritage of the country's Indian majority. In his first discourse as president-elect on 18 December, Morales emphasized the indigenous character of his new government and the formidable challenge ahead. 'We have won, and I tell you that the Aymaras, Quechuas, Chiquitanos, and Guaranis will be present ... but now the problem is no longer winning, but governing ...'[14]

The enormous challenge of governance was intimately linked to the role of new social movements. They had brought Morales to power and would be critical if he were to advance his agenda and theirs, especially within a truly democratic structure and process. From the outset, Morales listed the central goals of his new pro-people, pro-indigenous administration: the nationalization of oil and gas (hydrocarbons); a Constitutional Assembly to redraft the founding state Constitution, giving more rights and power to 'original peoples'; and a national referendum on regional autonomy.

After less than six months of Morales' government, a new Hydrocarbon Law 'renationalized' oil and gas resources. This meant that potentially some 25–50 trillion cubic feet of natural gas and approximately $70 billion in future revenues would accrue to the Bolivian state. In his May Day speech to cheering crowds, Morales stated that 'the state recovers ownership, possession and total and absolute control of these resources.'[15, 16] However, for the most part the new decree did not confiscate privately owned foreign properties outright, but required foreign oil corporations to renegotiate their contracts and royalty agreements on terms more beneficial to Bolivia. Within a year, the majority had done so through new joint venture or partnership agreements.

This fact and the strong profits that both foreign investors and the Bolivian government earned over the next years, as well as the government's overall support of socially productive private property rights generally, drew the criticism of more ideological class-struggle observers abroad. Rather than popular social movements supporting an avowed and long-standing presidential policy, these critics turned the situation around and emphasized that the so-called nationalization policy was 'clearly dictated by pressures from the popular movements,' so that the Morales government 'had no choice in the matter.'[17] On the other hand, Morales pursued the only form of 'renationalization' politically, economically and strategically possible for Bolivia. Moreover, across Bolivia the indigenous and the social movement base celebrated the hydrocarbon nationalization as a revolutionary act and decisive demonstration of the state's sovereignty over resources and independence from multinational control. In the final analysis, the new hydrocarbon law was a great success, more than doubling Bolivia's share of revenues and generating a fiscal surplus through 2008 and beyond.

A more difficult task was constitutional reforms. While still a candidate, Morales had outlined his revolutionary, socialist and indigenist program: 'The Constituent Assembly is our number one priority ... The majority of people in this country – people from more than 30 indigenous groups – did not participate in the foundation of Bolivia in 1825. We have to re-found Bolivia in order to end the colonial state, to live united in diversity, to put all our resources under state control, and to make people participate and give them the right to make decisions.'[18] However, Morales' efforts to 'refound Bolivia' on a foundation of indigenous cultural identity, democratic populism and communitarian socialism unleashed a firestorm of conservative class- and race-based regional opposition. Although described by some as fundamentally a class struggle, it was closer to civil warfare over both the body and soul of the country – its nationhood, and territorial, cultural and ethnic integrity – as well as its state structures and rich resources. The contention centered around two remaining reforms at the very heart of the Morales revolution: the definition and implementation of autonomy, and the redistribution of power in the new constitution, especially as these validated and empowered indigenous peoples. Thus, for the first time in decades, ethnicity and race emerged as a powerful unifying force within the new social movements, often compounding and even dominating traditional class and regional disputes.

Social movements and the struggle over autonomy

Throughout Bolivia's history as a new nation, secession had loomed as a constant threat; indeed, Bolivia was conceived as a buffer between more rapacious neighbors, and periodically its subtropical lowland provinces had toyed with annexation. Especially since the 1980s the lowland eastern departments (Santa Cruz, Beni, Pando, and Tarija), comprising 70 percent of the country, had lobbied for greater regional autonomy. Disaffected by Morales' election and his radical reforms, this largely non-indigenous, prosperous and more conservative region, called the Media Luna because the territory formed a half-moon or crescent on a map, demanded self-rule and even threatened secession. Regional disputes over natural gas revenues, land reform, autonomy referenda, and a new constitution provoked protests, roadblocks and armed clashes across the country, but especially in the Media Luna.

Even after the new state Constitution was approved by 61 percent of the voters in January 2009, the autonomy war raged on, stoked by seemingly irreconcilable socioeconomic class and ethno-cultural divisions. Even after Morales' reelection in December 2009 with an even greater governing mandate, the struggle over regional autonomy has continued with social movements once again playing prominent roles. Although there have been fewer clashes in the streets and more in the Congress and departmental governments, the Media Luna agro-business and landed elites have not given up the fight. Their class- and race-based opposition to Morales has been persistent and longstanding.

Already by the 2002 presidential election, the urban elites of the resource-rich eastern departments were mobilized in opposition to Morales and the MAS party, which had come in second. Regional, ethnic, and ideological tensions were already elevated. The lowlander social movements feared Morales' indigenist, reform agenda. So when he won in 2005, opposition to the new social and political order that he began to implement soon climbed off the charts. Without a majority in the national legislature, which was controlled by the MAS and pro-Morales social movements and indigenous representatives, the Media Luna agribusiness and political elites were unable to block reforms on the national level. They seized on autonomy and constitutional guarantees to protect their regional power base and economic interests from encroachments by the indigenous MAS-controlled central government. During most of 2005–08, much of the discord centered on the elections for the Constituent Assembly and its deliberations. When opposition parties, regional civic committees and conservative social movements were unable to control these outcomes, regional elites increasingly employed the same direct action tactics against the government as those of Morales' supporters – roadblocks, demonstrations, strikes, and other mass social mobilization. Consequently, for most of 2007–09, Bolivia was in virtually constant conflict bordering on chaos.

The center of the Media Luna pro-autonomy social movement is in the city and department of Santa Cruz. The influential Pro-Santa Cruz Civic Committee (Comité Cívico Pro-Santa Cruz, CPSC), a citizens' organization dominated by the Cruzeño oligarchy – rich entrepreneurs, cattle barons, and agribusiness elite – has promoted the autonomy revolt. The shock forces for the Civic Committee are the Union of Cruceño Youth (Unión Juvenil Cruceñista, UJC), a militant student group. Also, the National Democratic Council (Consejo Nacional Democrático, CONALDE), a coalition of five anti-Morales prefects and their departmental civic committees, has coordinated strikes and demonstrations in the Media Luna.

Control over the region's lucrative resource – oil and natural gas – is a major factor in the autonomy war, especially since profits doubled after nationalization. Moreover, the Gas Wars intensified the autonomy dispute for several reasons. First, lowlanders, who had supported the neoliberal privatization of hydrocarbons, vehemently opposed Morales' nationalization. Second, their idea of regional autonomy entailed a sizeable share, if not control, of the windfall oil and gas money. Consequently, in December 2007, the four Media Luna departments (plus Cochabamba department, or the Media Luna Ampliada) passed autonomy statutes giving them two-thirds of the hydrocarbon tax revenues. Fights over this money continued unabated in 2008/09. The regional elites rejected the Morales government plan to use a large chunk of the revenues to fund old age pensions. The regional *autonomistas* (autonomy supporters) were also determined to control the region's other important resources, particularly land, hardwoods, and semi-precious stones.

Without Media Luna-style autonomy, the region's Landless Movement (Movimiento Sin Tierra, MST), strongly supported by the MAS–Morales government and other progressive social movements, as well as protected by provisions in the new Constitution, poses a real threat to the large latifundios in the Media Luna. The autonomy war has also sought to undermine pan-Indian solidarity by pitting eastern indigenous groups against those of the western regions. Since the 1980s the Landless Movement, representative of lowlander peasants and indigenous peoples (*campesinos, indígenas* and '*pueblos originarios*'), has gathered momentum and been strengthened by Morales' election and the indigenous resurgence in the highlands. The 2009 Constitution has reduced large landholdings in the Media Luna (and the country) by half. Progress on land reform in Morales' second term has the potential to ensure that lowlander Indian loyalties and interests will favor ethno-cultural over a more reactionary form of regional autonomy. The controversial passage of autonomy and decentralization legislation in July 2010, and laws against discrimination and racism in September, has helped.

Indigenous and ethno-cultural autonomy presents a different dimension to the autonomy struggle – clearly one that the Media Luna elites reject. Greater self-rule and cultural and economic rights for Bolivia's thirty-six recognized indigenous groups are protected in the new 2009 Constitution, which extends earlier decentralization reforms. As a result, Bolivia's indigenous resurgence is not only in the highlands and valleys. In the eastern lowlands, the list of peasant and indigenous organizations aggressively and successfully promoting the interests of their communities has grown. Among major organizations are the Confederation of Indigenous Peoples of Eastern Bolivia (Confederación de Pueblos

Indígenas del Oriente Boliviano, CIDOB; later known as the Confederación de Pueblos Indígenas del Oriente, Chaco, y Amazonía de Bolivia); the Confederation of Indigenous Peoples of Bolivia (Confederación de Pueblos Indígenas de Bolivia), representing both highland and lowland indigenous groups; Assembly of Guaraní People (Asamblea del Pueblo Guaraní, APG); and Aid for Peasants-Indigenous of the Oriente (Apoyo para el Campesino-Indígena del Oriente Boliviano, APCOB).

Critics fear that indigenous autonomy will further balkanize the country and complicate jurisdictional, sovereignty, and territorial issues; for example, the right to indigenous 'communitarian justice' ('*justicia comunitaria*') has created problems of due process, judicial consistency and fairness, and offended Western-based legal sensibilities. On the other hand, non-indigenous authorities may find it more difficult to 'recolonize' indigenous communities and infiltrate and demobilize grassroots social movements. Moreover, even the pro-indigenous Morales government has been torn between efforts to encourage and support Indian land rights, and the necessity to discourage and restrain informal land takeovers in order to prevent violent confrontations and maintain orderly governance and respect for private property.

In early 2009, final passage of Article 398 of the new Constitution limiting agricultural holdings offered a green light to lowlander indigenous communities. Some of these moved aggressively to expedite land reform and autonomy over natural resources. At the outset, President Morales attempted to appease heightened indigenous expectations, and he personally distributed land seized from larger holdings to lowlander Guaraní farmers in a highly publicized and symbolic ceremony that March. Nevertheless, frustrated peasant-indigenous-based organizations, the CSUTCB, CIDOB, MST, and Tierra y Territorio (Land and Territory movement) turned up the pressure in 2010 with several nationwide marches for territory and autonomy.

Thus the competing interests of Morales' disparate constituency and protests over the slow pace of land reform and the protection of native peoples' land rights remained sources of friction between the government and social movements during Morales' second term. Increasingly social movements were at odds, such as when the claims of highlander coca-growing peasant groups and colonists clashed with those of local native peoples over protected territories and conservation preserves. Struggles over the biodiverse habitats and rich natural resources of the tropical lowlands even pitted eastern indigenous communities against the policies and fiscal necessities of Morales' highlander-based central government.

Complicating the situation, and even inviting criticism of hypocrisy, have been Morales' global crusade to protect the planet's environment from the ravages of capitalism and polluting and unsustainable economic development, and his promises to implement these ideals at home. On the one hand, Morales hosted the celebrated first Peoples' World Conference on Climate Change and the Rights of Mother Earth (Pachamama) in April 2010 in Tiquipaya, a small town outside the city of Cochabamba. On the other, his administration's policies clashed with the lowlander confederation of indigenous peoples (CIDOB) over seismic testing, drilling and mining, as well as planned construction and hydroelectric projects on indigenous lands. CIDOB and eastern indigenous groups have denounced the government's pursuit of mega development projects and lax protection of their rights against local and foreign industries.[19] For its part, the MAS government – its environmentalist sloganeering and anti-neoliberalism and anti-market rhetoric notwithstanding – was becoming desperate for more foreign investment by late 2011 as the fiscal surplus of Morales' first term steadily dwindled and economic growth slowed.

Thus far, despite Morales' praise for Bolivia's grassroots environmentalist social movements and high-profile international lobbying on behalf of global stewardship at the United Nations and international forums in 2010 and 2011, the Bolivian president's tangible support has remained limited and inconsistent at home. And as both political pressures and economic exigencies have increased during his second term, it has become less clear whether Morales can fulfill the elevated desires and demands of his diverse social movement and indigenous constituency for more rapid and radical land reform and environmental protectionism.

Indigenous resurgence and the struggle for the new Constitution

'The 500 years of Indian resistance have not been in vain. From 500 years of resistance we pass to another 500 years in power.' Evo Morales[20]

When Evo Morales, forty-seven years of age, of indigenous descent, and from a small Altiplano village in the department of Oruro, won 54 percent of the popular vote on 18 December 2005 to become president, Bolivia's race problem could no longer be ignored. Since colonial times the 'Indian Question,' or who was an Indian, and how to assimilate and acculturate the Indian, had bedeviled Bolivia's intellectual and governing class. Morales embodied these doubts. Although hailed by most as the country's first 'Indian' president, Morales' claim to indigenous identity was not unchallenged. Among the early critics were indigenous leaders themselves – Felipe Quispe Huanca, Aymara chief of the Pachakuti Indigenous Movement, and Víctor Hugo Cardenas, Aymara vice-president in the 1990s. On the other hand, opponents (predominately mestizo and non-indigenous, and middle- and upper-class) pejoratively called him 'that [expletive deleted] Indian.'

Indeed, Morales' pro-indigenist politics raised these questions of identity and the complexities of race and class in Bolivia to a higher level. Based on the 2001 census, 62 percent of Bolivians over fifteen years of age self-identified as indigenous. The National Revolution in 1952 banned the term '*Indio*,' which had historically pejorative connotations, and substituted '*campesino*' or 'peasant,' and 1952 reforms abolished the worst abuses against the indigenous peoples. The 1994 constitutional reforms, which affirmed Bolivia's multi-ethnic heritage, reflected a positive change in attitudes. However, Morales' election evoked a special pride in identity and culture among indigenous peoples. Their prominent role in the Constituent Assembly – for example, Silvia Lazarte, a Quechua woman and leader of Bolivia's federation of peasant women, served as its president – and in drafting the new Constitution served as a tutorial in democracy as well as in the rough-and-tumble politics of social movements.

Elected in July 2006, the 255-member Constituent Assembly was dominated by Morales supporters – MAS and social movements representing women, peasants, indigenous and coca leaf growers (*cocaleros*) organizations. This heavily 'Indian' pro-government majority was critical to drafting radical reforms. However, regional, ethnic, and class tensions led to rancorous and chaotic sessions. There were deadlocks and suspensions, and its deadline had to be extended three times. In November 2007, protests and violent confrontations among opposing citizens groups and social movements camped out in the colonial city of Sucre (where the assembly first met) resulted in several deaths. The Assembly was temporarily suspended and finally was reconvened in Oruro, a highland mining town near Morales' staunch indigenous base in El Alto/La Paz. Opposition delegates and anti-Morales parties and social movements boycotted the final sessions. Nevertheless, the proposed constitution was passed in December 2007.

However, the opposition delegates rejected the draft charter as illegal because the final draft was passed in their absence. And in May and June 2008, Media Luna departmental referendums also rejected the draft charter and pushed for autonomy. For most of that year, the Morales government battled the fierce opposition to the constitutional reform organized by the Media Luna prefects and pro-autonomy social movements. In September there were some thirty deaths across the region, with the worst violence in northern Pando department, where eleven Morales supporters were killed and President Morales was forced to impose martial law.

Bolivia was mired in a protracted constitutional crisis over competing models of economy and governance and which of these models the new Constitution would reflect. On the one hand, there was the established model of limited neoliberal democracy based on a capitalist, private-sector-dominated economy and an elitist party-controlled political order. On the other, there was Morales' more inclusive socialist and populist model of a state-directed, social welfare economy and a pro-indigenous, citizens-based, social movement democracy. In effect the struggle over the country's legal and governing structures initiated a second constitutional war, not unlike the one in 1899 that shifted power from the old silver oligarchy in the southern valleys of Sucre to the new tin oligarchy of the northern highlands of La Paz. In both cases regionalism and class conflict played a role; as did racism, and an indigenous awakening and struggle for communitarian autonomy.[21]

Ultimately the contention and violence between pro- and anti-government groups, parties and social movements failed to derail the Bolivian Congress's ratification of a revised constitutional draft on 21 October 2008. After over two years of wrangling and conflict, President Morales and his pro-indigenist, MAS–social movement base were able to claim another success in refounding the country. On 25 January 2009, over 61 percent of Bolivian voters approved the new Political Constitution of the State (*Constitución Política del Estado*, CPE) in the nationwide constitutional referendum. However, in three Media Luna departments (Beni, Santa Cruz, and Tarija) a defiant and angry, and largely non-indigenous, majority rejected the new Constitution. Consequently social movement agitation and street violence, fiercely polarized along racist lines, once again escalated during the hectic months preceding the December 2009 presidential elections when the opposition still hoped to defeat Morales and reverse the constitutional reforms. After Morales' decisive reelection, however, constitutional opponents emphasized a strategy of parliamentary manipulation and obstruction of enabling legislation in order to stall and hobble reforms.

At the same time race continued to play a critical role not only in the relations between the government and the opposition, but also within the government's own support base. Indeed, throughout

Morales' second term, complex and contested issues of identity and race contributed to volatility in the social movements' support of and loyalty to the Morales–MAS government. In addition to high-profile indigenous figures like Quispe and Cardenas, who remained strong opponents of Morales, new local and regional indigenous leaders – many proclaiming more authentic indigenous credentials – emerged to criticize and challenge Morales' leadership, as well as capitalize on differences among themselves and their peasant-indigenous support-ers. In the 2009 presidential elections, for example, three indigenous-peasant candidates ran against Morales; and in mid-2010 peasant and indigenous-led protests erupted over the continued poverty and limited economic development in the mining region and city of Potosí. Splits also developed within the MAS political coalition and other indigenous-based political parties, unions and movements. Thus, for much of 2010 and 2011, the government confronted demonstrations and roadblocks by the historically militant Bolivian Workers' Central (COB), whose members demanded higher wages than Morales was willing to concede.

Most new Indian leaders of social movements operated more like a Quispe than a Cardenas, and fixated on the interests and goals of their own ethnic communities, class and regions, at times testing the pan-Indian and multi-ethnic and pluricultural reality of Morales' Bolivia.

Social movements and the drug war

'The fight for coca symbolizes our fight for freedom.' ... 'Coca growers will continue to grow coca. There will never be zero coca.' Evo Morales[22]

The 2005 election of Evo Morales delivered a former coca grower and long-time leader of the Cochabamba coca growers' unions (Federation of Coca Growers of the Tropical Region of the Chapare, and the Six Federations of the Peasants and Coca Growers of the Tropical Region of Cochabamba) into the country's highest office. In fact, Morales directly credited his political ascendancy to the support of the peasant coca growers' movement and other progressive social movements that had lobbied and demonstrated against repressive coca eradication policies, and forged a political alliance with the MAS party. Morales himself admitted as much in a rally in fall 2006, stating: 'The coca leaf made me president.'[23] These social movement ties and the new president's refusal to step down from his leadership role in the coca growers' associations raised concerns abroad – notably in Washington – over the future of Bolivia's anti-narcotics policy.

Indeed, Morales' overall response to the United States-inspired drug war policy indicated that his primary sympathies and loyalties have remained with his class and indigenous, social movement base. Nevertheless, he has had to manage a difficult situation as a friend and ally of the coca growers' movement, on the one hand, and as the country's highest official responsible for the reduction and regulation of coca leaf production, on the other. Moreover, despite tensions and clashes between his government and the growers, on balance Morales has occupied the driver's seat in his relationship with the coca growers' unions (one of the country's most powerful social movements), and has not been a mere hostage to the growers' interests and demands. Perhaps for all these reason his administration's anti-drug policies have been more successful in reducing violence and human rights violations, as well as illegal cultivation, than those of all previous governments.

During most of the Andean drug war years, Bolivian governments generally pursued aggressive – often coercive and violent – coca leaf eradication and anti-narcotics policies. Especially between 1985 and 2005, stricter legislation and militarized enforcement heavily controlled and criminalized the cultivation and distribution of coca leaf throughout the country with disastrous social and economic consequences. Aggressive anti-narcotics trafficking measures impoverished and incarcerated countless traditional and innocent coca growers not involved in the drug trade. Most were indigenous peasant farmers and former mineworkers – many migrants from the economically depressed highlands – who were connected, if at all, only indirectly on the growing end of the drug trade as a way to sustain their families. Few of the estimated 1,500–2,000 extended families in the main coca-leaf-growing area of the Chapare of Cochabamba department actually processed the leaves or supplied illegal coca paste to the cocaine production networks of the Andean drug cartels. Nevertheless, external drug reports tended to eschew fine distinctions and portrayed these growers as living 'off the cocaine business.'[24]

The increasingly combative Andean drug war served Evo Morales and the *cocalero* social movement politically and contributed overall to indigenous resurgence and grassroots organizing. At first the goal of coca leaf activists and indigenous peasant growers was to defend the people's right to cultivate the 'sacred coca leaf.' However, as localized resistance to militarization of Bolivia's drug war and coca leaf eradication erupted into ever more violent confrontations, the struggle mushroomed into a sweeping national social movement. In turn, the initially limited agenda to protect peasant growers and Bolivia's cultural heritage of the coca leaf from foreign threat expanded into an all-encompassing social movement for indigenous rights, empowerment and autonomy. The impressive political and electoral success of the MAS in the last two decades can be attributed as well to the party's avowed opposition to coca leaf eradication, and its close alliance with Morales' peasant and growers' unions and other progressive social movements. At times, these government–party–movement alliances have been strained as President Morales has had to insulate coca leaf growing from anti-drug enforcement.

The drug war has never been popular in Bolivia. For the majority of Bolivians the drug problem was primarily one of demand (by US and European markets) rather than supply. Still, most governments responded to pressure and aid from Washington, and readily supplemented strapped policing and military budgets with US anti-narcotics funding. Morales' policy has eschewed US aid, and focused more on economic development and the 'nationalization' of Bolivia's anti-drug policy. Also, the official Morales–MAS strategy (*'Estrategía de Lucha Contra el Narcotráfico y Revalorización de la Hoja de Coca'*) has stressed local 'social control' and self-verification of legal cultivation limits by farming communities and local federations. Morales popularized self-policing of coca production instead of centrally enforced eradication with the slogan 'no to zero coca leaf, yes to zero cocaine.'[25] He has implemented 'rationalization' (another official term) of coca leaf production or cooperative reduction of excess coca by limiting plots to one fourth of a hectare, or one *cato*, down from one hectare. The Morales government regulates the merchandizing of coca leaf by quantity and the markets where it can be sold legally and has negotiated agreements with the unions and legal producers' associations to respect the rules. Nevertheless, even the more relaxed official policy provoked tensions and sometimes outright conflict with the coca growers' federations, especially with non-unionized growers in areas of illicit coca cultivation, primarily the remote national parks.

In September 2006, two coca growers were killed in a confrontation with the Bolivian military eradication forces in the Carrasco National Park in the Yungas region north of La Paz. These peasant farmers were 'freelancers' and not affiliated with the coca growers' federations, especially the six federations of unionized coca growers in the Chapare with which the Morales government had an agreement. The government characterized these unaffiliated growers as drug traffickers. The landless peasant subsistence farmers insisted that the area was a permitted, traditional growing area according to an agreement with the previous Mesa government. The Morales–MAS government disagreed and argued that the area was very remote, without roads and markets, and that therefore the coca leaf was being grown for cocaine production. The government even suggested – as had many previous governments in similar situations in the past – that the growers were being armed by foreign narcotraffickers. Moreover, the events surrounding the deaths were contradictory, with the military forces claiming self-defense from 200 coca growers armed with guns and dynamite, and the growers insisting that the army had fired on them, and that they had been armed only with sticks, and had even tried to negotiate with the government for over a month.[26]

In meetings with Cochabamba's six coca growers' federations over the incident, the union leadership resolved to 'support the politics of the fight against narcotrafficking and the control of the government of our friend Evo Morales over coca plantations.'[27] From a cynical perspective, the federations' support of the Morales policy not only protected the Chapare growers' interests financially by limiting the supply of coca leaf and preventing a potential drop in price by over-supply, but also permitted the policy of 'coca yes, cocaine no' to work, thereby legitimizing only unionized activity and insulating it, and the Chapare region, from forcible eradication. Indeed, Law 1008, which had criminalized coca leaf cultivation in 1988, had considered the Chapare a zone of excess and illicit production, subject to eradication and strict production limits. However, an agreement that Evo Morales, as president of the Six Federations of the Tropics of Cochabamba, signed with former president Carlos Mesa in October 2004 recognized the Chapare cultivations as legal.[28]

Morales' policy of 'zero cocaine' has been applied strictly in the protected natural parks where no coca leaf or cocaine production has been tolerated. The Morales government has maintained that cultivations in remote park territories are illegal, and aggressively pursued eradication of thousands of acres of coca leaf plantings and dismantled thousands of unlawful squatter settlements. Although generally reluctant to negotiate with 'freelance,' non-unionized growers, the government sometimes agreed to dialogue, largely to prevent violence from escalating. Often authorities had to intervene to maintain peace between the highland indigenous coca growers and the lowland Indian peoples native to the parks, whose lands were being invaded and despoiled. In September 2009, a conflict between the native Indian communities and peasant coca growers erupted in the Isiboro Sécure National Park and Indigenous Territory (located in northern Cochabamba and southern Beni departments). There was a death and several wounded when the lowland Indians tried to expel the coca colonizers who had illegally occupied their lands, which were specially protected under the new Constitution. The indigenous vice-president of the Central Indígena de Pueblos del Oriente Boliviano (CIDOB) demanded that President Morales remove the *cocaleros* and drug traffickers from the area, or the thirty-four different lowland indigenous peoples would assert their rights and force the intruders out. And a leader of the National Confederation of Indigenous Women of Bolivia (Confederación Nacional de Mujeres Indígenas de Bolivia) complained that 'It would be grave if the president failed to defend the rights of indigenous peoples.'[29]

President Morales responded quickly, commenting that 'Something strange was occurring in Bolivia. Before confrontations were of the landless movement or over insufficient land or the indigenous against landowners ... Now confrontations were among compañeros.'[30] He called the illegal coca growers 'false' or 'pseudo *cocaleros*' and 'enemies of the defense of the coca leaf.'[31] He blamed the Isiboro Sécure confrontation on narcotraffickers – although he also lashed out at the US Agency for International Development, which had been ousted from Bolivia in 2008.[32] Indeed, twenty coca paste factories had been busted in the vicinity outside the park since the beginning of the year. The president ordered the eradication of the coca plantings and the relocation of the colonizers to other areas where land was available. Similar clashes occurred among lowland native communities, coca colonizers and anti-drug forces in Carrasco National Park in Cochabamba and other dense tropical forest regions like the remote South Yungas (La Paz department) town of La Asunta, considered a '*zona excedentaria*,' or an area of excess outside of a legal coca cultivation zone. Land where peasant growers could legally cultivate coca was indeed becoming a critical problem.

This forcible eradication policy in the national parks and other illegal and excess growing areas was criticized by unfederated growers and certain social movements and human rights groups as hypocritical because on the presidential stump candidate Morales had promised non-violent and negotiated eradication. However, lowland Indian communities not engaged in coca production approved and supported Morales' hard-line policy of forcible eradication. The 'divide and conquer' strategy was also acceptable to Cochabamba's six federation union leaders, who were not impacted by the crackdown on non-unionized growers. Indeed, they agreed not only to support but to assist the eradication efforts by the army and anti-narcotics police in the national parks.[33] Some critics concluded that the Morales anti-drug policy represented but another example 'of populist candidates who come to office only to turn on their most faithful followers.'[34] Although repression and violence – largely sporadic and limited – against coca growers are deplorable, this reading of the Morales–MAS strategy failed to credit its complexities and contradictions both domestically and internationally. Abroad, President Morales pushed his 'coca is not cocaine' campaign and he petitioned the UN Commission on Narcotic Drugs to decriminalize the coca leaf.

When the UN International Narcotics Control Board recommended even criminalizing coca chewing and tea in March 2008, Bolivians protested. In line with his 'yes to coca, no to cocaine' policy, President Morales responded and fiercely defended the coca leaf as 'an important symbol of the history and identity of the indigenous cultures of the Andes,' in a *New York Times* op-ed piece. At the same time, Morales stressed his administration's commitment to domestic and international anti-drug trafficking enforcement.[35] The result is that the MAS government has been reticent to eradicate coca crops outright (except in limited and non-sanctioned areas), instead emphasizing cocaine seizures, destruction of coca paste processing sites, and the interdiction of drugs and precursor chemicals.

The consequent decline in illegal coca leaf eradication, according to US and international anti-narcotics enforcement agencies, has been contested by the Morales government.[36, 37] In part, behind the numbers dispute is disagreement over how much coca leaf is and should be illegal, and if, where, and how it should be eradicated. As much for political as for practical reasons, the Morales government has pursued non-repressive and voluntary methods, insisting that negotiated agreements with the coca growers' unions and the direct collaboration of growers made eradication more effective. According to Washington, there was a significant increase in coca leaf cultivation in 2006–09, especially in the nontraditional coca-growing regions of Cochabamba and the Chapare, where Morales was reelected president of the *cocalero* federations. The Morales government countered that increased cultivation has supplied alternative products and traditional needs, which have increased significantly since the legal limit (12,000 hectares or 29,640 acres) was established in a 1971 study (and incorporated into Law 1008 in 1988), when the country's population was half its size and legitimate demand much lower. The Morales government insisted that after nearly forty years the legal limit almost needed to be doubled. The US administration was not persuaded and in 2009 blacklisted Bolivia for the first time as a major drug-producing country.[38]

In summary, the Morales–MAS government has persisted with its less repressive counter-drug strategy, largely avoiding eradication and confrontation with the unions and growers wherever and whenever possible, often balancing the competing interests of grassroots social movements representing growers and native peoples. The strategy stresses the 'fight against drug trafficking' and the 'revalorization of coca,' and focuses on five main areas: coca industrialization, integral development, voluntary and negotiated coca crop reduction, interdiction of drug trafficking, and drug use prevention.[39] The ultimate goal is to commercialize and market alternative coca leaf products, such as teas, foods, medicines, pharmaceuticals, and cosmetics, internationally. The European Union's support for alternative uses and commercialization of coca leaf for overseas markets provided hope in early 2009. Still, the defense of the coca leaf will continue to be an uphill battle for Morales and his indigenous and social movement supporters. If the strategy is to succeed, the 1961 UN Convention that prohibits coca production, industrialization and trade for export must be revised. And despite vigorous diplomatic efforts, Morales has made little headway on this front.

Whether the pro-coca-leaf campaign succeeds abroad or not, at home it has been enormously successful politically. The Morales policy, even as it tested relations between the reformist government and its popular social movement base, has tapped into Bolivian and indigenous nationalism and strengthened ethnic and class solidarity. President Morales, for example, increased his political and social capital with his supporters and Bolivians generally when he terminated the US Drug Enforcement Administration (DEA) operations in Bolivia in November 2008. The Morales–MAS anti-drug strategy, with its ability to influence and maneuver across the competing interests of diverse social movements, has been successful on the whole in reducing significantly conflict among peasant growers, indigenous organizations and the government. Nevertheless, the strategy has also exposed tensions and contradictions among social movements of the highlands and the lowlands, competitive and conflicting interests in how coca eradication, land reform, indigenous autonomy and environmental policies are implemented, as well as cross-purposes among the policies themselves.

Evo and social movements: here to stay (for now)

'.... and Evo Morales of Bolivia, is a new face of the utopian-revolutionary dreams ...'[40]

Bolivia's new social movements opened up political space for more radical parties such as the Movement toward Socialism and the

Pachakuti Indigenist Movement, and a multitude of alternative forms of political organization and civil society representation. By giving voice to popular and excluded groups, social movements 'democratized democracy,' to use a term President Morales has popularized. In turn, the new Constitution encouraged a unique form of social movement advocacy, representation and direct action that has been integral to Morales' style of populist leadership. The water and gas wars were prototypes of the radical new model. The nationalization struggles were won because mass social movements like the Coordinating Committee in Defense of Water and Life, and the Federation of Neighborhood Councils of El Alto stood up to injustice and misrule.

Bolivia's social movements remained engaged in the struggle over the implementation of regional and indigenous autonomy and the popular legalization and democratization of coca leaf cultivation. Opinion polls in fall 2009 indicated that eight of Bolivia's nine departments (except Oruro) favored some form of autonomy from the central government,[41] and over Morales' second term autonomy negotiations and disputes continued, as contentious enabling legislation and autonomy provisions were passed and implemented. In fact there were persistent strains and divisions in almost every aspect and sector of Bolivian society. Throughout it all, President Evo Morales has had to juggle multiple and at times competing roles and personas: populist reform president, defender of global indigenous and environmental rights, Aymara Supreme Leader, MAS party chief, and head of the Cochabamba coca leaf growers' union. And despite being a social movement, indigenous and *cocalero* president, Morales has not had a completely free hand with these activist, and often competing, constituencies, nor has his administration been immune to social movement protests.

In 2009, for example, militant coca growers demonstrated and raised roadblocks to protest coca criminalization and quotas. In July, with national elections on the horizon, President Morales called for a national referendum to establish a new coca policy for the country. He was responding directly to the demands of the *cocalero* movement and other progressive groups to reform Law 1008, which had established production quotas (based on decades-old census and consumption data) and originally criminalized coca leaf cultivation in nontraditional growing regions of the country. In the end, although Morales retained the support of the growers and the majority of the electorate, the strains within MAS and between the MAS government and President Morales' indigenous and social movement adherents were more pronounced beginning in 2009, especially over containment of coca leaf cultivation, the future role of popular movements, and the implementation of the new Constitution.

During the agitated campaigning for the 2009 elections, candidate Morales remained very sensitive to the demands of his indigenous, peasant, labor, and radical social movement base. For example, he launched his campaign in the Media Luna capital of Santa Cruz, timing the event to coincide with the twenty-seventh anniversary celebration of the lowlander Confederation of Indigenous Peoples of Bolivia (CIDOB). Still, there were disagreements as social movements and indigenous groups complained about Morales' concessions to opposition parties and the compromises that were struck in order to ensure passage of the new constitution and effective implementation of key structural reforms. Indigenous organizations were especially disappointed over the low number of special congressional seats reserved to leaders of indigenous and native peoples in the new constitution.[42]

In one sense, one may read these tensions as indicative of a healthy give and take or co-dependency, reciprocity and openness within Morales' indigenist populism and social movement style of democracy. Morales needed the social movements and they needed him; he could not always command the allegiance of indigenous organizations and social movements outright, and in turn these could not simply dictate government policy (even if they could agree on policy). To one degree or another, these actors were mutual stakeholders in the survival and success of the Morales–MAS government. But because these relations were complex and not always equal or complementary, frustrations and strains were to be expected. The fact that in 2006 the Aymara Indian community proclaimed Morales their Supreme Leader (*Apu Mallku*) did not translate simply or directly into automatic and limitless indigenous support.[43] Bolivia's indigenous and native peoples – some thirty-six distinct groups – are extremely diverse, with constantly shifting and often conflicting interests and alliances. Even between the two main highlander groups – the Aymara and Quechua – as well as within various native communities, squabbles and disagreements have been endemic. There are further divisions among mestizo rural and urban groups that may self-identify as indigenous but may differ in concerns and allegiances from less assimilated community-based indigenous organizations.

Consequently, it was no surprise that there were sporadic clashes among potential indigenous contenders and candidates at every governing level and in every region of the country. In one news-making incident in March 2009, indigenous Morales supporters (ostensibly without the support of the government, which criticized the over-zealous followers) attacked the home of Bolivia's former first Indian vice-president, Víctor Hugo Cárdenas. An outspoken critic of Morales, Cárdenas was a potentially formidable presidential challenger until the Aymara candidate of the Gente (People) citizen's association suddenly withdrew from the race in September. For much of the spring and early summer, Cárdenas had been a strongly favored opposition candidate, who many believed could split the indigenous vote and unseat Morales. However, a series of opinion polls indicated otherwise as he soon trailed badly behind other proposed candidates. Briefly, at one point there were three other peasant indigenous presidential candidates in the running. In the end, neither Cárdenas nor other indigenous leaders, most of whom lacked Cárdenas' high profile, stature and national experience, were able to seriously weaken or threaten Morales' significant following and persistent influence among indigenous groups and grassroots social movements.

In part, Morales' success lay in his deft maneuvering and populist charisma, and the loyalty and trust of his highlander (Aymara and Quechua) indigenous supporters. These shared a similar popular class status and identity, and a tradition of collectivist (communitarian) and syndicalist solidarity that peasant, mining, and coca growers' associations had developed over decades of social struggle. However, most important and central to Morales' success were his ethno-socialist ideology and ethno-cultural agenda. His first presidency had increased Indian nationalism and legitimized indigenous rule. In 2009 an unprecedented number of indigenous-peasant candidates ran for office and more indigenous citizens than ever voted in the December elections, upping Bolivia's overall voter participation rate to over 90 percent. Morales' success in enacting and implementing fundamental reforms, which directly benefited and empowered his social base, also energized and further mobilized them. These achievements created a collective interest and responsibility to defend Morales against the threatened counter-revolution by opposition parties and class and ethnic enemies on the right, if not always on the left. Still, in the polarized pre-electoral climate everything seemed reducible to the simple logic of 'us' versus 'them.' The alliance formed between President Morales and his social movement and indigenous supporters persisted 'for better or worse' because of a shared solidarity – class, ethno-cultural, and revolutionary. This solidarity, which never completely shielded Morales or his government from the criticism and grievances of supporters, seemed to peak in 2009, and became markedly strained during his second term.

The day that the new Constitution of State became law, 25 January 2009, marked a major achievement of this solidarity. In the words of President Morales: 'The colonial state ends here'; the refoundational Constitution enshrines 'the deepest aspirations of the most neglected sectors, such as the workers and indigenous peoples.'[44] However, both Morales and social movement activists recognized that the battle over Bolivia's new Constitution and pluricultural state structure was not over; indeed, pro-government supporters were forced to defend the Constitution on repeated occasions. Critical to that defense were the passage and implementation of enabling legislation which would determine how and if there would be elections under the new constitutional provisions. In April 2009, social movement protests finally secured passage of the fiercely contested Transitional Electoral Law No. 4021 by the opposition-controlled Bolivian Senate. The law favored MAS, as many critics charged, but more importantly the law facilitated independent citizens' associations and indigenous and social movements to nominate and elect their own candidates.

Despite passage of the electoral law, the path to the December elections was not all smooth for Morales and MAS. There were repeated challenges to the new 'biometric' or electronic electoral registration system instituted to prevent fraud, and the massive registration of nearly five million voters, including for the first time thousands of Bolivians living abroad, primarily in the United States, Spain, Argentina, and Brazil. Moreover, once the organizing and politicking in the many local, regional and national electoral campaigns across the country heated up, complaints quickly surfaced among the MAS-allied social movements and indigenous organizations. Discontent was largely over the formal party lists and charges that the MAS had favored more politically prominent and better-funded urban and middle-class candidates over poorer rural and indigenous ones. In a press interview in September, an indigenous deputy grumbled that across the country 'brothers from various social sectors were upset' because 'white people' (*'la gente blancoide'*) and upstarts had displaced them on MAS party lists.

The Bartolina Sisa Federation of Campesina and Indigenous Women (Federación de Mujeres Campesinas Bartolina Sisa, popularly known as the 'Bartolinas') also charged that the women's movement's representatives had been passed over.[45] Its president, Leónida Zurita Vargas, an internationally recognized leader and advocate for indigenous women and leader of the women's branch of the peasants' and coca growers' unions of the Cochabamba tropics, criticized the party list as a *'chairo'* (a popular Andean mixed vegetable soup) – in other words, a hetero-geneous mishmash without clear principles or ideological criteria of selection. Unfortunately, MAS may not have been completely at fault here as there was a chronic problem of gender inequality among indig-enous communities in Bolivia and elsewhere in the region.[46] Still, these complaints from grassroots supporters embarrassed the governing party. President Morales' response to discontent among social move-ment and indigenous supporters was to remind them that Bolivia was 'plurinational' and that no revolution had ever been successful without the support of the middle class. Therefore, his goal was an inclusive 'social pact' allying all social sectors behind revolutionary change.[47]

In contrast, the main opposition parties remained severely divided and flailing against the more coherent MAS campaign. Eventually, the conservative politicians' fanatical opposition to Morales and his social movement agenda brought about a strange and largely expedi-ent pro-autonomy coalition. Campaigning feverishly, the opposition forces appeared panicked that summer and fall, as a steady stream of opinion polls favored Morales by 20–40 percentage points over the seven other political fronts and coalitions fielding presidential candidates. Many believed that the desperate *autonomista* coalition of Manfred Reyes Villa and Leopoldo Fernández Ferreira of the Progress Plan for Bolivia–National Convergence (Plan Progreso para Bolivia–Convergencia Nacional, PPB–CN) would not attract sufficient votes for the presidency under any conditions. So the back-up plan was to secure enough legislative seats to impede reform.

Still, Reyes and Fernández, the two ex-prefects (governors) of Cocha-bamba and Pando departments, represented the Media Luna's last hope, and were heavily financed by powerful regional, conservative and elite interests. According to charges by the Morales government, money from exiled former president Gonzalo Sánchez de Lozada and USAID also found its way into conservative coffers. Nevertheless, the pro-autonomy ticket never gained legitimacy throughout the country, and was unfavorably linked to the return of neoliberalism. Questions of character swirled around both candidates as well: Reyes was associated with past military dictators and oligarchs, and Fernández was arrested for the dozen or so deaths in sectarian violence (which opponents labeled 'genocide') between pro- and anti-Morales groups in the small Pando town of Porvenir in September 2008.

The pre-electoral strategy of the two major political fronts demon-strated a somewhat cynical pragmatism. While social movements of every stripe (ideological, class, ethnic, and regional) typically sought to appeal to traditional supporters and loyalists, the major political contenders focused on expanding and diversifying the voter base. Thus the MAS electoral front curried favor with the urban middle class and largely took its traditional indigenous and social movement base for granted. In turn, the Media Luna coalition courted the popular rural classes, and backed the candidacies of a record number of indigenous peasants and lowland Indians. Party platforms were also moderated and pitched to target audiences. The Reyes–Fernández electoral convergence, for example, promised increased development and investment in the economy to attract poorer voters. All of the seven anti-government contenders in the race proposed revisions to the 2009 Constitution. On the other hand, the official MAS coalition used the opposition groups' promised constitutional modifications to instill fear of unrest if activist social movements and civil society were thwarted by a reversal of reforms.[48] Capitalizing on this threat of counter-revolution, Morales and his running mate, Alvaro García Linera, warned voters (and any potentially disaffected supporters) that victory by the parties of the right meant the return of neoliberalism and neocolonialism. And the gains that the popular classes and indigenous sectors of society had achieved with the Morales Revolution, and still hoped to achieve, would end with the defeat of the Morales–MAS coalition.

Once again the electoral outcome was a historic and decisive victory for Evo Morales and the MAS. Nevertheless, despite the impressive voter turnout and support, especially among the indigenous and social movements, a number of difficult and contentious problems dogged Morales' second term. A majority of the eastern and southeastern lowlanders of the Media Luna remained deeply suspicious of, and disaffected by, Morales' indigenous and revolutionary populism. Angry and frustrated Camba (lowlander) patriots continued to demand regional autonomy (even outright secession) to protect their way of life, vast land and rich hydrocarbon resources from the grasp of the highlander- and Indian-dominated central government.

Clearly class conflict played an important, but not always dominant, role in the regionalist struggle against Morales. For the reactionary lowlander oligarchy – the few wealthy and powerful landowning families, cattle barons, and agro-business entrepreneurs and exporters of the Media Luna – there were no contradictions between Camba nationalism and their class interests. However, for many middle-class and poor and rural lowlanders, who supported the reactionary *autonomistas* and voted against the Morales–MAS reforms, their fierce regional loyalties and racist sentiments seemed to outweigh their true class interests.

These contradictions indicated that Bolivia remained sharply polarized not simply over class and competing political-economic orders (revolutionary versus reactionary), but also over competing regionalist nationalisms and ethnic identities (Camba versus Kolla).

In mid-July 2010, the comprehensive Framework Law of Autonomy (*Ley Marco de Autonomías*) was passed. The legislative autonomy package encompassed five specific laws establishing how autonomy would be implemented in the departments, municipalities and indigenous territories, and applied to key governing structures and functions – the judiciary, constitutional court, electoral body, and electoral procedures – including suspension of officials for corruption and malfeasance. There had been months of bitter wrangling and stalemate as parliamentarians endlessly debated every aspect of these laws. Meanwhile, opposing social movements again resorted to marches, protests and hunger strikes (including several threatened by President Morales) to influence the lawmakers and express support for and against the legislation. Finally a majority coalition of MAS, MSM (Movement without Fear) and indigenous legislators provided the decisive support.

The 2010 enactment represented a significant achievement not only because it had to overcome intractable opposition from conservative sectors, but also because of disagreement among pro-government deputies and lowlander indigenous groups. The indigenous and El Alto-based Movement without Fear has had differences with MAS, especially during the April departmental and municipal elections, and these persisted into 2011. There was also the threat of another massive march on La Paz by the Confederation of Indigenous Peoples of Eastern Bolivia (CIDOB) over the autonomy of native lands. As expected, reaction to the new autonomy legislation was highly polarized. An opposition commentator criticized the autonomy statutes as an unwarranted expansion of the MAS party's power from the control of government to the usurpation of total power. On the other hand, a pro-government Quechua congresswoman stressed how the autonomy provisions were inclusive and recognized everyone's interests.[49] The Media Luna departments, meanwhile, denounced the autonomy law and proceeded to follow their own regional autonomy statutes. These divisive issues continued to be hammered out and disputed in 2011 and 2012, as regional legislatures and opposition leaders persisted in defying the central government in La Paz however and whenever they could, while the MAS government steadily and relentlessly forged ahead with the implementation of one constitutional reform law after another.

During his second term, President Morales has been challenged as well by his own supporters and social movement base, making the task of governing especially difficult. Early on, the first Morales–MAS administration recognized the necessity of managing the new social movements, and established the office of Vice-Minister of Coordination with Social Movements (Coordinación con los Movimientos Sociales), and the National Coordination for Change (Coordinadora Nacional para el Cambio, CONALCAM). In 2010, the government described CONALCAM as an 'anti-imperialist, anti-neoliberal, and anti-colonial' entity in support of the plurinational state and Constitution, and communitarian socialism.[50] The political opposition criticized it as an extra-constitutional, 'superpower'-like arm of the MAS government, or a kind of high command for the popular forces ('*estado mayor del pueblo*'). And in the government's maneuvers with recalcitrant social movements, CONALCAM has served as officialdom's loyal 'shock troops' ('*aparato de choque*').

In 2011, Vice-Minister Navarro, a former MAS deputy, was returned to his post in the Coordination with the mandate to improve the deteriorating relations between the government and the country's unions and allied social movements. Navarro was central in orchestrating the government's hard-line response to the protracted confrontation with the main labor union, the Bolivian Workers' Central (Central Obrera Boliviana, COB). The union, which represented most Bolivian workers other than the coca growers and peasants, such as teachers, state employees, transportation and factory workers, artisans and miners, insisted on a higher wage increase (15 percent to cover a steadily rising cost of living) than the government offered (10 percent to keep down the deficit). Navarro – echoing Vice-President García Linera and Morales himself – denounced the COB protests, roadblocks and strikes as 'reactionary' and 'counter-revolutionary.'[51]

As the tense situation escalated in April and May, ideology, class, and race further complicated the union–government stand-off and pitted the pro-government social movements of the CONALCAM, primarily the peasant unions, *cocaleros* and 'Bartolinas,' against the workers' movements. The COB, historically aligned with socialist and Marxist parties, was supported on the left by (the Trotskyite) Revolutionary Workers' Party (Partido Obrero Revolucionario, POR) and the Movement without Fear (Movimiento Sin Miedo, MSM), which had defected from the MAS governing coalition. Rather than concentrate their attack on Morales directly, the COB, which also represented a pro-indigenous and progressive rank and file, blamed García Linera (the typical response of opponents and critics alike), and called for the vice-president's impeachment. During more collaborative meetings, the government emphasized points of agreement, such as the co-sponsorship of legislation to revoke the despised Supreme Decree 21060, which had established the neoliberal state and economic structures of 1986–2005, and launched the massive privatizations that had devastated workers and peasants. After more conflictive ones, Morales excoriated the COB and pro-labor social movement sympathizers for playing into the hands of the anti-indigenist and conservative opposition. The whole affair was sadly reminiscent of the old-style, pre-1992 clientelist politics of the MNR and the military–peasant pact against miners and workers that had divided (and weakened) the popular and progressive forces during the years of military dictatorship.

To date, Bolivia's highly participatory social movement democracy has had a serious downside: it has been too contentious and disruptive. In part, Evo Morales was first elected in 2005 because voters believed (and hoped) that he could bring an end to the cycles of protests, violence and governing instability that had prevailed since 2000. The Morales–MAS ticket was reelected in 2009, perhaps also in part because voters may have believed that, with the refounding of the new state, the worst was behind them. However, chronic protests and roadblocks have persisted into Morales' second term by opponents and social movement allies alike. High fuel prices and the government's attempt to end an energy subsidy set off a mini gas war, the 'Gasolinazo,' in December 2010. Unrest remained unabated in the tropical lowlands, where indigenous communities clashed with local groups over land reform and autonomy. And, just as in the past, the COB–government strife of 2011 disrupted economic activity and daily life with major roadblocks around the capital and country.

What will happen during the rest of Morales' second administration is sure to have decisive consequences for social movement democracy, the future of Morales and the MAS, and the continued progress for indigenous peoples. Thus far the crowning achievement of Evo Morales' social movement presidency and refounding revolution remains the progressive 2009 Political Constitution of the State (*Constitución Política del Estado*, CPE). Years in the making and overwhelmingly approved despite often violent opposition, the radical new charter extends sweeping political, social and economic rights to all Bolivians – especially those previously excluded for reasons of class and/or race. As long as the new Magna Carta is the law of the land, the promises of social welfare, land reform, environmental protection, sovereignty over natural resources, economic development, and greater legal protections and self-governance remain achievable. The new constitutional order has succeeded in reinforcing the importance of elections and democracy in determining the country's policies and future path. Indeed, the new constitution has fundamentally 'democratized' Bolivian democracy, and furthered the goal of the Morales government to establish 'a new state, a new economy, and a new society.'[52]

Central to this revolutionary goal has been the innovative blending of Western-style representative democracy and a more participatory and communitarian form of Andean democracy.[53, 54] Foremost in this hybridization process have been the activism of grassroots social movements and their complex relationships (both complementary and conflictive) with a movements-based president, party and government. Evo Morales, as an Indian and social movement president steadily advancing an ambitious populist and indigenous agenda against virulent opposition, has served an important mobilizing and catalytic role within Bolivia. He also has been a role model and example of a new form of socio-political leadership that has been more responsive to popular demands. Like a number of new social movements and indigenous community leaders, Morales developed his political leadership skills and credentials working his way up from grassroots advocacy and organizing. This bottom-up process, versus the exclusionary top-down old party system model, represented a new and alternative paradigm that has been particularly effective in developing new indigenous leaders and mobilizing Bolivia's ethno-political forces.[55] Moreover, Morales' presidency has been unique among Latin American leaders, providing an instructive lesson on how building trust and a working alliance between social movements and a progressive, like-minded executive can advance fundamental reforms within the democratic process and without destructive violent revolution.

The continued support of Bolivia's new social movements may allow President Morales' indigenist and populist revolution to consolidate its gains in the years ahead and fulfill many of the lofty promises of the new Constitution, especially comprehensive land reform and socio-economic redistribution and development. However, these goals will not be achieved easily or always peacefully. Indeed, the late sociologist Ralf Dahrendorf held that 'democracy is "about organizing conflict and living with conflict."'[56] The new plurinational Bolivia remains a land of instability and conflict, where civil discord has been inherent to democratization and social and revolutionary change, and Bolivia's indigenous and popular social movements are integral to that ongoing process.

Notes

1 James Petras and Henry Veltmeyer, *What's Left in Latin America? Regime Change in New Times* (Burlington, VT: Ashgate, 2009).

2 Moisés Naím, 'From normalcy to lunacy,' *Foreign Policy*, March/April 2004, www.foreignpolicy.com/story/cms.php?story_id=2522 (accessed 17 July 2009).

3 Ibid.; Petras and Veltmeyer, *What's Left in Latin America?*; Douglas Farah, 'The ghost of Che,' *Foreign Policy*, 17 July 2009, www.foreignpolicy.com/articles/2009/07/17/the_ghost_of_che (accessed 21 July 2009).

4 Petras and Veltmeyer, *What's Left in Latin America?*.

5 Sergio Berensztein, 'The closing of the Argentine mind,' *Foreign Policy*, January/February 2004, www.foreignpolicy.com/story/cms.php?story_id=2449 (accessed 17 July 2009).

6 Naím, 'From normalcy to lunacy.'

7 Donna Lee Van Cott, *Radical Democracy in the Andes* (New York: Cambridge University Press, 2008), pp. 44–5.

8 Waltraud Q. Morales, 'Bolivia,' in Harry E. Vanden and Gary Prevost (eds), *Politics of Latin America: The Power Game* (New York: Cambridge University Press, 2009), pp. 557–8; p. 576.

9 Oscar R. Olivera, *Cochabamba! Water War in Bolivia* (Cambridge, MA: South End Press, 2004).

10 Willem Assies, 'David versus Goliath in Cochabamba: water rights, neoliberalism, and the revival of social protest in Bolivia,' *Latin American Perspectives*, 30, 2003, pp. 14–36.

11 Benjamin Dangl, *The Price of Fire: Resource Wars and Social Movements in Bolivia* (Oakland, CA: AK Press, 2007), p. 150.

12 Martin Mendoza-Botelho, 'Quality of democracy in Bolivia: national contestation and grassroots popular participation,' in Daniel Levine and José Molina (eds), *Evaluating the Quality of Democracy in Latin America* (University Park: Penn State University Press, 2010).

13 Rodrigo Vazquez, 'Viewpoint: a new nationalism,' *BBC News*, 9 October 2007, news.bbc.co.uk/go/pr/fr/-/2/hi/americas/7035944.stm (accessed 16 March 2009).

14 Elizabeth Paravincini G., 'Indígena con mayoría absoluta asumirá gobierno el 22 de enero,' *Los Tiempos USA*, 23–29 December 2005, p. A8.

15 Chris Sweeney, 'Bolivia: between popular reform and illegal resistance,' Council on Hemispheric Affairs, 24 June 2008, www.coha.org/bolivia-straddles-between-popular-reform-and-illegal-resistance/ (accessed 11 October 2009).

16 Gaceta Oficial de Bolivia, Decreto Supremo no. 28701, 'Heroes del Chaco,' 1 May 2006, Agencia Boliviana de Información: Documentos-Decreto Nacionalización, www.constituyentesoberana.org/noticiasdeldia/mayo2006/010506_4.htm (accessed 11 October 2009).

17 Petras and Veltmeyer, *What's Left in Latin America*, p. 107.

18 America Vera-Zavala, 'Evo Morales has plans for Bolivia,' *In These Times*, 18 December 2005, www.inthesetimes.com/site/main/print/evo_morales_has_plans_for_bolivia/ (accessed 2 February 2006).

19 Katherine Charin, 'A belated happy World Environment Day, President Morales,' Council on Hemispheric Affairs, 23 June 2010, www.coha.org/a-belated-happy-world-environment-day-president-morales/ (accessed 7 July 2010).

20 Jonathan Rugman and Dan Glaister, 'Thousands throng streets as Bolivian leader sheds tears but talks tough at inauguration,' *Guardian*, 23 January 2006, www.guardian.co.uk/world/2006/jan/23/topstories3.mainsection (accessed 2 February 2006).

21 Waltraud Q. Morales, *A Brief History of Bolivia* (New York: Checkmark Books, Facts on File, 2004), pp. 87–90.

22 Steve Boggan, 'Coca is a way of life,' *Guardian*, 9 February 2006, www.guardian.co.uk/world/2006/feb/09/features11.g2 (accessed 12 February 2006).

23 April Howard, 'Bolivia: coca growers killed in action approved by Morales administration,' Global Research, 14 October 2006, taken from UpsideDownworld.org, www.globalresearch.ca/index.php?context=va&aid=3481 (accessed 7 September 2009).

24 Danna Harman, 'In Bolivia, a setback for U.S. anti-coca drive,' *Christian Science Monitor*, 22 December 2005, www.csmonitor.com/2005/1222/p04s02-woam.html (accessed 17 October 2009).

25 International Crisis Group, 'Bolivia's rocky road to reforms' (Bogotá/Brussels: International Crisis Group), *Latin America Report*, 18, 3 July 2006, pp. 1–37; p. 27, www.crisisgroup.org/library/documents/latin_america/18_bolivia_s_rocky_road_to_reforms.pdf (accessed 27 March 2009).

26 Howard, 'Bolivia: coca growers killed in action approved by Morales administration.'

27 Ibid.

28 La Prensa, 'Viceministro de la Coca asegura que la hoja chapareña es legal,' 17 October 2009, www.laprensa.com.bo/noticias/17-10-09/noticias.php?nota=17_10_09_poli6.php (accessed 18 October 2009).

29 La Razón, 'Indígenas piden a Evo respeto a la ley y control de cocaleros,' Edición Digital, 28 September 2009, www.la-razon.com/versiones/20090928_006864/nota_249_886164.htm (accessed 28 September 2009).

30 El Deber, 'Indígenas exigen el desalojo de campesinos del Isiboro Sécure,' 29 September 2009, www.eldeber.com.bo/2009/2009-09-29/vernotanacional.php?id=090929002527 (accessed 29 September 2009).

31 La Razón, 'Indígenas piden a Evo.'

32 Jornada, 'Evo: USAID causa conflicto por tierras para debilitar al Gobierno,' 2 October 2009, www.jornadanet.com/n.php?a=37997-1 (accessed 2 October 2009).

33 Howard, 'Bolivia: coca growers killed in action approved by Morales administration.'

34 Ibid.

35 Evo Morales Ayma, 'Let me chew my coca leaves,' *New York Times*, 14 March 2009, p. A17.

36 International Crisis Group, 'Bolivia's reforms: the danger of new conflict' (Bogotá/Brussels: International Crisis Group), *Latin America Briefing*, 13, 8 January 2007, pp. 1–15; p. 13, www.crisisgroup.org/library/documents/latin_america/b13_bolivias_reforms___the_danger_of_new_conflicts.pdf (accessed 27 March 2009).

37 United Nations, *World Drug Report 2008*, United Nations Office of Drugs and Crime, www.unodc.org/unodc/en/data-and-analysis/WDR-2008.html (accessed 12 March 2009).

38 Tejas Kadia, 'Drug enforcement in Bolivia: yes to coca, no to cocaine,' Latin America Information Office, 1 January 2009, pp. 1–6; p. 4, www.lataminfo.org/post/wp-content/uploads/2009/01/bolivia-drug-fact-

sheet-final.pdf (accessed 30 March 2009).

39 International Crisis Group, 'Bolivia's reforms: the danger of new conflict.'

40 Douglas Farah, 'The ghost of Che,' *Foreign Policy*, 17 July 2009, www.foreignpolicy.com/articles/2009/07/17/the_ghost_of_che (accessed 21 July 2009).

41 Los Tiempos.com, '8 departamentos ya aceptan autonomía,' 12 October 2009, www.lostiempos.com/diario/actualidad/nacional/20091012/9-departamentos-ya-aceptan-autonomia_40349_68270.html (accessed 12 October 2009).

42 Erin Hathaway, 'Morales leads undefined Bolivian presidential race,' Andean Information Network, 20 August 2009, ain-bolivia.org (accessed 13 September 2009).

43 Charin, 'A belated happy World Environment Day, President Morales.'

44 BBC News, 'New Bolivia Constitution in force,' 7 February 2009, news.bbc.co.uk/2/hi/america/7877107.stm (accessed 30 March 2009); and 'Bolivians "back new Constitution,"' 26 January 2009, news.bbc.co.uk/2/hi/americas/7849666.stm (accessed 30 March 2009).

45 La Razón, 'En el MAS hay molestia por las candidaturas,' Edición Digital, 9 September 2009, www.la-razon.com/ versiones/ 200 90910_006846/nota_249_876356.htm (accessed 10 September 2009).

46 Ramiro Escobar, 'Indigenous women: invisible citizens,' *Latinamerica Press*, 2 July 2009, www.lapress.org/articles.asp?art=5894 (accessed 16 July 2009).

47 Alcócer Caero Gisela, 'Masistas buscan seducer a clase media,' *Los Tiempos*, 13 September 2009, www.lostiempos.com/diario/actualidad/nacional/20090913/masistas-buscan-seducir-a-clase-media_36331_59975.html (accessed 13 September 2009).

48 Rosario Paz Monasterios, 'A excepción del MAS, todos los frentes proponen ajustes a CPE,' *La Prensa*, 5 October 2009, www.laprensa.com.bo/noticias/05-10-09/noticias.php?nota=05_10_09_poli5.php (accessed 5 October 2009).

49 Mery Vaca, 'Bolivia concluye el rediseño del Estado,' BBB Mundo, 18 July 2010, www.bbc.co.uk/mundo/america_latina/2010/07/100718_bolivia_ley_autonomias_amab.shtml (accessed 19 July 2010).

50 Cambio, 'Navarro: Conalcam solo será un organismo de coordinación,' 9 January 2010, www.cambio.bo/noticia.php?fecha=2010-09-01&idn=26830 (accessed 8 May 2011).

51 Página Siete, 'César Navarro dice que cúpula sindical es "reaccionaria,"' 20 April 2011, www.paginasiete.bo/2011-05-01/Nacional/Destacados/02Nalo2010511.aspx (accessed 12 May 2011).

52 El Día.com, 'García Linera ve muy bien las cosas en el país,' 12 October 2009, eldia.com.bo/?cat=148&pla=3&id_articulo=17103 (accessed 12 October 2009).

53 Mendoza-Botelho, 'Quality of democracy in Bolivia.'

54 David Booth, Suzanne Clisby and Charlotta Widmark, *Popular Participation: Democratising the State in Rural Bolivia* (Stockholm: Swedish International Development Cooperation Agency [SIDA], 1997).

55 Mendoza-Botelho, 'Quality of democracy in Bolivia.'

56 William Grimes, 'Ralf Dahrendorf, sociologist, dies at 80,' *New York Times*, 22 June 2009, p. A19.

4 | Dilemmas of urban popular movements in popular-sector *comunas* of Santiago, Chile

EDWARD GREAVES

This chapter on contemporary political battles in Santiago, Chile fits well into the overall theme of this volume: the challenge that progressive social movements face when parties of the left hold power. Because the left came to power earlier in Chile than elsewhere in the hemisphere, it is possible to draw up a longer balance sheet on the effect that prolonged government power from the left has on social movements. The Chilean left is the Chilean Socialist Party, which entered government in coalition with Christian Democratic presidents in the 1990s and then with its leaders, Ricardo Lagos and Michelle Bachelet, assuming the presidency within the *concertación* coalition in the 2000s. This long period of social democratic rule, following the era of Augusto Pinochet, has resulted in profound challenges for the social movements that developed during the dictatorship. The chapter will demonstrate how especially urban social movements were drawn into projects of the social democratic government that compromised the independence of these groups while giving them some channels for redress of their grievances. In early 2010 Chilean politics shifted to the right with the election of Sebastián Piñera. The return of the right to power by democratic election may result in a repositioning of the social movements, but full exploration of that question will require further research.

> Chile is the most neoliberalized country in Latin America. They are now neoliberalizing our community and our city ... our struggle is about the right of *pobladores*[1] to the city. Are we going to quietly let them move us all to the urban periphery, where we will be invisible and have long commutes to work? The *pobladores* built Peñalolen, and now they want to take it away from us. This struggle is difficult because popular culture has also been neoliberalized. *Pobladores* have lost the sense of solidarity and collective struggle that they once had. The problems of the *pobladores* have been individualized so that they view their struggles in individual terms.[2]

Introduction: socio-spatial struggle in the neoliberal era

The above statement was made by Lautaro Guanca, an activist in Peñalolen, a *comuna*[3] (commune) in the eastern sector of Santiago. This chapter examines the efforts of the Council of Social Movements of Peñalolen (CMSP) to mobilize the urban popular organizations of the *comuna* in opposition to the efforts of the Municipality of Peñalolen to modify its *Plan Regulador* (the zoning ordinances and regulations regarding the use of space). The goal is to shed light on many of the dilemmas that have confronted urban popular movements in post-dictatorship Chile.

Over the last decade, urban growth and the outward expansion of Santiago have been a catalyst for a number of spatial conflicts, which are conflicts that pit local communities against urban planners and large and politically influential '*inmobiliarias*' (construction firms that specialize in building apartments) over the use of space. In the more affluent *comunas* of Santiago, urban spatial conflicts have generally pitted well-to-do 'NIMBY' activists who oppose the construction of '*torres*' (high-rise apartment buildings) in their neighborhoods or the construction of major thoroughfares near their homes. Local groups in some of the older neighborhoods of Santiago have also organized and mobilized to preserve the traditional architecture, which in some areas of the city has also been a catalyst for urban gentrification.

In the low-income *comunas* of Santiago, by contrast, many spatial conflicts continue to be associated with more fundamental issues that have to do with access to adequate housing, community infrastructure (parks, etc.) and much-needed social services. Thirty years of neoliberal housing and urban development policies, however, have transformed the dynamics of urban spatial conflicts. The massive construction of small and often shoddily built low-income social housing in the peripheral *comunas* of Santiago (San Bernardo, La Pintana, Puente Alto, La Granja) over the last twenty-five years has been quite successful in significantly alleviating the chronic housing deficit in the city. Indeed, from 1985 to 2005, 200,000 'social homes' (*viviendas sociales*) were built in Santiago. As a result, nearly one fifth of the population of Santiago – 1.5 million people – now lives in subsidized social housing, much of which is concentrated in the urban periphery.

The housing question in contemporary Chile, then, has less to do with a chronic deficit of affordable housing for the urban poor than it does with the problems and contradictions created as a result of the successful drive to eradicate Santiago's squatters' settlements. In the latter 1970s, the Pinochet regime began to eradicate illegal squatter settlements (*campamentos*) by moving them to subsidized 'social housing,' which was built by private construction companies that had purchased large tracts of cheap land in the urban periphery of Santiago. With minor modifications, the policy that was adopted by the Pinochet regime was continued through the two decades of *concertación* rule.

In the last decade, however, it has become increasingly evident that the policy of warehousing the urban poor in shoddily built, poorly equipped, and overcrowded social housing blocks on the periphery of the city has given rise to a particularly 'malignant'[4] form of socio-spatial segregation that is accompanied by a number of undesirable social side effects. Among these are domestic violence that stems from extreme overcrowding and an absence of sociability owing to the destruction of community and social networks and the lack of public space. Indeed, the densely packed blocks of 'social housing' that paint a bleak urban landscape in many *comunas* of Santiago's urban periphery can be seen as the uglier side of the neoliberal miracle in Chile – the side that the tourists don't see.

Some analysts have argued that the 'social housing' blocks built over the last two decades have also been a species of social incubator for the transformation of urban poverty. The 'new urban poverty' that emerged in these areas, argue some analysts, has much more in common with the 'underclass' of the cities of the United States and Europe than it does with the poverty of the Third World squatter settlement.[5] In sum, housing policies during the neoliberal era were a catalyst for the transformation of urban poverty.[6]

As private banks have begun to assume responsibility for the debts of the beneficiaries of subsidized 'social housing' programs, the issue of debt and the prospect of eviction has also emerged. In some areas, the prospect of eviction has become an acute problem for many residents of low-income social housing. This led to the creation of the National Association of Home Debtors (Asociación Nacional de Deudores Habitacionales – ANDHA Chile), an organization that has emerged in the last decade to demand a moratorium on evictions and action from the government to ameliorate the problem. An activist in ANDHA Chile stated the matter bluntly: 'The government would forgive the debtors who owe money on their homes. The banks don't forgive anything ... they will come here and evict you and sell your home ... all they care about is money.'[7]

Moreover, as Santiago has expanded outward and space in many of the inner *comunas* of the city has become scarce and more expensive, communities in many low-income *comunas* have also begun to feel the forces of urban gentrification as many of these areas have suddenly become attractive to middle- and upper-middle-class families seeking housing. In the last decade in particular, construction companies and urban developers have also begun building 'fortified' enclaves – gated communities and condominiums – in *comunas* that have traditionally been seen as low-income areas.[8] The construction of highways and the extension of Santiago's subway system made these *comunas* more attractive to middle- and upper-middle-class families seeking afford-able housing. Urban gentrification, moreover, is changing the political calculus of municipal governments that seek to expand their revenue bases by attracting more affluent residents to their *comunas*.

Urban socio-spatial conflict in Peñalolen

As a socially heterogeneous and rapidly growing *comuna* of 240,000 nestled against the base of the foothills of the Andes cordillera, Peñalo-len can be seen as a microcosm of urban socio-spatial conflict in the era of neoliberal hegemony. Peñalolen has had a long history of social conflict that pits squatters' organizations and urban popular movements seeking access to land on which to build homes against the Chilean state. In the 1960s and 1970s, Peñalolen was the site of several large '*tomas*' – land seizures that were carried out by organized squatters' movements. Once seen as a peripheral *comuna* made up largely of low-income *poblaciones* and shantytowns, Peñalolen's relative proximity to downtown Santiago and its location adjacent to the more affluent *comunas* of Nuñoa, La Reina, and Las Condes, combined with the dynamics of urbanization and the growth of Santiago, have made it an attractive site for the construction of more affluent and upscale housing. Since the transition to democracy in 1990, Peñalolen has once again become an epicenter of urban socio-spatial conflict in Santiago. Indeed, since the transition, Peñalolen has been the site of the only successful large-scale *toma* in Santiago.

In the early morning of 4 July 1998, 1,800 *allegado*[9] families and committees organized a *toma* on Nasur, a tract of unused land in northeastern Peñalolen that had once been used as a sports field. The shantytown that gradually took shape there over the next few months has since become known simply as the '*toma* of Peñalolen.' When it happened, the *toma* garnered national attention because it was seen as an assault on private property. Thirteen years later, however, approx-imately four hundred families continue to live in relative obscurity in the flimsily built shacks of the *toma*. The *toma* is now surrounded by twelve-foot-high steel fences that were erected by the municipality and the police. Police guard the entrances to the *toma* in order to make sure that nobody is able to bring in the kind of building materials that can be used to begin to build viable long-term homes. Indeed, in order to bring in any kind of non-food items, the *pobladores* of the *toma* must obtain written authorization from the municipality. The fence is also part of a campaign by the municipality that is designed to harass, socially isolate, and stigmatize the residents of the *toma*. In this species of twenty-first-century ghetto, the *pobladores* of the *toma* wait for what they refer to simply as a '*solución*' – a 'solution' to their demands for a home.

Since the 1998 *toma*, moreover, many of the approximately 19,000 *allegado* families that currently live in Peñalolen have organized the 'Unitary Movement of Allegados' (Movimiento Unitario de Allega-dos – MUA), to demand that a housing solution be found for them in Peñalolen. Many of the *allegados* were born in Peñalolen and thus see Peñalolen as their home, and therefore do not want to be moved to *comunas* in the urban periphery (La Pintana, San Bernardo, Puente Alto) in order to obtain a solution to their housing problem. As comments by the president of MUA suggest, many *allegados* see their struggle in class terms and their demand for a home in Peñalolen through the prism of a right to the city:

> We have the same right to the city that the *cuicos* do. Why should we
> have to move to the urban periphery in order to obtain a *solución*?
> Peñalolen belongs to us. Let the *cuicos* go and find homes somewhere
> else, we were here first. Our families built Peñalolen, and now the *cui-*
> *cos* want to move us out.[10]

Paraphrasing Henri Lefebvre,[11] the French analyst of urban space, Lautaro argues that urban socio-spatial conflict in Peñalolen is a class conflict over 'the right to the city,' a key dimension of which involves the right to define how urban space will be organized and used.

Demands for a housing solution in Peñalolen, and more broadly for the right to a voice in determining how urban space is organized and used, were catalysts for the creation of the Council of Social Move-ments of Peñalolen (Consejo de Movimientos Sociales de Peñalolen, CMSP). The CMSP is a small network of *poblador* (i.e. urban poor and shantytown dwellers) organizations that has emerged in Peñalolen over the last year in order to oppose a set of proposals put forth by the municipality in 2009 which would modify the *comuna's* 'plan regulador.' The *plan regulador* is the set of ordinances and regulations regarding the use of space; these include zoning and land-use ordinances, ordinances regarding transportation networks, and regulations that establish population densities and building heights of residential areas. CMSP activists want to derail the municipality's proposals to modify the *plan regulador*, which they believe serves the interests of the rich and powerful *inmobiliarias* at the expense of the *allegados* and the poor. Their demands call for designating much more space for the construction of social housing for the *allegados* of Peñalolen.

The CMSP is a loosely knit, horizontally structured coalition of local popular organizations and social movement organizations. The most important of these is the Movement of Pobladores in Struggle (Movimiento de Pobladores en Lucha – MPL). Created and led by Lautaro Guanca in 2005, the MPL was formed to help *allegado* families in Peñalolen obtain subsidized low-income 'social housing' (*vivienda social*). Since its creation, the goals of the MPL have evolved and changed in a number of ways. A second local organization in the coalition is the Unitary Movement of Allegados (Movimiento Unitario de Allegados – MUA), which represents a network of *allegado* committees (*comités de allegado*) in Peñalolen. Finally, a number of cultural groups that seek to 'recover' popular identity through popular education are also affiliated to the CMSP. In addition, some of Peñalolen's neighborhood councils have also participated in the CMSP's activities, but only a small number have become formally affiliated with the CMSP.

Also participating in and supporting the CMSP are the Peñalolen chapters of a number of national organizations involved in the struggle for the right to a 'dignified home' (*vivienda digna*): the National Federation of Pobladores (Federacion Nacional de Pobladores – FENAPO), the Movement of Peoples without a Roof (Movimiento de los Pueblos Sin Techo – MPST), and the National Association of Home Debtors of Chile (Asociación Nacional de Deudores Habitacionales de Chile – ANDHA Chile). These organizations are also supported by the Institute of Housing (Instituto de la Vivienda – INVI) of the University of Chile, a university center that analyzes urban planning and housing policies, as well as by a number of university students who donate their time to the CMSP. Many of the students who support the CMSP are associated with the Corporación Educacional Poblar, an NGO that specializes in popular education, which is associated with the MPL.[12] INVI, Poblar, and the students provide logistical support, legal advice, education, and coordination. CMSP activists also have linkages to *poblador* movements in other Latin American countries through the Latin American Secretariat of Popular Housing (Secretaría de Vivienda Popular – SELVIP), an umbrella organization that has its origins in the popular housing movement in Brazil.

CMSP activists see the proposed modifications to the *plan regulador* that were put forth in 2009 by the municipality with the help of Urbe – a consulting firm specializing in urban planning with ties to the *inmobiliarias* – as part of a broader strategy that is designed to socially 'sanitize' Peñalolen and thereby make the *comuna* attractive for the construction of more upscale housing. If adopted by the municipal council, the proposed modifications would tend to restrict the construction of low-income social housing in Peñalolen. Since it was created, one of the CMSP's main goals has been to ensure that the estimated 19,000 *allegado* families living with family members in the *comuna* stay in Peñalolen. The CMSP wants as much of the land that is still available for development in the *comuna* as possible earmarked for the construction of low-income 'social housing' for the *allegado* families of Peñalolen. The construction of social housing, however, is not a high priority for a municipality that is seeking to attract more affluent and upscale home buyers to the *comuna* and for it to become more like Las Condes and Vitacura. Indeed, the goal of Peñalolen's mayor, as he said at a meeting with the community leaders of the *comuna*, is that 'Peñalolen have no reason to envy Vitacura and Las Condes ... Peñalolen will be just like them.'

If the construction of social housing were to be limited in Peñalolen, however, many of the *allegado* families of the *comuna* who apply for a subsidy for 'social housing' would more than likely be required to relocate to *comunas* in the southern periphery of Santiago (San Bernardo, Puente Alto, and La Pintana) – where the bulk of new social housing projects are built. Many of these *comunas* are far from job sites in the more affluent *comunas* and social services in the center of Santiago. Located at the farthest extremes of the city, many of these housing developments lack basic community infrastructure (parks, community centers, public spaces, etc.) as well. *Allegado* families, however, began mobilizing in order to be able to stay in Peñalolen. The MUA, which was originally created with the blessing and support of the municipality, began to oppose the mayor – a Christian Democrat – when the proposed modifications to the *plan regulador* were unveiled. They began their campaign against the *plan regulador* by addressing the municipality's claim that there was not enough land in Peñalolen to accommodate the demands of all of Peñalolen's *allegado* families. *Allegado* committees began publicizing their grievances by putting up notices in the bus stops of Peñalolen, which contained a list of their demands and used maps to show the location of available land and to point out that there is 'enough land in Peñalolen for all of the *allegados.*'

Much of the land that would be available for social housing, however, is located adjacent to the well-to-do communities of 'upper Peñalolen.' These more affluent communities have organized to resist efforts to build social housing adjacent to their communities. For example, in 2009 the municipality began exploring the possibility of building 200 social housing units on a strip of land adjacent to the 'ecological community' of Peñalolen in order to house some of the 1,800 families living in the *'toma* of Penalolen.' The ecological community is a group of affluent environmentalists, or *'ecolitistas'* (ecolitists – ecological elitists), as Lautaro calls them, that built a community oriented toward 'ecologically sustainable housing and living' in upper Peñalolen. When residents found out about the municipality's plans to build social housing on land adjacent to the ecological community, they organized and mobilized against the proposal, arguing that the presence of social housing would be damaging to the environment and to the 'social and cultural fabric'[13] of the area. The ecological community finally ended up buying the land as a way to derail the social housing project.

The conflict between *pobladores* and the residents of the ecological community over the social housing proposal reveals a broader division between a 'popular left,' which is focused on traditional 'material' demands associated with class (housing, healthcare, education, incomes, etc.), and a more middle-class, upscale, and affluent left that is much more focused on 'postmaterial' issues (the environment, women's rights, gay rights, indigenous rights, etc.). The division between the popular (material) left and the affluent (postmaterial) left has become increasingly pronounced in Chile over the twenty years of *concertación* rule. The schism between a popular left and an affluent postmaterial left has also been one of the vehicles that right-wing parties with a populist discourse, such as the Independent Democratic Union (UDI), have used to penetrate the *poblaciones* and further divide the popular sectors.

Housing and urban development policies, which for all practical purposes require *allegado* families who apply for a housing subsidy to move to *comunas* in the urban periphery in order to obtain access to a *'vivienda social,'* are framed by CMSP activists in terms of the 'expulsion of the urban poor from the city.' The process of 'expelling the urban poor,' they argue, began in the late 1970s during the Pinochet dictatorship with the eradication of illegal squatter settlements in Santiago. The process continued after the transition to democracy in 1990 with the mass construction of subsidized social housing in the peripheral *comunas* of Santiago. The position of CMSP activists has been that Peñalolen 'belongs to the *pobladores* who built the *comuna*, and not to the large *inmobiliarias* and the rich who want to expel us.'[14]

CMSP activists frame the *plan regulador* put forth by the municipality within the context of a broader dynamic: the 'neoliberalization' of urban space. Pointing to a large map of the *comuna* of Peñalolen on a table, the president of the MUA explained that the 'expulsion' of the popular sectors to the urban periphery and the social segregation of the city are important dimensions of the 'neoliberalization' of urban space:

> The municipality and the *inmobiliarias* are trying to neoliberalize the urban space of Peñalolen. This requires expelling *pobladores* out to the urban periphery in order to make the *comuna* attractive for rich communities. The *'cuicos'* don't want *poblaciones* next to their homes. They don't want social housing anywhere near them. During the dictatorship they would use soldiers and trucks to move the *pobladores* out to the periphery. Today, they use the *Plan Regulador* and market forces to move us out, and highways and other structures to isolate, divide, and fragment us.[15]

Spatial segregation, then, is a mechanism for socially cleansing urban space in order to make it available for the construction of modern, neoliberal space. Building the modern neoliberal city requires the exclusion or expulsion of marginal groups that do not fit within the neoliberal paradigm.[16] Since the neoliberal paradigm views everything through the prism of a market transaction devoid of cultural and social meaning, the social impact of housing policies that separate families and destroy social and community networks is not taken into consideration.

Other dimensions of the neoliberalization of urban space involve policies and strategies that can be described in terms of the 'cultural reorganization' of public spaces: the suppression, relocation, regulation, or transformation of activities and behaviors that do not fit within the imaginary of neoliberal modernity – street vending, open-air markets, begging, etc. These activities, which are expressions of popular culture, are viewed by many political elites through the prism of 'disorder.' That is, left unregulated, the proliferation of these activities distorts the rational, ordered, bourgeois conceptualization of space that is at the heart of neoliberal ideology.[17] The effort to neoliberalize urban space is seen by CMSP activists as one of a number of fronts in a broader class struggle, which they define in both cultural and material terms.

The CMSP's objectives and strategies: 'from social movement to communal power'

The organizations of the CMSP adopted a variety of strategies to press their demands. One strategy has been to publicize their demands, first by putting up signs, posters, and banners in public spaces in order to counter claims by the municipality that there is not enough land available for social housing in Peñalolen. Members of MUA and other CMSP organizations periodically engage in '*pegatones*,' which involves festooning bus stops and other public places in Peñalolen with signs that claim that there is enough land in the *comuna* to accommodate the *allegados*. In this way activists hope to mobilize the organizations that represent the *pobladores* of Peñalolen (neighborhood councils, women's organizations, cultural groups, etc.) to put pressure on municipal officials to withdraw what is described as 'the Plan Regulador of the "*cuicos.*"'

Activists have also organized meetings with neighborhood councils and other community organizations in an effort to raise awareness of the broader issues that are associated with the neoliberalization of urban space. However, in bringing these issues up and discussing them with leaders of Peñalolen's social organizations (neighborhood councils, women's organizations, cultural groups, sports clubs, etc.), activists had to go to great lengths to camouflage any sort of political motivations because many *dirigentes* (organizational leaders) in Peñalolen are very wary of getting involved in anything that is perceived as 'politics' or in open confrontations with the municipality or the authorities. Nevertheless, by publicizing their grievances and educating community leaders about the implications of the neoliberalization of urban space, CMSP activists hope that they will garner the support of other popular organizations in the *comuna*.

The reluctance of organizational leaders to get involved in anything that could be perceived as 'politics' and to avoid anything that might entail confrontation with the municipality or the state, however, led the MPL to realize that there was much cultural and discursive groundwork to be done before a sustainable social movement could be constructed. This sobering realization led the MPL to broaden its efforts into the realm of popular education, a strategy that in Peñalolen was initiated jointly by the MPL and the Corporación Educacional Poblar. Poblar uses popular education as a strategic tool to rebuild a popular culture that activists argued has been transformed by thirty years of neoliberalism. The object of popular education is to contest neoliberal hegemony at the cultural and discursive levels by working through organizations in civil society to develop an alternative understanding of contemporary reality. In essence, then, popular education is a Gramscian strategy, the object of which is to challenge the state's hegemonic project and build counter-hegemony on the terrain of civil society. Working together with Poblar, in 2010 the MPL created a school for organizational leaders (*escuela para dirigentes*). The school seeks to provide organizational leaders with an alternative view of housing policy, and a variety of other issues, by exploring these issues through a critical lens. Housing policies, for example, are examined through the prism of the neo-liberalization of urban space.

The goal of the school for *dirigentes* is to carve out an autonomous space for dialogue and debate among the leaders of Peñalolen's social organizations, thus reclaiming a civil society that in the view of CMSP activists is on a daily basis shaped, molded, and undermined into quiescent conformity by an ever present municipality and by the agencies of the central government. One of the sociologists associated with Poblar alluded to the municipality's constant presence within civil society and its discursive effect on popular movements:

> The only real voice that the *pobladores* hear is the voice of the municipality. The municipality and the agencies of the central government were the only actors that were talking to popular organizations. This 'conversation' was rarely a dialogue, mostly it was a monologue. *Pobladores* had no space within which they could meet to discuss issues autonomously. Political parties no longer provide a space for debate and dialogue. We realized that we had to create spaces to build consciousness and change a culture that was being transformed by neoliberalism.

Popular education, then, is an effort to create what Nancy Fraser has called a 'subaltern counterpublic,' a space where the popular sectors can develop their own understanding of their interests, a space that has been sorely lacking in post-transition Chile.

The object of creating a subaltern counterpublic is to counteract the state's discursive 'monologue' and the discursive and cultural strategies that are woven into the social policies of municipalities and agencies of the central government. The myriad social programs that target material assistance to different segments of the population (the poor, women, children, indigenous groups, etc.) are also part of a neoliberal cultural project, the object of which is to transform popular culture. Most of the major social programs that are offered through the ministries and agencies of the central government have a strong pedagogical element. For example, one of the three pillars of *Chile Solidario*, a multi-dimensional program created during the Lagos government through which a number of different benefits are distributed to the poorest segments of Chilean society, is 'psycho-social' and involves 'shaping attitudes and dispositions through which families can become agents of their own development.'[18] Similarly, during the government of Michelle Bachelet (2006–10) the Ministry of Housing built an educational component into its social housing policies that involves 'social habilitation' and the 'formation of future property owners.'[19] The imagery that has provided the underpinning for these kinds of educational efforts is deeply embedded in an individualistic, middle-class, consumer-oriented culture.

These kinds of educational efforts are also targeted at popular organizational leaders. Urban popular organizations are viewed by the *concertación* as vehicles through which to attempt to transform a popular culture that was seen as far too accustomed to looking to the state for solutions to problems. Since the latter 1980s, municipal governments and the Division of Social Organizations (DOS), an agency of the Ministry of the Secretary General of Government, have jointly and separately sponsored a variety of courses, seminars, workshops, and schools with the object of training organizational leaders. The DOS has also developed and distributed an array of manuals, booklets, and pamphlets to leaders of popular organizations that instruct *dirigentes* in 'the factors that make a good *dirigente*,'[20] and inform them of their scope of action and responsibility. The manuals also provide a guide to the kinds of projects that are made available to popular organizations by the different ministries and agencies of the government. *Dirigentes* must apply for these projects by filling out a project proposal form. Guidelines for writing project proposals are also provided.

The DOS manuals provide important insights into how policymakers define and understand 'participation,' the role of civil society, and the relationship between the state and civil society. Two of the more consistent themes that can be found throughout the manuals are: (1) the cooperative and harmonious nature of the relationship between the state, local government, and 'social organizations' and (2) the 'apolitical' and autonomous mission of social organizations. *Dirigentes* are cautioned that their 'participation' should remain separate from any kind of political activities. The good *dirigente* is portrayed in the manuals as an apolitical actor whose sole focus is his or her community. The most effective way of assisting the community is to help the municipality and the central government in their tasks by providing information and feedback to the government, and by helping government agencies in the implementation of policy.

Some manuals also make reference to a number of provisions and clauses in the laws governing social organizations that receive funding from the state (which government agencies can use to marginalize unruly organizations). The general thrust of these legal provisions is an attempt to separate the 'social' sphere of the *dirigente* from a 'political' sphere that is reserved for elites, to localize and territorialize the scope of concerns of the *dirigente*, and to sever tangible and often legitimate demands from any sort of broader political discourse or ideology.[21]

The pedagogical effort deployed by the *concertación* in social programs can be seen through the prism of what one analyst[22] calls the 'resignification' of civil society. Instead of constituting a space for the formulation of alternative political projects, for questioning and holding the state accountable, or for the expression of unrepresented, postponed, or ignored social demands, neoliberal discourse envisions civil society (or what in neoliberal idiom is often called the 'third sector') as largely the apolitical – and junior – partner of the state.[23] Thus, the resignification of civil society involves transforming urban popular movements that articulate claims, which if adopted would expand the state's role in addressing redistributive social demands, into associations that pursue largely apolitical goals or that assist the state in implementing social policies that are in part designed to adjust popular organizations to neoliberal reality. This involves the implementation of policies and actions that have the object of embedding, reproducing, and legitimizing the neoliberal order at the societal level by *mobilizing and redirecting* a potentially oppositional civil society in the service of adjusting the popular sectors to neoliberal rule.

Resignifying civil society was one of the core objectives of the *concertación*'s policies vis-à-vis urban popular organizations. Indeed, a sociologist who worked with the Division of Social Organizations, the agency that coordinates the relationship between the government and civil society, for several years during the *concertación* era described the goals of the DOS thus:

> Our task at the DOS was to mobilize popular organizations, not to transform the neoliberal system, *but rather to mobilize them to support and*

deepen the neoliberal system … this required patient work. The culture of organizations had to be changed, which meant that *dirigentes* had to be educated and learn their role. *Our goal was to transform popular organizations and by extension popular culture … not the other way around.* We didn't create spaces so that they could penetrate and change the state, *these spaces were created in order to rebuild linkages, to penetrate their networks, and to provide a platform through which to transform them.*[24]

One of the key missions of the DOS, then, was to 'assist the organizations of civil society in adjusting to the neoliberal reality.'[25]

CMSP activists, however, view the policies and actions of the government as an effort to train a cadre of what Lautaro disparagingly dismissed as 'docile political eunuchs.'[26] Nevertheless, the courses offered by the municipality and the DOS present a tangible manifestation of the degree to which municipal governments and agencies of the central government have been able to penetrate and shape civil society. In the absence of spaces for dialogue that are outside the glare of powerholders, this multifaceted penetration of civil society undermines the notion of an autonomous civil society. Indeed, in the view of CMSP activists the 'autonomy' of organizational leaders, which is consistently stressed and celebrated in DOS manuals as the mark of a good *dirigente*, is merely a rhetorical illusion. Although most popular organizations may have no formal political affiliations or loyalties, and thus appear 'autonomous,' they are nevertheless not autonomous in the sense that they are able to form their own independent judgments and assessments of contemporary reality. In the absence of spaces where people can engage in debate and dialogue, *dirigentes* will remain embedded in a context in which they hear only one dominant discourse – a discourse that stresses conformity, de-politicization, a focus on the tangible and the immediate, and which disarticulates participation from the sphere of politics. In short, they will be beholden to the state's discursive monologue.

Popular education is viewed by CMSP activists as a vital dimension of a broader effort to empower social movements in Peñalolen, and to turn the Council of Social Movements into a more permanent organizational structure capable of acting as a referent through which to channel *poblador* demands and grievances in the *comuna*. The slogan written on the posters of the MPL captures the long-term objective: 'From social movement to communal power.' The long-term goal, then, is to build a coalition of urban popular movements that can eventually 'conquer the municipality.' In this context, the question of the *plan regulador* is 'one of a number of issues. For us it is more important to give the council permanence so that it can channel all of the demands of the *pobladores*. Our goal is to create an entity that is not merely "conjunctural" and that can sustain itself over time.'[27]

'We see the conflict over the *plan regulador*,' added another activist, 'as one step on the way toward empowering the *pobladores* to take control of and administer the affairs of their own *comuna*.' Activists, in sum, want to turn the CMSP into an organizational structure that is capable of participating directly in the making of municipal policy.

In attempting to build a more permanent council to represent popular movements, the CMSP seeks to subvert a consistent and troubling pattern that has defined social movements in post-transition Chile, in which movements occasionally are able to mobilize and burst onto the public stage with great fanfare, only to be quickly absorbed, disarticulated, and demobilized by the state within a few weeks, or even a few days (which speaks to the strength of the Chilean state). Acutely aware of this lack of staying power, the CMSP wants to use the momentum gained from a successful struggle over the *plan regulador* to build a sustainable coalition of movements. On this view, then, the struggle over the *plan regulador* can also be understood as part of the process of popular education, a sort of 'live fire' exercise in public contestation and popular mobilization. If successful, the CMSP believes that the struggle over the *plan regulador* will demonstrate to *pobladores* that there are ways to break down the barriers that separate popular organizations from public policymaking.

The dilemmas of popular movements in the context of 'neoliberal society'

The difficulties that CMSP activists have encountered in their efforts to build a network of social movements in Peñalolen shed light on the dilemmas that confront the myriad urban popular 'micro-movements' that exist on the margins of neoliberal society in Chile since the transition to democracy. Indeed, since the advent of democracy, across Santiago a fragmented archipelago of small urban popular social movements – i.e. micro-movements – have been involved in a number of struggles that give expression to grievances and demands across a range of material issues, such as housing, education, and healthcare. As the case of the CMSP suggests, some micro-movements, disillusioned with a representative democracy dominated by elites and technocrats, have also begun demanding greater participation in public policymaking. However, save for those few brief and fleeting occasions when they have been able to mobilize large numbers of organizations to burst onto the public stage and capture the spotlight, 'micro' popular movements have remained marginalized, navigating in the relative obscurity of the nooks and crannies of a neoliberal hegemony.

The fundamental challenge that confronts the CMSP is similar to that of many other urban popular micro-movements: transforming a network that is made up of a small number of permanent activists supported by a relatively small number of base-level popular organizations into a broad-based and sustained organizational network. Building this kind of network, however, can be an extremely daunting challenge. To build a broad-based popular movement or coalition of popular movements in Peñalolen, the CMSP must find ways of overcoming the crippling effects of a segmented democracy that gives the state a formidable capacity to neutralize and marginalize potential challengers by addressing demands in a selective and piecemeal fashion.[28] The dynamics of Chile's territorially and institutionally segmented democracy have made it very difficult for the CMSP to extend its support base in the *poblaciones* of Peñalolen. In a word, the municipality of Peñalolen and the central government have the institutional capacity and the resources to dispense a range of selective benefits – community development projects and social programs – to base-level organizations (neighborhood councils, women's organizations, cultural groups, etc.). The municipality of Peñalolen uses its institutional capacity to dispense selective benefits to co-opt and shape the organizational leaders of the *comuna*.

Indeed, the CMSP has encountered significant difficulties in trying to mobilize the neighborhood councils and other organizations of Peñalolen in support of their demands. For a number of reasons many of the urban popular organizations in Peñalolen are extremely wary of involvement with the CMSP or with the MPL. First, many *pobladores* support the mayor and echo the claims advanced by the municipality that the construction of more affluent housing in Peñalolen will bring jobs and other economic benefits in the form of projects to Lo Hermida and the other low-income *poblaciones* of the *comuna*. Moreover, even the *allegado* organizations in the *comuna* are split: some support the MUA and the CMSP, while many other *allegado* organizations are extremely reluctant to take on the mayor and a formidable institutional apparatus that has at its disposal a variety of bureaucratic and legal tools that it can use to marginalize challengers and troublemakers.

Even the families that are living in the *toma* of Peñalolen are divided: some have begun to give up their demands for a home in Peñalolen and are willing to move to the urban periphery. With the mayor's blessing, the Department of Community Initiatives of the municipality began working with residents of the *toma* to create and support its own *allegado* committees in a classic exercise of 'divide and conquer.'[29] The municipality sought to diminish and marginalize the influence of the Movement of Peoples without a Roof within the *toma*. These efforts have been very successful in peeling away support for the MPST.

One problem that has hampered the CMSP's efforts is that, unlike in the 1960s and 1970s, Peñalolen's neighborhood councils now represent homeowners, most of whom have legal title to their home and thus do not feel threatened by the proposals to modify the *plan regulador*. Indeed, many *pobladores* who in the 1960s and early 1970s participated in the *tomas* that took place in Peñalolen have since been given legal titles to their homes, making eviction without compensation impossible. More broadly, the conferral of legal ownership through the granting of titles to land, argues one neighborhood council president, was crucial in demobilizing the *poblador* movement and in reshaping the identity of the *poblador*:

> The key to the destruction of the *poblador* movement was to turn them
> into property owners. Once they became property owners, many began
> to think like the *cuicos*. *Pobladores* began to see themselves as part of
> the middle class. Once the *pobladores* were given title to their land and
> their homes, popular organizations began to die out. This was the first
> step in the individualization of collective problems. It began to change
> popular culture and identity. The solidarity that we once felt toward
> one another disappeared. Many of the *pobladores* who own their homes
> identify more with the *cuicos* than with the *allegados*.[30]

This same council president later noted that 'rather than participating in the *junta de vecinos*' (neighborhood council) or in a women's organization, *pobladores* prefer to spend their free time 'in the malls and the home centers buying things ... on credit,' a comment that is indicative of the extent to which the consumer culture of neoliberal society has penetrated the *población*. Another member of the council pointed to the individualization of problems that has taken place over the last two decades:

> Since everyone in the *poblacion* now owns their home, and they also
> have basic things like water, gas, and electricity, the *junta de vecinos* has
> lost relevance. The problems that people have are now individual prob-
> lems. For example, they can't pay their electric bill or their water bill,
> so they go to the municipality for help. They feel that organizations like
> the *junta de vecinos* are not very useful anymore.

Moreover, while some in the *poblaciones* have been able to benefit from the economic policies of the past twenty years, others have lagged behind. As a result, the sense of collective solidarity that once existed among *pobladores* has begun to fray and break down.

These comments suggest that the difficulties confronting urban popular movements in Chile since the transition must be analyzed in the broader context of the 'neoliberalization' of Chilean society over the last twenty-five years. Indeed, in a number of ways, the four consecutive center-left *concertación* governments that ruled Chile from 1990 until the election of Sebastián Piñera in 2010[31] consolidated, extended and deepened neoliberal hegemony in Chile, integrating the popular sectors into the dynamic of what José Bengoa[32] calls 'compulsive modernization' – a pattern of unbridled modernization which obliterates memory and identity, and transforms culture.

In the late 1970s, during the Pinochet dictatorship, neoliberalism evolved to become much more than a mere set of economic policies and a mode of capitalist development and accumulation.[33] Neoliberalism became institutionalized in a way that transcended the dictatorship, acquiring a powerful social base of support in a wealthy and influential business class that emerged largely as a result of structural adjustment policies that privatized economic assets and social services (such as healthcare and pensions). Neoliberalism, then, also has a powerful support base in Chilean society. It was in the latter half of the dictatorship that neoliberalism became what Evelina Dagnino calls a 'project,' i.e. a 'set of beliefs, interests, conceptions of the world, and representations concerning what life in a society should be like, which orient the political actions of different actors.'[34]

In contrast to a set of economic policies, 'projects' are characterized by their societal scope and their hegemonic ambitions. In the latter 1970s, neoliberalism came to acquire social and cultural dimensions that provided the blueprint for the construction of what analysts have called 'market society,'[35] or 'neoliberal society.'[36]

While the dictatorship laid the foundations upon which to construct a market society, however, it would be during the two decades of *concertación* rule that neoliberalism would evolve to encompass all of Chilean society and become hegemonic. As one analyst writes, 'if Pinochet is the father of today's Chile, the *Concertacion* has been a most capable stepfather.'[37] By making limited, but critical, economic, social, and institutional modifications to the 'savage neoliberalism' of the Pinochet dictatorship (which nonetheless did not compromise the key pillars of the model), the *concertación* was able to demobilize anti-neoliberal urban popular movements.[38] More important for the long term than the immediate demobilization of popular movements, however, was the extension and deepening of the neoliberal project in ways that permeated all social groups, producing a profoundly neoliberalized culture, economy, politics, and citizenry.

During two decades of *concertación* rule, increasing integration into the vortex of 'compulsive modernization' and consumer capitalism structurally and culturally transformed the popular sectors. As several analysts have noted, the multifaceted integration of the popular sectors into the market economy over the last two decades has been a catalyst for a transition from 'political citizenship' to 'credit card citizenship.'[39] That is, as the popular sectors became increasingly integrated into the consumer market (in large part through credit mechanisms), they also began to turn away from politics. Indeed, in the last two decades, an entire credit industry that is targeted at the lower-middle-class strata of Chilean society – i.e. the C2 and D segments – has emerged and flourished. The development of a credit industry targeted at low-income groups has been a vehicle for further integrating these segments of the population into the consumer market, which has allowed many to acquire the trinkets of modernity (cell phones, laptop computers, LCD TVs, brand-name clothing, etc.).

The extension of credit instruments to the lower-class segments of Chilean society was made possible by the creation of mechanisms and institutions that are capable of quickly and effectively punishing – and thus deterring – those who do not pay credit card bills. These mechanisms are used by numerous institutions in assessing whether or not to provide services and credit to people. For example, private hospitals check a person's creditworthiness before admitting him or her to the hospital. In short, credit has become a critical component of citizenship.[40]

The integration of *pobladores* into the consumer market, however, began with home ownership. Many *pobladores* who own their homes do not have to pay any kind of mortgage or rent. Thus, what people would otherwise have to spend on rent or a mortgage can be spent on other things. Moreover, because there are often several people, or even families, living in the home – most of whom are working – costs of living are reduced even further by sharing basic expenses. The ability to participate in the consumer capitalist market has created the perception among many who live in the *poblaciones* that they are part of a 'middle class,' even if by the standards of their income they would be considered poor. Indeed, an important contemporary marker of status in the *poblaciones* of the urban periphery is how much credit a person is able to qualify for.[41]

As the popular sectors were increasingly integrated into the market economy, a new social class – the so-called 'aspirational'[42] class (*clase aspiracional*) – also began to emerge. The aspirational class is that segment of the popular sectors that benefited from the *concertación*'s 'pragmatic neoliberal' policies, and in the process became integrated into the market economy. Employment opportunities, increases in the minimum wage, an array of targeted social programs and benefits, and increasing access to a variety of credit mechanisms expanded the purchasing power of families in the *poblaciones* of the urban periphery, giving many people a sense that things were improving for them and their families, while at the same time integrating them into the market economy.

Penetrating the popular sectors and 'resignifying' civil society

After taking office in 1990, against the broader backdrop of the transformational forces of compulsive modernization, the *concertación* built linkages to urban popular organizations that served to institutionalize the social dispersal, fragmentation, and segmentation created by the market liberalization policies of the dictatorship. These linkages were also used as vehicles in an effort to resignify civil society and to elicit what Antonio Gramsci called the 'passive consent' of the popular sectors. Indeed, the integration of the popular sectors into market society went hand in hand with the reorganization of state–society relations and the space of participation. Somewhat paradoxically, in the context of an increasingly 'neoliberalized' society, one of the key difficulties that have confronted urban popular micro-movements is a strong, legalistic, bureaucratic, complex, and multi-tiered state that extends its presence deep into civil society to dispense an array of targeted, focalized social programs to a number of different groups, and which is capable of shaping political and associational space.

Over the last two and a half decades, the Chilean state has developed a formidable capacity to penetrate deep into the interstices of civil society to shape the terrain on which social movements act. The state's capacity to penetrate and shape urban popular organizations is rooted in the latter 1970s, when the 'new right' that emerged during the dictatorship began to use municipal governments as an institutional vehicle through which to articulate linkages to the popular sectors.[43] One of the main goals of the party that would eventually become the standard-bearer of Chile's new right – the Independent Democratic

Union (UDI) – was to penetrate the popular sectors in order to build a base of support within them and to overcome the dynamic of class struggle that had characterized Chilean politics from the 1960s until 1973.[44] During the latter half of the dictatorship, after the 1980 Constitution came into effect, municipal governments became focal points for a form of 'popular participation' that was narrowly focused on the immediate, the specific, the tangible, and the particular. As municipalities became increasingly adept at addressing these kinds of narrowly framed demands, they began developing a formidable capacity to co-opt popular organizations and build clientelist communal networks.[45]

Concertación governments used the institutional capacity of the state to penetrate society that was developed during the dictatorship, as well as many of the techniques that were deployed by *Pinochetista* mayors and right-wing movements, to co-opt popular organizations, to isolate and marginalize micro-movements and deprive them of political and associational space, and to begin to implement policies designed to resignify civil society. The effort to 'localize' popular participation continued after the transition as *concertación* governments – supported by NGOs – encouraged popular movements to focus their energies and efforts on 'conquering the *comuna*.'[46] The increasing evidence during and after the transition that *concertación* elites were becoming increasingly distant and inaccessible to popular organizations also provided many movement leaders with an incentive to begin shifting their attention to the local level. It is important to keep in mind, however, that the fact that elites were becoming more distant from urban popular movements does not mean that the state was becoming more distant. To the contrary: during the twenty years of *concertación* rule, as elites became more disconnected from popular movements, the state's linkages to civil society expanded considerably, in a way that gave the state the capacity to make considerable progress in the effort to resignify civil society.

Indeed, shifting the focus of collective action toward the local required a discursive shift that dovetailed neatly with efforts to resignify civil society. The volunteer mode of participation encouraged by the neoliberal project has a strong localist orientation. Although often viewed as largely apolitical, volunteer type activities (neighborhood clean-up drives, tree-planting campaigns, neighborhood watch campaigns, educational campaigns to promote healthy lifestyles or cleanliness, volunteering to build housing for the poor, dog-vaccinating drives, etc.) often serve as vehicles for imparting a specific – in this case neoliberal – vision of the 'good society.'[47] Moreover, by teaching people how to live and behave in the context of a leaner state, these activities help 'adjust' people to neoliberal reality. The volunteer mode of participation, as Nina Eliasoph[48] points out, can also be conducive to a dynamic of 'political evaporation' – i.e. the silencing of critical and public-minded speech. Municipal governments also play an important role as an institutional platform for 'spatial targeting'[49] – i.e. mobilizing and implementing social policies at a specific scale of abstraction with the object of transforming the social terrain.

Municipal governments at the base of the state's institutional hierarchy played a key role in channeling, containing, and shaping popular collective action during the two decades of rule by the *concertación*. A statement made by the president of the neighborhood council of La Victoria *población*, one of Santiago's older and most militant shanty-towns, hints at the role played by the trenches and dispersed field offices of the state in shaping popular collective action:

> The government's strategy is to *divide and conquer* the working class and the poor. It has been this way ever since the dictatorship. This is why popular movements seem to have disappeared. In reality, popular movements did not disappear. Many were absorbed into municipalities, which turned them into small organizations that chase after the little projects that are are offered by the government, and that really don't change our reality. Those few who continue to resist or who don't play by the rules are marginalized and either worn down or repressed.[50]

Her comment points to the role that municipal governments and the social protection network have played in shaping and managing popular collective action. One of the many 'social assistants' who work in the Municipality of Peñalolen's Department of Community Initiatives put a more positive spin on the relationship between the municipality and popular organizations:

> When we got here, we had no one in the community with whom we could talk. Our first day here, we were confronted with protesters at the gates of the municipality. Today, we have many organizations in the *comuna* that have a very good relationship with the municipality. In the years since we arrived here we have been able to establish a very cooperative relationship with the *dirigentes*, who have played an indispensable role in the municipality's success. *You could say that we were able to organize and build a civil society in Peñalolen.*[51]

In a somewhat incremental fashion, *concertación* governments also built and developed a 'social protection network' (*red de protección social*),[52] an array of ministries, agencies, councils, directorates, divisions, offices, and services that design and implement social programs and dispense selective benefits to specifically targeted segments of the population (women, indigenous groups, youth and children, different segments of the poor, etc.). In addition, a number of institutions that deal with specific issue areas (the environment, drugs, consumer rights, etc.) were also created.[53] In terms of their impact on urban popular micro-movements, the effect of the agencies of the social protection network has been to extend the reach of the state outward and downward into society. The increasing 'embeddedness' of the state at the grassroots level of civil society transformed the terrain on which urban popular organizations build networks in a way that severely undermines their capacity to mobilize sustained and broad-based challenges to the state's policies.

Over the last decade, many of these agencies have built collaborative partnerships with municipal governments in socially vulnerable *comunas*, which has enabled them to establish branch offices in local space and to create an institutional network that projects the state deep into the interstices of the urban popular-interest regime. For example, *Chile Solidario*, a poverty alleviation program developed during the Lagos government (2000–06) that is designed and administered by the Ministry of Planning (Mideplan), maintains 'Units of Family Intervention' in low-income municipalities to work with families receiving assistance.[54] Similarly, the National Service for Women (SERNAM) has joined with municipal governments to build women's centers in a number of Santiago's poorer and more vulnerable municipalities. Many of the women that have been hired to staff women's centers in low-income municipalities are or have been activists in women's organizations and NGOs.[55] Hiring activists to staff these agencies is one way in which municipalities have been able to co-opt potentially troublesome micro-movements. Because the activists that are hired by municipal governments do not have formal contracts and are hired on a temporary basis, they can be fired at any time. Indeed, these centers can be defunded at any time, which gives municipalities and the central government considerable leverage over their activities.

These agencies have also provided institutional vehicles for establishing and deepening direct linkages with an array of base-level urban popular organizations (neighborhood councils, housing committees, cultural groups, women's organizations, local indigenous organizations, etc.). The fact that they are often staffed by community activists, moreover, endows these institutions and their actions with an

110

important degree of legitimacy in the community. The linkages to popular organizations that were established through these agencies and institutions greatly amplified the state's capacity to coordinate and shape popular collective action and discourse, while making it very difficult for the archipelago-like array of micro-movements that continues to exist at the margins of neoliberal hegemony to penetrate and mobilize urban popular organizations. Indeed, many popular micro-movements have been integrated into this institutional network. Thus, the triad that was forged by linking (1) municipal governments, (2) the network of 'social protection' and issue-specific agencies created by the *concertación*, and (3) base-level urban popular organizations was quite effective in incorporating the urban popular-interest regime and in depriving micro-movements of potential support from neighborhood councils and other base-level organizations.

The linkages articulated at the local level between these agencies and urban popular organizations also played an important role in the institutionalization of associational dispersion and segmentation. Because these linkages were established largely at the local level, where demands can be neutralized and depoliticized by processing them in a selective, piecemeal, and particularistic fashion, micro-movements have had a difficult time building strong cross-communal linkages. In a unitary and centralized polity – such as Chile – where most major policy decisions are made in a top-down fashion by a fairly narrow circle of political party elites and technocrats in ministries and think tanks, trans-communal linkages are crucial in the building of social movements that are capable of mobilizing pressure on the apex of the state. Indeed, trans-communal networks allow for cross-spatial collaboration, and provide vital spaces for theorization – i.e. the 'generalization and abstraction of a core causal idea from a particular reality into a general frame that can be applied to other realities.'[56] Trans-communal networks are also sites for articulation. Trans-communal horizontal networks, particularly in the absence of formal institutions that can link organizations (such as political parties or unions), provide key sites for 'upward scale shift.'[57]

Municipalities and the institutions of the social protection network were able to penetrate the urban popular-interest regime to build the kind of state–society linkages that act as a brake on the kinds of processes that are conducive to 'upward scale shift.' Upward scale shift, a 'change in the number and level of coordinated contentious actions to a different focal point, involving a new range of actors, different actors and broadened claims,'[58] is crucial to the emergence of transition from micro-movements to broad-based social movement. Upward scale shift, then, is the dynamic that occurs when urban popular movements begin brokering cross-spatial horizontal alliances and coordinating collective action across spaces (communities, neighborhoods, etc.) and institutional jurisdictions (communes, districts, etc.) to mobilize against targets situated at higher levels in the state's administrative hierarchy. Such an upward shift in the target of contention generally also entails a broadening and expansion of claims. Thus, upward scale shift is usually accompanied by claim shift, i.e. a broadening of once narrow and particular claims, and in some cases by identity shift.[59]

Rather than upward scale shift, however, the institutionalization of associational dispersal and segmentation was a catalyst for the opposite dynamic: 'downward scale shift.' One of the effects of the dynamic of downward scale shift was to segment, localize, and cage popular organizations, distancing them from the 'commanding heights' of the state. Downward scale shift insulated the commanding heights of the state from direct popular pressure. Indeed, urban popular micro-movements lack the kinds of durable cross-communal horizontal linkages that will allow them to put sustained and direct popular pressure on the state. Beyond the level of the *comuna*, associational networks tend to be very weak and tenuous. Cross-communal linkages and networks, when they exist, are in many cases organized and coordinated through agencies of the state or NGOs that are contracted by the state. Thus, the practical effect of institutionalizing dispersal and segmentation, and of caging popular organizations in local spaces, was to severely undermine the mobilizational capacity of the urban popular-interest regime.

Conclusion

Rather than provide an institutional environment open to and supportive of urban popular movements, then, *concertación* governments combined neoliberal economic policies with social and institutional reforms to consolidate, extend, and deepen the hegemony of the neoliberal project. The increasing integration of the popular sectors into market society that has occurred over the last two decades transformed the popular sectors in ways that make it more difficult for micro-movements to build social movement networks in popular-sector *comunas*. Moreover, the increasing penetration of the state into popular civil society has also resulted in the increasing marginalization and fragmentation of urban popular micro-movements.

Notes

1 '*Poblador*' is a term coined in the 1960s, which was used to refer to the urban poor, many of whom were migrants, who lived in shantytowns, and who mobilized to press the government for a solution to the housing problem or who engaged in '*tomas*' (land occupations). In the late 1960s, the *pobladores* emerged to become a significant political force that would align itself with the left. During the Pinochet dictatorship the *pobladores* were also an important part of the movements that emerged to oppose the regime.

2 Statement made by Lautaro Guanca, leader of the Movimiento de Pobladores en Lucha (MPL) and member of the Municipal Council of the Municipality of Peñalolen, 8 April 2011, at a meeting of the Secretaría Latinoamericana de Vivienda Popular (the Latin American Secretariat of Popular Housing).

3 *Comuna* (commune) is the territorial unit of space over which a municipal government has jurisdiction. The city of Santiago is divided into thirty-two *comunas*, each of which has its own municipal government.

4 Francisco Sabatini, Gonzalo Caceres, and Jorge Cerda, 'Segregación residencial en las prinicipales ciudades chilenas: tendencias de las últimas tres decadas y posibles cursos de acción,' *Revista EURE* v, XXVII(82), December 2001.

5 Eugenio Tironi, *Radiografía de una Derrota o Como Chile Cambio sin que la Concertación Se Diera Cuenta* (Santiago: Uqbar, 2010).

6 Alfredo Rodriguez and Ana Sugranyes (eds), *Los Con Techo* (Santiago: LOM, 2005).

7 Interview with an activist in the National Association of Home Debtors of Chile – ANDHA Chile.

8 Sabatini, Caceres, and Cerda, 'Segregación residencial en las prinicipales ciudades chilenas.'

9 *Allegados* (the 'arrived') are people – generally families – who do not have a home of their own and thus must live with relatives (parents generally). *Allegados* either live in the same home as the primary family (i.e. in a bedroom or the living room), or in a makeshift home that is built on the back patio of the main home. Thus, although the housing deficit has been reduced, it nevertheless remains a significant problem. There are approximately 19,000 *allegado* families in Peñalolen.

10 Interview with the president of MUA, 28 April 2011. *Cuico* is a slang term used to refer to members of Chile's upper class.

11 Henri Lefebvre, *The Production of Space* (Oxford: Blackwell, 2001).

12 Two university centers provide support for the CMSP: the Housing Institute of the University of Chile, and the Urban Observatory of the Catholic University. In addition, a number of NGOs also provide support: ECO, Poblar, SUR, etc.

13 Letter sent from the Comunidad Ecológica to the mayor and the Municipal Council of Peñalolen, November 2010.

14 Interview with the president of the Unitary Movement of Allegados, Santiago, 6 April 2011.

15 Interview with CMSP activist, 7 April 2011.

16 Sabatini, Caceres, and Cerda, 'Segregación residencial en las prinicipales ciudades chilenas.'

17 Some municipalities have engaged in concerted efforts to eradicate street vendors and open-air street markets (*ferias*). Some of these efforts have been the catalysts for

small-scale – yet at times intense – protests. In the southern city of Temuco, for example, recent efforts by the municipality to move street vendors out of the downtown area produced violent protests by street vendors. In the *comuna* of El Bosque, in southern Santiago, the mayor's effort to relocate the open-air market led to a protest in which *feria* women stripped naked and lay down in the street in an effort to draw attention to their grievances. In downtown Santiago, the police routinely make anti-street vendor patrols.

18 Osvaldo Larrañaga and Dante Contreras, 'Chile Solidario y el combate a la pobreza,' in *Las Nuevas Políticas de Protección Social en Chile* (Santiago: Uqbar, 2010).

19 *Fondo de Solidaridad de Vivienda Manual para el Diseño y Ejecución de Planes de Habilitacion Social* (Santiago: MINVU, 2007).

20 *Manual para dirigentes.*

21 The legal depoliticization of popular organizations by creating a juridical wall between a 'social sphere' and a 'political sphere' began during the dictatorship. After the 1980 Constitution came into effect in 1981 municipalities became defined as the focal point of citizen participation. Municipalities, which have limited jurisdictions over issues, became the space through which citizens would participate, leaving broader political questions to elites. See Verónica Valdivia Ortiz de Zarate, 'Cristianos por el gremialismo: la UDI en el mundo poblacional,' in Verónica Valdivia, Rolando Álvarez, Julio Pinto, Karen Donoso, and Sebastián Leiva, *Su Revolución contra Nuestra Revolución: La Pugna Marxista-Gremialista en los Ochenta* (Santiago: LOM, 2008).

22 Evelina Dagnino, Alberto J. Olvera, and Aldo Panfichi, 'Para otra

lectura de la disputa por la construcción democrática en América Latina,' in Evelina Dagnino, Alberto J. Olvera, and Aldo Panfichi (eds), *La Disputa por la Construcción Democrática en América Latina* (Veracruz: Fondo de Cultura Económica, 2006).

23 Ibid.

24 Interview with a sociologist in the Division of Social Organizations, July 2008.

25 *Temas de Participación*, División de Organizaciones Sociales, 1995.

26 Conversation with Lautaro Guanca, 15 April 2011.

27 Statement by Cristobal Saez, municipal assistant to Lautaro Guanca, at a meeting of the CMSP, 7 May 2011.

28 Kenneth M. Roberts, *Deepening Democracy? The Left and Social Movements in Chile and Peru* (Stanford, CA: Stanford University Press, 1998).

29 Interview with an activist who represents the CMSP and is a member of the Movement of Peoples without a Roof in the *toma* of Peñalolen, 9 May 2011.

30 Interview with a neighborhood council president of Población Simón Bolívar in Lo Hermida, 15 April 2011.

31 Patricio Aylwin, PDC (1990–94), Eduardo Frei, PDC (1994–2000), Ricardo Lagos, PS (2000–06), and Michelle Bachelet, PS (2006–10).

32 Compulsive modernization is a term used to describe a situation of unbridled consumption in which to consume more things is a good in and of itself. Compulsive modernization is also a dynamic that destroys popular culture and identity. See José Bengoa, *La Comunidad Perdida: Nación y Desigualdad en Chile* (Santiago: Catalonia, 2009).

33 Verónica Valdivia Ortiz de Zarate, 'Los guerreros de la política:

la Unión Democratica Independiente, 1983–1988,' in Verónica Valdivia, Rolando Álvarez, Julio Pinto, Karen Donoso, and Sebastián Leiva, *Su Revolución contra Nuestra Revolución: La Pugna Marxista-Gremialista en los Ochenta* (Santiago: LOM, 2008).

34 Dagnino et al., 'Para otra lectura.'

35 Eduardo Silva, *Challenging Neoliberalism in Latin America* (Cambridge: Cambridge University Press, 2009).

36 Juan Carlos Gomez Leyton, 'Chile 1990–2007: una sociedad neoliberal avanzada,' *Revista de Sociología*, 21, 2007.

37 Navia, *El Díscolo: Conversaciones con Marco Enriquez Ominami* (Santiago: Debate, 2009), p. 35

38 Silva, *Challenging Neoliberalism.*

39 Tomas Moulian, *Chile Actual: La Anatomía de un Mito* (Santiago: LOM, 1999).

40 Ibid.

41 Interview with a sociologist in the municipality of Peñalolen.

42 Eugenio Tironi, *Radiografía de una Derrota* (Santiago: Uqbar, 2010).

43 Valdivia, 'Cristianos por el gremialismo'; and Carolina Pinto, *UDI: La Conquista de Corazones Populares* (Santiago: A&V, 2006).

44 Angel Soto Gamboa, 'La irrupción de la UDI en las poblaciones 1983–1987,' Paper delivered at the Latin American Studies Conference, September 2001.

45 Carlos Huneeus, *El Regimén de Pinochet* (Santiago: Editorial Sudamericana, 2004).

46 *Cal y Canto Revista de Movimientos Sociales*, June 1990.

47 Julia Paley, *Marketing Democracy: Power and Social Movements in Post-Dictatorship Chile* (Berkeley: University of California Press, 1998).

48 Nina Eliasoph, *Avoiding Politics: How Americans Produce Apathy in Everyday Life* (Cambridge: Cambridge University Press, 1998).

49 Neil Brenner, *New State Spaces: Urban Governance and the Rescaling of Statehood* (Oxford: Oxford University Press, 2004), p. 81.

50 Statement made by a neighborhood council president in La Victoria *población*, Pedro Aguirre Cerda *comuna*, Santiago, July 2008.

51 Statement by a municipal official in the Department of Community Initiatives, Municipality of Peñalolen.

52 Osvaldo Larrañaga and Dante Contreras, *Las Nuevas Políticas de Protección Social en Chile* (Santiago: Uqbar, 2010).

53 Since 1990, the *concertación* has created the National Service for Women (SERNAM), the National Council for Indigenous Affairs (CONADI), the National Service for Minors (SENAME), the National Council on Drugs (CONACE), the National Council on the Environment (CONAMA), the National Consumer Service (SERNAC), the Division of Social Organizations (DOS), and a range of other agencies.

54 Larrañaga and Contreras, 'Chile solidario y el combate a la pobreza.'

55 In the municipalities of El Bosque and San Ramon, two of the poorer municipalities in southern Santiago, women's centers were created in which activists from EPES (Educación Popular en Salud) and Llareta, a woman's healthcare network, were hired as staff.

56 Sidney Tarrow, *The New Transnational Activism* (Cambridge: Cambridge University Press, 2005), p. 122.

57 Doug McAdam, Sidney Tarrow, and Charles Tilly, *Dynamics of Contention* (Cambridge: Cambridge University Press, 2001).

58 Ibid.

59 Tarrow, *The New Transnational Activism.*

5 | Social movements and the government of Rafael Correa: confrontation or cooperation?

MARC BECKER

On 10 August 2009, the bicentennial of Ecuador's first declaration of independence from Spain, Rafael Correa was inaugurated for a second term as the country's president. Correa had gained broad popular support through a combination of nationalist rhetoric and increased social spending on education and healthcare. His meteoric rise to power and consolidation of political control over this systemically unstable country has been truly remarkable. He is the first president in Ecuador to win a sequential term in office.[1] His rise to power came in the context of the complete collapse of the old political establishment. Correa championed his victory as the second liberation of Ecuador.

While many international observers and solidarity activists either bemoaned or cheered Correa's triumph as part of Latin America's move to the left, many social movement activists in Ecuador were much less convinced that the actions of his government would benefit them. Despite Correa's claims that under his administration the long dark night of neoliberalism was finally over, Indigenous peoples[2] condemned him for continuing these same policies through large-scale mineral extractive enterprises, particularly of petroleum in the ecologically delicate eastern Amazonian basin. His populist posturing appeared to be part of a long Latin American tradition of appealing to the left to win election, only to implement policies once in office that favored the traditional oligarchy in order to retain control over the government.

Equally surprising as Correa's rapid rise to power has been the rapid collapse of social movements. Since a 1990 Indigenous uprising that challenged elite exclusionary power structures, Ecuador had been positioned as a leading model for how to organize a grassroots social movement. The largest and best-known Indigenous organization was the Confederación de Nacionalidades Indígenas del Ecuador (CONAIE, Confederation of Indigenous Nationalities of Ecuador), founded in 1986 as an umbrella group of regional Indigenous organizations intended to represent all Indigenous peoples in Ecuador. CONAIE emerged on the national scene through a 1990 uprising for land and Indigenous rights that shook the country's white elite to its core. In addition to CONAIE, two competing Indigenous organizations were the Confederación Nacional de Organizaciones Campesinas, Indígenas y Negras (FENOCIN, National Confederation of Peasant, Indigenous, and Negro Organizations) and the Consejo de Pueblos y Organizaciones Indígenas Evangélicas del Ecuador (FEINE, Council of Evangelical Indigenous Peoples and Organizations of Ecuador). FENOCIN has its roots in the Catholic Church's attempts in the 1960s to draw support away from the communist-affiliated Federación Ecuatoriana de Indios (FEI, Ecuadorian Federation of Indians). FENOCIN broke with the Church and became much more radical in the 1970s, assuming a socialist position. It allied with Correa in the 2009 elections, and some of its principal leaders, including President Pedro de la Cruz, served as Acuerdo País (AP) deputies. FEINE tended to be much more conservative, and allied with former president Lucio Gutiérrez. From this perspective, FEINE also criticized Correa for his failure to incorporate broader participation in his government.[3] In the past, the three organizations (CONAIE, FENOCIN, and FEINE) sometimes collaborated to advance Indigenous interests and at other times they have bitterly competed with each other for allegiance to their Indigenous base. After Correa's rise to power, they remained as fractured as they ever had been.

Complicated relationships between social movements and elected governments, along with the disruptions they create for Indigenous organizing strategies, are not new. Lucio Gutiérrez allied with Indigenous activists to claim the presidency in 2003, but then managed to cripple the movement that was largely responsible for bringing him to power. Correa moved much more quickly than his predecessor to usurp the leadership of social movements, removing a force that could challenge his hold on power. Notably, Ecuador had failed to produce national-level social movement leaders who were capable of realizing cross-class and cross-ethnic appeal similar to what Evo Morales achieved in Bolivia. Indigenous movements declined from being a leading actor in defining the direction of Ecuadorean politics to a marginal and bit player. Correa, with his eager desire to monopolize control in his own hands, appeared to be negating a strong opportunity for social movements to open up political spaces that would allow for a fundamental restructuring of Ecuador's historically exclusionary political system. Negotiating relationships with a seemingly sympathetic government points to the compromises and contradictions that a social movement faces in attempting to implement an agenda of improving the lives of marginalized peoples.

Rafael Correa

Correa was a young economist and university professor who wrote his dissertation at the University of Illinois at Urbana-Champaign, attacking the neoliberal economic policies known as the 'Washington Consensus.'[4] He did not emerge out of social movement organizing, but rather out of a Catholic left motivated by concerns for social justice. Correa first came onto the public scene in 2005 as the minister of finance in Alfredo Palacio's government after Gutiérrez fell from power when his neoliberal policies alienated a large segment of the population. Correa leveraged his popularity in that position to a win in the 2006 presidential elections. In power, Correa appeared to follow Venezuelan president Hugo Chávez's strategy of consolidating power through rewriting the Constitution. He could then call for new elections that would reaffirm him in office and provide for a more sympathetic legislature. Like Chávez, Correa had run as an independent without the support of a traditional political party. The existing 'party-ocracy' was severely discredited in both countries.[5]

On 15 April 2007, three months after Correa took office, 80 percent of the Ecuadorean electorate approved a referendum to convoke a Constituent Assembly. Correa created a new political movement called Acuerdo País (AP), which on 30 September 2007 won a majority of seats in the Assembly. A year later, on 28 September 2008, almost two-thirds of the voters approved the new Constitution, which had been drafted largely under Correa's control. As was the case with Venezuela's 1999 Constitution, Ecuador's new Magna Carta so fundamentally remapped Ecuador's political structures that it required new local, congressional, and presidential elections.

Lengthy and contentious debates in the Constituent Assembly resulted in a constitution that provided a basis for a more inclusionary and participatory political system. The new document rejected neoliberalism, and embraced increased resource allocation to education, social services, and healthcare. Like Venezuela's, it employed gender-inclusive language. It also expanded democratic participation, including extending the vote to those between sixteen and eighteen years of age, foreigners living in the country for more than five years, and Ecuadorean immigrants living outside the country. The Constitution also defended the rights of nature, Indigenous languages, and in a highly symbolic gesture, plurinationalism designed to incorporate Indigenous cosmologies into the governing of the country. The Constitution also borrowed from Bolivia's foreign minister David Cho-quehuanca the Quechua concept of *sumak kawsay*, of living well, not just better. *Sumak kawsay* includes an explicit critique of traditional development strategies that increase the use of resources rather than seeking to live in harmony with others and with nature.

Following Venezuela's lead, Ecuador also created five branches of government. In addition to the executive, legislative, and judicial, the Constitution added an electoral branch, the Consejo Nacional Electoral (CNE, National Electoral Council), and a 'Consejo de Participación Ciudadana y Control Social' or Council of Citizenship Participation and Social Control. The last branch was in charge of nominating officials, including the attorney general and comptroller general. Its purpose was to increase citizen participation and improve political transparency, although the opposition complained that it would concentrate more power in Correa's hands. Advocates argued that a stronger executive was necessary to bring stability to this chronically politically unstable country. Since 1996, not a single president in Ecuador had been able to complete a four-year term in office. Three presidents (Abdalá Bucaram in 1997, Jamil Mahuad in 2000, and Lucio Gutiérrez in 2005) were removed through massive street protests. Social movements, on the other hand, feared that a stronger executive would come at a cost to their ability to influence policy decisions.

2009 elections

Correa won the 26 April 2009 presidential elections with 52 percent of the vote.[6] With this victory, he promised to accelerate the pace of his 'citizens' revolution.' He 'dreamed of a scenario in which there is no misery, there is no inequality, there is no injustice.' To achieve these goals, he would pursue reforms that would expand the popular economy, including supporting informal businesses, micro-enterprises, artisans, and cooperatives.[7]

The significance of Correa's victory cannot be overstated. Most Latin American presidential campaigns are multi-party races that require either a run-off election between the top two vote-getters or a congressional decision to select the victor. Salvador Allende, for example, won the 1970 presidential race in Chile with only 36 percent of the vote. Evo Morales' 2005 victory in Bolivia with 54 percent of the vote was the first time in that country's history that a candidate had won the election with a majority of the vote. Correa's victory was the first time since Ecuador's return to civilian rule in 1979 that a candidate had won a high enough percentage of the vote to avoid a run-off election. Under the current Constitution, in order to avoid a second round a candidate must either win more than 50 percent of the vote, or gain at least 40 percent of the vote and outpace the nearest rival by at least 10 percentage points. In Ecuador's fragmented and contentious political landscape, it is unusual for any candidate to poll more than 25 percent of the vote in the initial multi-candidate round. For someone to win in the first round, particularly in the crowded field of eight candidates that Correa faced, is almost unheard of in Ecuador or anywhere in Latin America.

A variety of factors contributed to Correa's first-round victory. Unquestionably, he counted on broad public support for his political project. Correa also faced a weakened and discredited opposition, with many of the traditional political parties in complete collapse. The Ecuadorean electorate also suffered from fatigue from frequent and extra-constitutional changes in power, and many people welcomed the political stability Correa's first term (although truncated, owing to the calling of elections under the new Constitution) brought to the country. With Ecuador having run through ten chief executives in ten years prior to Correa's election, Correa appears positioned to remain in power for ten years if he can maintain his current coalition to win reelection in 2013.

Correa's closest competitor was the former president Lucio Gutiérrez of the relatively new centrist Partido Sociedad Patriótica (PSP, Patriotic Society Party), which won 28 percent of the vote. In 2003, in a seeming repeat of Hugo Chávez's rise to power in Venezuela, Gutiérrez was elected president after a failed 2001 military–Indigenous coup. He quickly moved in a significantly neoliberal direction, alienated his social movement base and finally fell in an April 2005 popular uprising known as the 'rebellion of the *forajidos*' or outlaws. In the 2009 election, Gutiérrez continued to draw a significant amount of support from his native Amazonian region, winning those provinces by a wide margin. He also polled well in evangelical Indigenous communities in the central highland provinces of Bolívar, Chimborazo, and Tungurahua. Even though Gutiérrez continued to identify himself as with the left, most of those on the left now denounced him as a center-right populist. Many people from the conservative opposition voted for him, including the most traditional sectors of the Catholic Church grouped into Opus Dei, who recognized him as the best opportunity to defeat Correa. Their opportunistic positioning led Correa to condemn 'the amorality of our powerful sectors, of the Ecuadorian right, because they put their interests before their principles.' No one, Correa claimed, 'can vote for a person with such serious moral and intellectual limitations as Lucio Gutiérrez.' Following this strategy, the old elite 'shot themselves in the foot, thank God.'[8] For social movements, even if they had misgivings about Correa's policies and his monopolizing their political spaces, their old ally Lucio Gutiérrez was a much worse option.

The third-place candidate was billionaire banana magnate Alvaro Noboa of the right-wing Partido Renovador Institucional Acción Nacional (PRIAN, National Action Party of Institutional Renewal). Noboa almost defeated Correa in the 2006 elections. In 2009, however, with the right completely discredited but still running on the same neoliberal agenda of privatization, opening up the country to foreign capital, and lowering taxes for the most wealthy, he only polled 11 percent. This was his worst showing in four attempts to win the presidency.

Traditional parties such as the Partido Social Cristiano (PSC, Social Christian Party) continued to lose support. In fact, all of the parties that largely defined the return to civilian rule in 1979 and had actively contested power over the last thirty years – the PSC, the Izquierda Democrática (ID, Democratic Left), the Democracia Popular-Democracia Cristiana (DP, Popular Democracy), the Partido Roldosista Ecuatoriano (PRE, Ecuadorean Roldosist Party) – had now largely disappeared. The PSC did not run a presidential candidate, instead focusing its energies on congressional and municipal elections. In the coastal commercial port city of Guayaquil, which has long been a bastion of opposition to Correa's left-populist government, the conservative PSC mayor Jaime Nebot easily won reelection. Despite its declining fortunes, the PSC still won eleven seats in the National Assembly, making it the third-most powerful party in Congress. Noboa's right-wing PRIAN won six seats. The right, however, was far from unified, with much of its program extending little beyond a stated opposition to Correa. Even in Guayaquil, however, political allegiances were constituted along class lines, with poor people strongly supporting Correa, including many of those who voted for Nebot as mayor.

The left did not fare any better than the right. Martha Roldós, the strongest left-wing competitor, won less than 5 percent of the vote. The daughter of the progressive president Jaime Roldós, who returned Ecuador to civilian rule in 1979 but was killed two years later in a mysterious plane crash, ran as a candidate of the Red Ética y Democracia (RED, Ethics and Democracy Network), which grouped labor leaders and other leftist militants. Her campaign was based largely on attacking Correa, without successfully presenting an alternative to his 'citizens' revolution' project. Longtime radical socialist leader Diego Delgado strongly questioned Correa's commitment to socialism, but his candidacy failed to gain 1 percent of the vote. Similarly to how conservatives had grouped much of their vote behind Gutiérrez to keep Correa out of power, many on the left preferred to opt for Correa instead of risking a conservative victory. Three other conservative candidates together won about 4 percent of the vote.

Many on the left had urged Alberto Acosta, the popular former president of the 2008 Constituent Assembly, to run. When it appeared unlikely that he could rally the left against Correa in the face of the president's overwhelming popularity, he declined to enter the race. The Indigenous party Pachakutik did not run a presidential candidate and refused to endorse any of the candidates. In the 2006 elections, when a possible alliance with Correa fell apart, Pachakutik ran their standard-bearer Luis Macas but polled only 2 percent of the vote. After that disappointing experience, Indigenous activists remained leery of venturing another bid for the country's highest office, preferring instead to focus their efforts on local races. Correa repeatedly used Macas's dismal showing in 2006 to argue that radical Indigenous movements represented an insignificant percentage of the population.

While Correa enjoyed majority support from the voters, the same is not true of his AP, which lost its control over Congress. The party won 59 of the 124 assembly seats, just short of the 63-vote majority needed to pass legislation. Even that figure was higher than the 55 that some observers had initially estimated. After campaigning in 2006 without the support of a political party or alliances with congressional delegates, Correa still had difficulty drawing his new party together three years later. The 25 January 2009 primaries for legislative and local races were fraught with difficulties and disorganization. The AP was by no means an ideologically homogeneous or coherent party, which may have been its greatest strength as well as its largest weakness. While it incorporated a broad range of people, that diversity also threatened to pull the party apart into left and right wings. In an attempt to strengthen the electoral fortunes of his congressional allies in the run-up to the April vote, Correa implemented several populist economic measures, such as restructuring the foreign debt. Even these efforts failed to extend his shirttails to congressional contests.

A string of high-profile dissidents left the party, complaining that Correa's authoritarian nature left no space to discuss or question the decisions that he made. In addition to Alberto Acosta, Mónica Chuji broke with the president over what she saw as his inadequate challenges to extractive neoliberal policies and a failure to provide strong support for Indigenous issues. In Correa's first government, Chuji had served as his communication secretary. In the 2008 Constituent

Assembly, Chuji won election as an AP delegate and effectively provided an Indigenous face for Correa's policies. In the April 2009 elections, Chuji joined Martha Roldós as the lead congressional candidate for the leftist RED coalition.

Adding an additional layer of complication to Correa's plans to consolidate power was the strong showing of Gutiérrez's party. The PSP won nineteen seats, making it the second largest and a very antagonistic presence in Congress. Correa's complications in controlling the Congress were further indicated by the delay in reporting the results of the congressional vote. It was not until 1 July, more than two months after the 26 April elections, that electoral officials released the results. This delay in reporting the vote, together with Correa's weaker than expected showing, took much of the shine off his victory. Gutiérrez claimed he had evidence of a monstrous fraud that denied him victory, although the electoral council rejected the charge. The electoral council contended that the delay in reporting the vote was due to Gutiérrez's politically motivated challenges to the electoral outcome. AP congressional leader Fernando Cordero, in turn, charged the opposition with fraud, including claims that they had moved votes from the AP to other small left-wing parties, in particular the RED.[9] International observers, meanwhile, criticized Correa's overwhelmingly dominant media presence as compromising the fairness of the poll.

Even though the AP fell far short of the two-thirds majority it enjoyed in the Constituent Assembly, it still remained the largest party in the Assembly. To gain a controlling majority would require building alliances with smaller leftist parties. Such alliances were sure to be fragile. Correa claimed that he should be able to secure a total of seventy votes in Congress, but he almost immediately lost the support of the Maoist Movimiento Popular Democrático (MPD, Democratic People's Movement), the strongest of the various left-wing parties, which had won five seats in Congress. The MPD moved into a position of determined opposition when Correa cracked down on its primary ally, the powerful teachers' union, the Unión Nacional de Educadores (UNE, National Union of Educators). Correa proposed a new evaluation system for teachers, designed to improve the quality of public education. The UNE, which represented about two-thirds of the country's teachers, strongly opposed the attack on its hegemonic power. They charged Correa with seeking to fire teachers in order to replace them with his supporters. The UNE responded with marches in both Quito and Guayaquil. Not being able to count on the aid of the MPD put additional pressure on Correa to build alliances with the remaining small left-wing parties that together controlled a total of thirty-one seats.[10] Nevertheless, the new Constitution significantly strengthened executive power at a cost to the Assembly, so losing congressional control did not prove a significant liability to Correa, who could still rule through decrees and referendums. It was a strong and increasingly antagonistic executive that so unnerved social movements.

Indigenous critiques

Many Indigenous militants on the left viewed Correa's government as highly contradictory. On one hand, he had promulgated a new constitution that codified plurinationalism and the *sumak kawsay*, two of their key and highly symbolic demands. Correa also spoke in favor of sovereignty and against payment of the foreign debt, which he saw as illegitimate. These were positions that Indigenous movements had long pressed. On the other hand, Correa repeatedly approved laws that went against the interests of Indigenous communities, including laws that expanded mining concessions, privatized water resources, and ended Indigenous control over bilingual education programs.[11]

Correa pursued an aggressive and combative policy against his opponents, but this attitude was not limited to those on the conservative right; he also relentlessly attacked progressive forces that were opposed to his policies. Correa dismissed groups that opposed him as part of an 'infantile left' comprised of 'fundamentalists' who should not be allowed to derail his programs.[12] Indigenous activist and CONAIE vice-president Miguel Guatemal retorted that 'this is a racist and rude government, and in the coming elections we will withdraw our support and void our ballots.'[13] Correa's attempts to restrict the actions of social movements led to charges that he was attempting to criminalize political protest. Under Correa's governance Indigenous movements had become increasingly fragmented, with militants accusing the president of attempting to destroy their organizational capacity.

A series of events contributed to the growing tensions between Correa and leftist Indigenous movements. To the consternation of many rural dwellers who might otherwise be strong government supporters, Correa sought to expand and develop mining industries and other extractive enterprises. He refused to grant communities prior and informed consent before mining activities could proceed on their lands. Correa argued that these types of economic development would grow the economy, provide more employment, contribute to spending for social programs, and that all of this could be accomplished without a serious environmental impact. Opponents were not so convinced

of the positive advantages and, given the dirty legacy of petroleum
extraction in the Amazon, recognized that often those who bore the
brunt of ecological impacts of extractive enterprises rarely realized any
of its economic benefits. Despite Correa's seemingly leftist credentials,
Ecuador's militant Indigenous movement moved deeply into the anti-
Correa camp.

CONAIE leader and 2006 Pachakutik presidential candidate Luis
Macas criticized Correa for pursuing a 'citizens' revolution' as part of
a fundamentally liberal, individualistic model that did not provide a
fundamental ideological break with the neoliberal past. In contrast,
Indigenous movements pressed in the 2006 electoral campaign for a
'constituent revolution' to rewrite the structures of government to be
more inclusive. Correa stole the thunder from Indigenous militants in
also pressing for a new constitution, and even going one step farther
in granting CONAIE their long-standing demand to have Ecuador declared a plurinational country. It was not without reason that CONAIE
resented Correa for taking over issues and occupying spaces that they
previously held. At the same time, Correa held those to his left hostage
because criticizing him played into the hands of the oligarchy, which
was equally anxious to attack him from the right.

On 20 January 2009, thousands of Indigenous activists took to the
streets in a 'Day of Mobilization for Life' against Correa's new mining
law, which was intended to advance extractive enterprises. Opponents
shut down the Panamerican Highway between the highland towns of
Latacunga and Ambato, and also led protests in Quito and Cuenca.
Although the marches were peaceful, the government responded with
force, firing tear gas and bullets that injured dozens of protesters. For
social movements committed to sustainable development, Correa's
repressive responses to resistance seemed little different from those
of previous right-wing neoliberal governments.[14] The president retorted
that the protesters did not have any significant support, and that their
leaders lacked genuine representation in the population. 'Three or
four people are enough to make a lot of noise,' he claimed, 'but, quite
sincerely, they don't have the popular backing.' Rather, he claimed that
he enjoyed broad popular backing for the mining law, and that this
translated into electoral support for his government, even in areas such
as Azuay that were strong centers of protest against mining operations.
Furthermore, he accused some of the leaders against large-scale mining
as having interests in small-scale mining, and contended that small-
scale mining had a much more negative impact on the environment.[15]

Seemingly in retaliation for Indigenous opposition to his economic

5 · Becker

development plans, Correa stopped funds for the Consejo de Desarrollo de los Pueblos y Nacionalidades del Ecuador (CODENPE, Development Council of the Indigenous Nationalities and Peoples of Ecuador) under allegations that its director and long-time Indigenous leader Lourdes Tibán had misused funds. CODENPE was an Indigenous-run government agency designed to give Indigenous peoples a larger role in development programs in their communities. Mónica Chuji retorted that, for Correa, 'like all neoliberal governments, we Indians represent *an obstacle to development*.' Chuji denounced Correa's arrogance, racism, and authoritarianism based on the principle of 'I am the state,' which allowed him to act unilaterally without considering the interests of other Ecuadoreans, or the impact his decisions would have on the country. He would not permit any opposition to his neoliberal policies. 'This is another example of the great lie that the *Citizens' Revolution* has become,' Chuji concluded.[16] Continuing his onslaught against Indigenous dissidents, Correa began to criticize Indigenous justice systems. He also removed control of the Dirección Nacional de Educación Intercultural Bilingüe (DINEIB, National Directorate of Intercultural Bilingual Education) from CONAIE, placing it instead under the control of the Ministry of Education.

Correa's attacks on Indigenous movements led CONAIE president Marlon Santi to state that, despite constitutional codification of plurinationalism, 'the government does not really want to recognize' those gains. Rather, Correa advanced a process of 'disaccreditation,' in which 'the movement loses representation and participation in whatever agenda or economic process [is] taking place through the state.' Economist Pablo Dávalos, who had long worked closely with Indigenous movements and briefly joined Correa in the Finance Ministry under the Palacio government, added that Correa's goal was 'to neutralize the ability of the indigenous movement to mobilize and to destroy it as a historic social actor.' Despite the apparent advances in the 2008 Constitution, 'the new political system is more vertical, more hierarchical, and more dependent on the president than before.' Dávalos argued that Correa's 'government is far from a leftist government and corresponds more closely to the interests of powerful groups that are emerging with the new mining and agro-fuels sectors.' In fact, Dávalos suggests that Correa's approach is closer to 'intervention strategies developed by the World Bank toward social movements in the 1990s through projects geared at specific groups including women, peasant farmers, youth and indigenous.'[17] Rather than addressing structural issues of oppression and exploitation, social movements suggested,

Correa was engaging in clientelistic strategies that played the interests of one group against another's with the goal of advancing the interests of a political leader.

At a 2 April assembly, CONAIE made its position crystal clear in a resolution that stated that 'Correa's government was born from the right, governs with the right, and will continue to do so until the end of his time in office.' They condemned the government for creating organizations parallel to CONAIE, and stated that they would evict anyone from their ranks who took positions in his government or worked with Correa's electoral campaign. The sanction would be due to 'their lack of respect for our organizational process.' In particular, CONAIE targeted Correa's extractive policies and especially large-scale mining and petroleum exploration efforts: 'because they go against nature and Indigenous peoples, they violate the constitution, and they threaten the governance of the *sumak kawsay*.' They charged Indigenous communities to no longer welcome government officials with their traditional symbols because of their lack of respect for 'our cultures and ancestral knowledge.'[18]

CONAIE stated that as an organization they would not support any presidential candidate in the 2009 elections, including the leftist Martha Roldós, despite earlier conversations with her. Humberto Cholango, president of CONAIE's highland regional affiliation Ecuarunari, said, 'We are not going to support any presidential candidate, because none represents a real alternative for the country.'[19] The refusal to endorse a presidential candidate was an explicit reversal of a policy in previous elections to support a candidate, because otherwise campaigns would prey on rural communities to gain the Indigenous vote.[20] In 1995, CONAIE helped found Pachakutik as a political movement for Indigenous peoples and their allies to contest electoral office. A short-lived alliance with Gutiérrez in 2003, however, was such a horrific experience that CONAIE and Pachakutik remained very wary of entering into another such similar alliance.[21] Nevertheless, CONAIE did urge support for local and congressional candidates running under the Pachakutik banner. In the 2009 election, Pachakutik suffered significant losses to the AP, and barely survived with a minimal presence of only four seats in the National Assembly. Timo Schaefer argues that Correa defeated Pachakutik by appropriating the Indigenous anti-neoliberal discourse that was least connected to their ethnic or cultural demands.[22] Even in their weakened state, Indigenous movements still influenced the outcome of the elections. Correa's withholding of support from CONAIE probably cost his party a majority in the Congressional Assembly.

Historically, Pachakutik has fared much better in local races than it has on a national level, and the same thing was true in the 2009 elections. Its most significant victory was that of Salvador Quishpe to the prefecture of the province of Zamora Chinchipe in the southeastern Amazon. Quishpe, who is of Saraguro descent, won in alliance with the leftist MPD party. Quishpe had a long trajectory in the Indigenous movement, previously serving as the leader of Ecuarunari and as a deputy for Pachakutik in the National Assembly. Despite Correa's claims that he had a strong base of support in areas of the most intense protests against mining, Quishpe won in such an area and precisely because of his long history of struggle against neoliberalism and extractive enterprises. Pointing to the significance of his victory, Quishpe noted that he defeated not a single candidate, but a coalition comprised of the Correa government, right-wing parties, and foreign mineral interests. 'It does not matter to the government or mineral interests who wins,' Quishpe said, 'as long as Salvador Quishpe does not win,' because they knew that 'with a Prefect such as myself it will not be easy to deliver our wealth to the hands of a group of Canadian mining companies.' He called for support of his candidacy, defending collective rights to water, nature, and food sovereignty, and the *sumak kawsay*. 'We know that large-scale mining will not guarantee these rights,' he said.[23] Quishpe's triumph heralded the possibility of advancing Indigenous political agendas through the avenue of electoral participation.

Twenty-first-century socialism

Correa was very eager to speak of socialism of the twenty-first century, but he was never very clear what precisely he meant by this term. During a January 2009 trip to Cuba, Correa rejected the 'dogmas history has defeated,' including 'the class struggle, dialectical materialism, the nationalization of all property, the refusal to recognize the market.'[24] Discarding key elements traditionally associated with socialism while failing to identify alternative visions raised questions as to what exactly Correa meant by twenty-first-century socialism. Hugo Chávez in Venezuela has faced similar criticisms. At the 2005 World Social Forum (WSF) in Porto Alegre, Brazil, where Chávez first spoke of the Venezuelan revolution as socialist, he said that new solutions must be more humanistic, more pluralistic, and less dependent on the state. Nevertheless, both Chávez and Correa have relied on strong governmental control in order to advance their political agendas.

In January 2009, Correa joined his fellow leftist Latin American presidents Luiz Inácio Lula da Silva of Brazil, Hugo Chávez of Venezuela, Evo Morales of Bolivia, and Fernando Lugo of Paraguay in a meeting with representatives of Vía Campesina, an international network of rural movements, at the World Social Forum in the Brazilian Amazonian city of Belém. Of the five, Correa was the president with the weakest links to civil society. Lula and Morales, of course, were labor leaders before becoming president. Lugo was a priest who, influenced by Liberation Theology, worked in rural communities. Chávez rose through the ranks of the military and used that experience to cultivate his popular support. Correa seemed to be the most eager of the five presidents to employ populist discourse in order to identify himself as with 'the people.' Correa spoke favorably of Indigenous movements and the history of exclusion that Afro-Ecuadoreans have faced.

In contrast to the other leaders, who rose through the ranks of social movements, Correa came out of the academic world. But of the five presidents at the forum he presented the deepest and most serious analysis of the current economic crisis. He began his talk with a challenge to neoliberalism and the Washington Consensus. 'We're living a magic moment, one of new leaders and governments,' he said. Correa noted that capitalism is commonly associated with efficiency, whereas socialism emphasizes justice. Nevertheless, Correa argued, socialism is both more just and efficient than capitalism. Latin American countries need national development plans in order to advance, and Ecuador's new Constitution was part of that process. He appealed for support for Indigenous cultural projects, the Pachamama (mother earth), and repeated the now common call for the *sumak kawsay*, to live well, not better. We need to be responsible for the environment, Correa said, and conserve resources for the next generation. Capitalism is in crisis, Correa argued, and Latin America is in search of new models, ones that would bring dignity to Latin American peoples. 'We are in times of change,' Correa concluded. 'An alternative model already exists, and it is the socialism of the twenty-first century.' Much of his rhetoric echoed the dominant leftist discourse at the forum, which had broadly shifted public sentiments away from neoliberal policies.

In a June 2009 interview with Amy Goodman on the news program *Democracy Now*, Correa strongly condemned capitalism as leading to greater inequality and more poverty. He denounced it 'as a vulgar instrument for capital accumulation' that destroyed nation-states through outsourcing, labor intermediation and other mechanisms of exploitation. Latin America was a victim of a crisis that it had not provoked, he said. Furthermore, the crisis of global capitalism had been created by factors that were 'the very essence of the system: exacerbated individualism, deregulation, competition and so on.'[25] As an economist, Correa provided a clear, compelling, and damning critique of capitalism.

Many leftist observers responded well to Correa's rhetoric and economic policies. In June 2009, Mark Weisbrot and Luis Sandoval of the liberal Washington, DC-based think tank Center for Economic and Policy Research (CEPR) released a report that was largely laudatory of Correa's economic performance during his first two and a half years in government. They pointed to economic growth, reductions in unemployment and poverty, increased government spending on healthcare and other social programs as a positive direction in Correa's policies. Furthermore, they applauded Correa on his expansionary fiscal policy, which led to a decrease in inflation and a significant reduction in the country's debt load. His most significant economic problems were due to factors beyond his control, most significantly the drop in oil prices, the global economic downturn, and the imposed limitations on his monetary policy owing to the dollarization of the Ecuadorean economy. Nevertheless, they concluded that even with limited monetary policy tools, Correa was implementing beneficiary trade and investment policies that were leading to economic growth.[26]

Even in the context of this positive economic news, Weisbrot and Sandoval acknowledged that Correa's policies were having a more beneficial impact in cities than on rural areas, where poverty rates remained high. Much of Correa's support came from urban professionals. While urban poverty rates were falling significantly, few of these gains made their way into rural areas, and even less so among Indigenous and Afro-Ecuadorean peoples, where poverty rates historically have been disproportionately higher.[27] It would appear that Indigenous movement bases received little of the benefit of Correa's government, therefore lowering their level of support. On the other hand, the experiences of poor urban dwellers, including those in the slums of the coastal city of Guayaquil, who began to move into the middle class, helped explain his strong performance among those populations.

After long holding off Venezuelan president Hugo Chávez's urging for Ecuador to join ALBA, Correa finally agreed to join on 24 June 2009. It was never entirely clear why he had long resisted pressure to come into the international alliance, nor was it necessarily apparent why he consented to sign up at this point. Some intimated that after winning reelection he felt he had sufficient domestic support to radicalize his 'citizens' revolution.' Alternatively, he perhaps made this move in order to solidify his support from the left, particularly from those who questioned his opposition to neoliberal economic policies. An alternative interpretation suggested that without majority control in Congress he was reaching out to regional allies in case he needed their support to push forward a more radical agenda.[28] Upon welcoming Ecuador and several Caribbean countries to the alliance, Chávez announced that the acronym ALBA would now stand for the Bolivarian Alliance for the Americas rather than Bolivarian Alternative for the Americas. With the Washington Consensus in complete collapse and nine countries now in ALBA, Chávez was leading what was no longer so much an alternative as the dominant discourse. Correa declared that 'ALBA is a political project based on solidarity, integration, and being the owners of our own destiny.'[29] He pointed to the significance of new mechanisms such as the Bank of the South in order to 'keep our money here in the region instead of sending it to the First World to finance the developed countries.'[30] Increasingly, ALBA was positioned to replace international organizations such as the United Nations or the Organization of American States, which had long been accused of serving imperial interests. When justifying his decision to join ALBA, Correa pointed to a need for a counterweight to provide alternative points of view in these international bodies.[31]

Indigenous intellectuals and their close allies, such as economist Pablo Dávalos, argue that once one looks beyond the rhetoric of socialism of the twenty-first century, regional integration, and the Bolivarian dream of a united Latin America, the reality on the ground often looks quite different. Yes, there has been state intervention in the economy, most notably in important areas such as health and education. But the basic economic model remains capitalist in its orientation. Not only did Correa continue to rely on extractive enterprises to advance Ecuador, but he used the repressive power of the state to attack anyone who dared to challenge his policies, including attempting to charge dissidents as terrorists. In one of the most high-profile cases, Correa sent the military into Dayuma in the eastern Amazon in search of these 'terrorists' who had opposed his extractive policies.[32] The environmental organization Acción Ecológica (Ecological Action) also faced a threat of removal of legal status, seemingly because of their opposition to Correa's petroleum policies. When faced with a massive outcry, Correa quickly backpedaled, claiming that the government was simply moving its registration to a different ministry, where it more logically belonged.

Although AP managed to liquidate the previous political system and emerged with a leftist discourse, Dávalos argued that 'in reality it represented a continuation of neoliberalism under other forms.' This is clear in its themes of 'decentralization, autonomy, competition, and privatization.' Correa continued to follow traditional clientalistic and populist policies far removed from what could be reasonably seen as radical or as a socialist reconstruction of society. Dávalos concludes that in no sense was Correa a leftist, nor could his government be identified as progressive. Rather, he 'represents a reinvention of the right allied with extractive and transnational enterprises.'[33] Dissidents also criticized Correa for proceeding with a free trade agreement with the European Union. Correa justified his discussions with the EU as being based on political dialogue, cooperation, and trade, emphasizing that Ecuador was pushing the idea of fair rather than free trade, designed to build economic development. 'We're not negotiating a free trade agreement with the European Union,' he claimed.[34]

After Correa's victory in the 2009 election, Luis Fernando Sarango, rector of the Amawtay Wasi Indigenous University, criticized the president's talk of radicalizing his programs. 'What socialism of the twenty-first century?' Sarango asked. 'What about a true socialism, because we have seen almost nothing of this of the twenty-first century.' Instead, Sarango proposed 'a profound change in structures that permits the construction of a plurinational state with equality, whether it is called socialism or not.'[35] Other Indigenous activists presented similar critiques. 'From the point of view of the social movements and the Indigenous movement in particular,' CONAIE president Marlon Santi declared, 'Correa's socialism is not socialism at all ... He waves the flag of socialism, but he does other things.'[36] For these Indigenous activists, Correa was not sufficiently radical.

All of this created the context of increasingly tense relations between Correa and social movements. Correa's failure to respond well to criticism and condemning what he termed as 'infantile' Indigenous activists and environmentalists further strained relations. CONAIE sent a letter to the 2009 WSF in Belém asking organizers to exclude Correa as a *persona non grata*, as someone foreign to social movement struggles. At the closing of the Indigenous tent three days after the presidential presentations, long-time leader Blanca Chancoso denounced the 'nightmare' that they were living with Correa, who was undertaking resource extraction 'at all costs.' Perhaps the only current Latin American president broadly identified with the left who would have received more vigorous denunciations at the forum was Nicaraguan president Daniel Ortega, who in particular has engaged in pitched battles with women's movements. While Correa positioned himself as part of the new Latin American left, he had alienated many social movement leaders whose decades of activism had made a twenty-first-century socialism possible.

Many lefts

Is Correa justifiably included as part of a leftward tilt in Latin America, or is his inclusion in this pantheon just a result of hopeful thinking? On one hand, analysts now talk of Latin America's 'many lefts,' ranging through Chile's neoliberal socialist president Michelle Bachelet, Bolivia's Indigenous socialist Evo Morales, and the state-centered socialism of Venezuela's Hugo Chávez. Following Chávez's lead, Correa sought to build his popularity on the basis of 'petro populism' in which he used income from oil exports to fund social programs. But the fall of the price of oil threatened to put those programs at risk. At the same time, a growing inflation rate jeopardized some of his government's accomplishments. Although Correa talked openly of embracing socialism for the twenty-first century, he made no move to nationalize industries. Building his government on economic development without proper concern for the environment and people's rights cost him support, while gaining him the label of 'pragmatic' from the business class.

Despite Correa's attempts to mimic Chávez's strategies, his policies were not nearly as radical as those of his counterpart. Of the many lefts that now rule over Latin America, Correa represented a moderate and ambiguous position closer to that of Lula in Brazil or the *concertación* in Chile than Chávez's radical populism or Morales' Indigenous socialism. The danger for popular movements was a populist threat, with Correa exploiting the language of the left but fundamentally ruling from the right. It was in this context that a historically mobilized and engaged social movement remained important as a check on a personalistic and populist government. If Correa followed through on any of the hopeful promises of his government, it would be due to this pressure from below and to the left.

On the other hand, Correa did follow through with enough of his policy proposals to ensure his continued popular support. He promised not to renew the US Forward Operating Location (FOL) lease on the Manta airbase when it came due in 2009, and the USA complied with his wish that they withdraw. In December 2008, Correa defaulted on more than $3 billion in foreign bonds, calling the foreign debt illegal and illegitimate because it had been contracted by military regimes.

Many people rallied to his defense, saying that he was safeguarding the country's sovereignty. In addition to tripling spending on education and healthcare, Correa increased subsidies for single mothers and small farmers. These steps played very well with Ecuador's impoverished majority.

Correa continues to enjoy an unusually large amount of popular support in a region which recently has greeted its presidents with a high degree of goodwill only to have the populace quickly turn on its leaders, who inevitably ruled against their class interests. Chávez (and, to a certain extent, Evo Morales in Bolivia) bucked this trend by retaining strong popular support through their connections with social movements, despite oligarchical attempts to undermine their governments. Correa is a charismatic leader, but in the Ecuadorean setting charisma does not secure longevity. José María Velasco Ibarra, Ecuador's classic caudillo and populist, was president five times, but was removed four times when he failed to follow through on his promises to the poor. More recently, Abdalá Bucaram was perhaps the most charismatic leader, but he lasted only seven months in power after winning the 1996 elections before his neoliberal policies alienated most of the country. Charisma alone does not assure political stability. Repeatedly throughout Ecuador's long twentieth century, the country seemed to be on the verge of deep political change, only for social movements to see the country slip back into oligarchical control under the guidance of a charismatic populist leader.

Correa has said that it will take eighty years for his 'citizens' revolution' to change the country. Leftist leaders need the support of social movements in order to make lasting changes. In sacrificing these alliances in order to solidify his control on power, Correa appears to be playing a dangerous game of consolidating short-term gains at the potential risk of the long-term prospects of his socialist policies. In quickly moving Ecuador from being one of Latin America's most unstable countries to maintaining a strong hold over executive power, Correa appears to have been able to mimic Chávez's governing style. Whose interests this power serves, and particularly whether it will be used to improve the lives of historically marginalized subalterns, is an open question that remains to be answered.

Notes

1 Other presidents have served multiple terms in office, most notably José María Velasco Ibarra, who served five terms between 1934 and 1972, although he was able to complete only one of those (his third, 1952–56). The

closest to being reelected was Juan José Flores, who served two terms from 1839 to 1843 and again from 1843 to 1845, although these were separated by two and a half months as interim president, for which he had not been duly elected. See Mark J. Van Aken, *King of the Night: Juan José Flores and Ecuador, 1824–1864* (Berkeley: University of California Press, 1989).

2 The use of a capital 'I' in reference to Indigenous peoples is intentional and based on (and in respect for) the stated preference of the board of directors of the South and Meso American Indian Rights Center (SAIIC) as a strong affirmation of their ethnic identities.

3 Kintto Lucas, 'Indigenous groups protest government policies,' www.ipsnews.net/news. asp?idnews=45513, 22 January 2009.

4 Rafael Vicente Correa, 'Three essays on contemporaneous Latin American development' (PhD dissertation, University of Illinois at Urbana-Champaign, 2001).

5 Greg Wilpert, *Changing Venezuela by Taking Power: The History and Policies of the Chavez Government* (London: Verso, 2007), p. 55.

6 Consejo Nacional Electoral, República del Ecuador, 'Resultados preliminares elecciones 2009, primera vuelta,' app.cne.gov.ec/resultados2009.

7 Rafael Correa, 'Interview with Ecuadoran President Rafael Correa,' *North American Congress on Latin America (NACLA)*, 18 June 2009, nacla. org/node/5900.

8 Ibid.

9 'Correa's victory starts to curdle,' *Andean Group Report*, RA-09-05, May 2009, pp. 10–11.

10 'Correa heaps pressure on teachers and banks,' *Latin American Weekly Report*, WR-0 9-22, 4 June 2009, p. 9.

11 Coordinadora Andina de Organizaciones Indígenas (CAOI), 'Firmes en nuestra defensa: Indígenas ecuatorianos deslindan con el gobierno de su país,' *Boletín Informativo de la Coordinadora Andina de Organizaciones Indígenas*, 3(9), May 2009, p. 17.

12 Raúl Zibechi, 'Ecuador: the logic of development clashes with movements,' in *IRC Americas Program* (Silver City, NM: International Relations Center, 17 March 2009).

13 'Indígenas no dejarán ingresar a las mineras,' *Hoy* (Quito), 28 January 2009.

14 Zibechi, 'Ecuador: the logic of development clashes with movements.'

15 Rafael Correa, 'Ecuadorian President Rafael Correa on global capitalism,' *Democracy Now*, 29 June 2009, www.democracynow. org/2009/6/29/ecuadoran_president_rafael_correa_on_global.

16 Mónica Chuji, 'El cierre del CODENPE: otro ejemplo del racismo y autoritarismo del presidente Correa,' *Llacta*, 27 January 2009, www. llacta.org/notic/2009/noto127a.htm.

17 Jennifer Moore, 'Swinging from the right: Correa and social movements in Ecuador,' *Upside Down World*, 13 May 2009, upsidedownworld.org/main/content/view/1856/49/.

18 'Resoluciones de la asamblea ampliada CONAIE 2 de abril del 2009,' www.conaie.org/es/ge_comunicados/20090402.html; Coordinadora Andina de Organizaciones Indígenas (CAOI), 'Firmes en nuestra defensa.'

19 'Ecuarunari no apoyará ninguna candidatura presidencial,' *Hoy* (Quito), 1 April 2009.

20 Mario Gonzalez, 'A la caza del voto indígena,' ecuador.nativeweb. org/96elect/caza.html, 13 June 1996.

21 Marc Becker, 'Pachakutik and indigenous political party politics in Ecuador,' in Richard Stahler-Sholk, Harry E. Vanden, and Glen Kuecker (eds), *Latin American Social Movements in the Twenty-First Century: Resistance, Power, and Democracy* (Lanham, MD: Rowman & Littlefield Publishers, 2008), pp. 165–80.

22 Timo Schaefer, 'Engaging modernity: the political making of indigenous movements in Bolivia and Ecuador, 1900–2008,' *Third World Quarterly*, 30(2), March 2009, p. 400.

23 'Salvador Quishpe Prefecto – Zamora Chinchipe,' salvadorprefectozch.blogspot.com, 16 June 2009.

24 'Correa attempts to define modern socialism,' *Latin American Weekly Report*, WR-09-02, 15 January 2009, p. 3.

25 Correa, 'Ecuadorian President Rafael Correa on global capitalism.'

26 Mark Weisbrot and Luis Sandoval, *Update on the Ecuadorian Economy* (Washington, DC: Center for Economic and Policy Research [CEPR], June 2009), www.cepr.net/documents/publications/ecuador-update-2009-06.pdf.

27 Ibid., p. 15.

28 'Correa's Codelco accord risks upsetting Shuar,' *Latin American Weekly Report*, WR-09-23, 11 June 2009, p. 4.

29 'Alba expands to include Ecuador and Caribbean states,' *Latin American Weekly Report*, WR-09-26, 2 July 2009, p. 16.

30 Rafael Correa, 'Interview with Ecuadoran President Rafael Correa.'

31 Rafael Correa, 'Ecuadorian President Rafael Correa on global capitalism.'

32 Milagros Aguirre, *Dayuma: ¡Nunca más!* (Quito: CICAME, 2008).

33 Pablo Dávalos, 'Alianza País o la reinvención de la derecha,' alainet.org/active/29776.

34 Correa, 'Ecuadorian President Rafael Correa on global capitalism.'

35 Luis Fernando Sarango, 'Triunfo histórico, dialogo y radicalización de la revolución,' *Boletin Digital Universidad Intercultural Amawtay Wasi*, 12 May 2009, p. 2.

36 Jennifer Moore, 'Swinging from the right: Correa and social movements in Ecuador,' *Upside Down World*, 13 May 2009, upsidedownworld.org/main/content/view/1856/49/.

6 | Venezuela: movements for rent?

DANIEL HELLINGER

Venezuela's Bolivarian Constitution of 1999 seeks to institutionalize *democracia participativa*, including a 'protagonistic' role for social movements and organizations in determining governmental policy. That Venezuela's oil export economy gives rise to a state with extraordinary economic resources relative to those of civil society complicates this task. By definition, petrostates are rent-seeking in their outward face, rent-dispensing inwardly.[1] Accomplishing this latter goal requires that popular power be formally articulated with the apparatus of the state but at the same time avoiding its subordination to the economic, bureaucratic, and technocratic power of the state.

The goal of building *democracia participativa* grows out of frustration with the failure of a modernizing project based on appropriation and 'sowing' of international oil rents. The collapse of this project in the 1980s gave rise to social movements whose original intention was to contest the power of a hyper-autonomous state but now find themselves in a new relationship with the state. The mass urban rebellion, known as the Caracazo, followed by the failed coups of 1992, the first led by current president Hugo Chávez Frías (a lieutenant colonel at the time), did give rise to a decade-long surge of social movement activity. The years from 2002 until 2004 saw intense conflict, with massive marches on the part of both pro- and anti-Chávez movements. After defeating a coup in April 2002, surviving an economically devastating work stoppage organized by the management of the state oil company (PDVS), and finally *chavismo*'s landslide victory in the August 2004 attempt to recall the president, Venezuela seemed to enter a period of 'normalcy,' with much less obvious political tension.

However, according to data from the human rights group PROVEA (2008), protests did not abate (see Figure 1). In fact, the number of protests recorded by PROVEA shows a significant increase for the years subsequent to 2004. Note also, however, the small proportion of protests repressed violently by government forces – remarkable given the polarized state of politics.

The seeming contradiction is easily enough explained by the sense

137

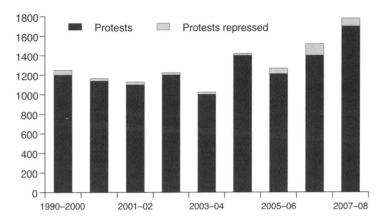

6.1 Protests and repressed protests (data from PROVEA annual reports)

of empowerment that ordinary Venezuelans have achieved in the last twenty years and the relatively restrained repression that the government has utilized against both supporters, who still take their grievances to the street, and opponents, still fearful (rightly or wrongly) that Chávez intends to impose the Cuban model. Movements on both sides of the political divide are wary of co-optation by parties and state, but none would give up access to the fiscal resources of government. The task of defining a relationship to the state that is neither liberal nor corporatist is made more difficult by acute political polarization, a situation made worse by the hostility of the United States.

Movements and the petrostate: from Gómez to the collapse of Punto Fijo

Venezuela fully entered the twentieth century in 1935, with the death of Juan Vicente Gómez, dictator from 1908 until 1935. Fledgling social movements had appeared earlier in the century in labor (funeral societies, some early union movements) and most notably among middle-class students at the Central University (UCV). Since 1928 student movements have retained an outsized importance in national politics, as became apparent again in 2007 when university students spearheaded protests against the government's decision not to renew the television broadcast license of RCTV (discussed below), which had played a leading role in the short-lived military coup against Chávez in 2002.

The death of Gómez in December 1935 unleashed a wave of protests and strikes demanding democracy the following year. More liberal- and secular-oriented leaders grouped around Rómulo Betancourt, eventually forming Acción Democrática (AD) in 1941. A more conservative reform movement, alarmed by the secular, positivist tendencies within AD, grouped around Rafael Caldera and in 1946 formed the Christian Democratic Party, COPEI (Independent Political Electoral Organizing Committee). AD sought to unite a variety of mostly middle-class and urban working-class movements behind a program of social reform, oil nationalism, economic planning for development, and democratization. A leftist reform party, AD competed with the communists, who had established a strong presence in the unions, especially in the crucial oil sector. During an abortive era of rule between 1945 and 1948, AD was able to wrest hegemony within the labor movement,[2] especially in the oilfields, from the third important mass political force, the communists.

From 1936 to 1948, the founders of AD and the Communist Party battled for control over student organizations, neighborhood groups, peasant associations, unions, and a variety of professional, middle-class organizations, and (especially) labor. Although control of the state ultimately determined the outcome of the battle for hegemony between AD and the communists in this era, we should resist the temptation to think that oil, today or in the past, determines that social movements are merely a 'top-down' construction. The breadth and coherence of the social movements associated with the rise of democracy are evident in the popular response to the oil workers' strike of 1936, in which both economic and political demands (organizing rights and democracy) were advanced. Centered in the Maracaibo region, the strike generated support throughout the country. The pages of *Ahora*, the Caracas newspaper that emerged as the key voice of Organización Venezolana (ORVE), show women playing a key role in organizing solidarity. Besides organizing relief, they took in the children of striking workers.[3]

Over the next decade, Betancourt worked to moderate peasant and worker actions in the interests of building a populist coalition to modernize the country. Although the *trienio* was a period of radical populism, Betancourt and his allies exerted party discipline to keep AD's left wing in check.[4] Still, in the context of the Cold War, suspicions of Betancourt and AD's leftist past contributed to a coup in 1948 and installment of a military regime between 1948 and 1958. When the government of General Marcos Pérez Jiménez fell in January 1958, Betancourt, Caldera and leaders of other non-communist parties agreed to a power-sharing pact at Caldera's home, the villa 'Punto Fijo,' in Caracas. The pact was not just inclusionary, guaranteeing all signatories influence over the new government after presidential elections (won by Betancourt) in December 1958; it also *excluded* the Communist Party. Other pacts among elites guaranteed that the post-1958 regime would not challenge fundamental interests of domestic businessmen, the military, and the Church.

These agreements, which formally expired five years later at the end of Betancourt's term, laid the basis of a political condominium, mainly between AD and COPEI, under which the two parties competed for influence not only in government (at national, state, and local levels) but throughout various social and economic sectors – including unions, professional associations, business confederations, student organizations, etc. Although providing for some alternation of power, the Venezuelan political system, *puntofijismo*, resembled in many respects the Mexican system in the era of PRI hegemony. This populist system of elite reconciliation[5] provided for competition mainly between AD and COPEI for access to oil rents, but also reinforced tight party discipline increasingly divorced from representation of social sectors. In such a context there was little political space for national social movements of the sort that emerged in much of Latin America in the struggles against military or other types of authoritarian regimes.

The oil boom of 1974–81 deepened the corporatist nature of *puntofijismo*. However, toward the end of this period the first stirrings of movements that would challenge the system began to appear in the form of a neighborhood association movement. The massive migration of people from countryside to town and the inadequate response of the state to the challenge of developing jobs and urban infrastructure to accommodate them led to a variety of forms of local organization in both the barrios and in middle-class areas. COPEI, which controlled the presidency between 1979 and 1983, saw an opportunity to neutralize AD's historic domination of organized labor by asserting influence over the neighborhood movement, but the collapse of oil prices (leading to devaluation in 1983) and the organizational response of AD frustrated the COPEI plan.

Steve Ellner points out that the neighborhood association movement never developed the political influence of organized labor because of divisions between the interests of lower-class and middle-class neighborhoods, and because the local nature of concerns inhibited national-level organization.[6] In some ways, however, these same factors mitigated the efforts of parties to subordinate them. In the 1980s middle-class groups, such as Queremos Elegir ('We want to choose'), advanced constitutional reform for political decentralization and a reform of the list-oriented system of proportional representation, vital to internal party discipline. Meanwhile, in some barrios, leftist survivors of the ill-fated armed struggle of the 1960s, though divided on tactics, joined with younger leaders to organize residents to make demands on political authorities. In his highly anthropological study of the 23 de enero neighborhood, historian Alejandro Velasco shows that even before the 1989 Caracazo riots, the mass rebellion that took place in twenty-two Venezuelan cities at a cost of perhaps one thousand lives in 1989, this massive neighborhood experienced a significant upsurge in autonomous organizing and direct actions that forced responses from government to problems such as garbage collection and other municipal services.[7]

Another notable pre-Caracazo development was the emergence of a union democracy movement in the Ciudad Guayana region in eastern Bolívar state. The city is the site of an array of heavy industries, mostly in the metallurgical sector, started in the late 1960s and drastically expanded during the administration of President Carlos Andrés Pérez. The new industries attracted hundreds of thousands of migrants to what had been little more than a village before 1968. Harsh working conditions, the weakness of AD hegemony in a relatively new labor sector, and inadequate municipal services presented an opportunity for organizers of Matancero, an insurgent labor movement that laid the basis for a new leftist party, the Causa R.[8] (Causa R also enjoyed some success organizing among students and in the urban slums of Catia in Caracas, not far from the 23 enero project.) Although the Causa would split in later years, it represented the first effort to develop a party linked organically to social movements. Its success influenced the political trajectory of the Movimiento Bolivariano Revolucionario (MBR) of Hugo Chávez within the military.

Social movements and the rise of Chávez

Margarita López Maya has argued that the Caracazo shares with other recent Latin American uprisings the nature of a protest by the poor against the erosion of a moral economy of inclusion (characteristic of Latin America in the populist era) and the amoral forces of the market. She asserts that the uprising must not be reduced thereby to an irrational reaction to modernization. Citing Fox and Piven's *Poor People's Movements*, López Maya argues that such revolts are the only response available to poor people when penury is imposed upon them by the authority's imposition of market forces.[9]

The collapse of the Venezuelan economy after the fall of oil prices in the early 1980s decisively broke the basis of a social pact promoted by AD's founders, especially Betancourt, in the period after 1935.[10] In short, AD's hegemonic bloc was formed out of a national project with three dimensions: (1) an anti-imperialist appeal by which AD promised to insist upon a 'fair' share of oil profits; (2) a promise to 'sow the oil' profits in a program of economic and social modernization that would lift Venezuelans out of the indolence of the past; and (3) institutionalization of democracy in the form of a polyarchy based on universal adult suffrage. Betancourt and his contemporaries contended that only a mass-based democratic state would have the will to confront 'imperialismo petrolero' and to sow the profits in way that improved the conditions of life for most Venezuelans.[11]

The persistence of urban protest traditions in places like 23 de enero (described in Velasco's study) and the regional success of Causa R in Bolívar have in common their location in what were perhaps the two most visible manifestations of failed attempts to realize the project of democratically capturing and sowing oil profits for modernization, with serious deprivations for those living out the consequences. The Caracazo of 1989 was the moment at which popular discontent became generalized.

Elsewhere I have suggested that we typically underestimate the importance of a third historical moment in the breakdown of *puntofijismo*: the nationalization of the oil industry in 1976.[12] With nationalization, no longer could Venezuela's ruling elites blame *imperialismo petrolero* for their failings, because these failings were being acutely felt. The percentage of families living in poverty rose from 17.7 percent in 1980 to 61.4 percent in 1996; those in extreme poverty rose from 9 percent to 35.4 percent in the same period.[13] In 1989, as he began to implement the provisions of a structural adjustment program negotiated with the IMF, neither CAP nor AD nor COPEI could blame foreign oil companies. The Venezuelan people responded with the Caracazo, support for the coup attempts of 1992, and then a surge in protest activity that was eventually galvanized behind the electoral challenge of Chávez.

Utilizing data gathered by PROVEA, the country's best-known and most comprehensive human rights agency, López Maya shows that from October 1989 through September 2003 nearly 13,000 protests took place, with peaks between 1991 and 1993, corresponding to the aftermath of two failed coups of 1992, the last years of the shortened Pérez term and the interim year of government under Ramón Velásquez. The number of protests subsided over the next eight years but markedly increased again in 1998, the year of Chávez's election.[14]

The most important social force behind neoliberalism could be found within PDVSA, by far the most influential business sector in the country. Promoting it as a 'meritocracy,' the PDVSA executives had sought systematically to take Venezuela out of OPEC, move profits out of the grasp of a discredited political elite through acquisition of foreign subsidiaries ('internationalization'), and gradually privatize oil production (if not PDVSA itself). As Bernard Mommer, a vice-minister for oil in the Chávez era put it, 'The military dreamt about saving the country; PDVSA executives dreamt about saving the oil industry from the country.'[15] The collapse of oil prices in 1998 played a role in discrediting the PDVSA's executives, but the executives remained in their suites at company headquarters, and the battle would be rejoined in the economic *paro* (shutdown) that they orchestrated in December 2002.

On the one hand, then, Venezuela resembles the rest of the region in the way that social movements surged in response to the consequences of neoliberal economic policies. However, we have to recognize some other characteristics of the Venezuelan case. Ethnic identity has played a less prominent role than in Brazil and in countries with larger indigenous movements. Afro and indigenous movements have tended to emphasize more particularistic demands than elsewhere. The Causa R enjoyed significant success in organizing a democratic labor movement but never came close to the national scope of organization achieved by the Workers' Party. PT also had the 'advantage' of serving as a rallying point for other movements opposed to dictatorship. Beyond PDVSA, business sectors highly dependent upon the financial resources of the petrostate enjoyed very limited autonomy and influence, in contrast to Mexico, where popular demand for change resulted in voters turning tactically to a conservative opposition (Vicente Fox, of the PAN, in 2000). Finally, while the military had thoroughly exhausted its political capital during the harsh years of dictatorship in most of the hemisphere, military rule never came to Venezuela. The popular opposition actually galvanized behind a military-led political opposition committed to profound institutional change and revenge against a rapacious ruling class.

If the country is bestowed with natural wealth, and the people are poor, then it must be the fault of the politicians, the reasoning went. By 1998 the most salient issue of the presidential campaign was political, not economic: how to replace the corrupt political class. Only Chávez unequivocally supported a Constituent Assembly to write a new constitution to replace the 1961 document, which had provided the foundation for the hegemony of AD and COPEI. Anti-party sentiment among social movements runs deep in most of Latin America, but nowhere else in South America have parties born in the populist era been so thoroughly routed from power in a single election.

Social movements in the Chávez era

Conservative Venezuelan elites from the 1930s down to the present day have always regarded such mass behavior as a sign of immaturity, and they lament the failure of modernization to take hold.[16] However, from the perspective of ordinary Venezuelans, oil wealth is a *natural* and a *national* patrimony. As Betancourt recognized in shaping AD's hegemonic project and strategy for economic development, the disposition of oil export earnings ought to be determined democratically. Venezuelans still adhered to this notion, but after bitter years of bust, impunity and corruption, and pain from structural adjustment, they began to question whether this particular set of democratic institutions was functional. Chávez recognized that most Venezuelans were ready to embrace an alternative political project – first articulated as *democracia participativa*, later as 'socialism of the twenty-first century.'

Mobilized to oust the old political class, Venezuelans were not content to return to their private lives, even if they supported the new president. While we do not have precise figures, qualitative analyses by academic observers and the narratives of protests from PROVEA's monthly and annual reports indicate that many of these protests, perhaps the majority, originated not with the opposition but with movements continuing to articulate grievances and demands to the government through direct actions commonly practiced in the post-Caracazo period.[17]

Given the central role of the state in accumulation of capital through appropriation of international rents, the notion that Venezuelan social movements can maintain autonomy only through a strict boundary between civil society and the state makes little sense. With a relatively small percentage of indigenous peoples, with a small formally employed, private sector proletariat (no matter how broadly or narrowly one defines the term), without the experience of struggle against harsh military dictatorship, and with a state that enjoys outsized economic resources in relationship to the productivity of labor, social movements in Venezuela are bound to be more state-focused than their counterparts elsewhere in the hemisphere. When Chávez moved in November 2001 beyond political reform and reasserted control over PDVSA, he challenged fundamental elite interests and gained the financial resources needed to carry out his ambitious programs. Hence, although oil did not directly figure as an object of social movements in the 1990s and early years of the Chávez administration, it became the common focus of both opposition and *oficialista* mass movements in the ensuing period.

Bolivarian Circles The popular mobilizations in defense of Chávez between 2002 and 2004 were largely organized autonomously by leaders of the movement to form 'Bolivarian Circles.' These 'Circles' began to form in the 1990s as the organized expression of civilian support for the MBR. In 1997, the MBR changed its name to the Movimiento V República (MVR) with the decision of Chávez to abandon his calls for abstention and directly seek the presidency. While the political strategy had changed, the notion of a civic–military movement had not. The MVR explicitly defined itself, among other things, as an anti-party 'movement' whose first goal would be calling for a Constituent Assembly to write a new constitution, a direct response to growing popular clamor for reforms beyond the modest ones implemented as partial fulfillment of recommendations from a reform commission report of the late 1980s.

The Constitution itself, it should be noted, was not simply dictated by Chávez (though the president exerted strong and decisive influence over much of its content), but was the result also of significant input from a number of movements, including the women's movement, indigenous groups, Afro-Venezuelan groups, human rights organizations, micro-broadcasters, and others. Although support for Chávez has always been more pronounced among the poor, class and political polarization accelerated after the president announced in November 2001 a series of decrees (authorized by the National Assembly) that aimed to reassert state control over PDVSA, implement land reform, and accelerate redistribution of oil rents toward the poor.

The opposition's response in the streets led to President Chávez's call in December for his supporters to organize in response. Also, his more ambitious social and economic agenda required more active public involvement and expansion of the Circles. As Medina and López Maya put it,

> Among the functions being assumed by the Bolivarian Circles the most important would be as intermediaries between government organizations and neighborhoods in support of community activities, help in transmitting micro-credits, the establishment of small cooperative markets, help in the creation of health services, etc. In addition to the

foregoing [was] added ideological work that took as its reference the text of the Bolivarian Constitution.[18]

The critical role played by the Bolivarian Circles in rescuing Chávez from the coup of 2002 inspired a dramatic expansion of the *misiones* and the Circles. The *misiones* involve much more than simple allocation of budgetary resources to education, health, housing, nutrition and grassroots economic projects; they require the organization of community-based committees to carry them out. A great deal of work is demanded of local community activists, and in some cases stipends are allocated. Not surprisingly, activists are favored in selection processes, e.g., for education programs. Although social movement leaders frequently express misgivings about being co-opted, they also feel deserving of compensation and recognition. At all levels, from the highest to the lowest, then, social movement leaders often feel it appropriate to accept posts in government or compensation for their work.[19]

The polarization and successive crises – the coup of April 2002, the opposition *paro* and oil industry shutdown later that year, and finally the *revocatorio* (recall) referendum of August 2004 – shaped relations among the state, *oficialista* party and social movements. Despite characterizing itself as an 'electoral movement' rather than a party, the MVR took on different trappings as it contested elections. Its upper ranks were populated by politicians who quickly changed their clothes or who emerged from below as part of an insurgent new political class. The gap between the Circles and the professional politicians of the MVR became evident when Chávez changed his campaign strategy for the *revocatorio*, reducing his reliance on the MVR politicians and successfully appealing to his supporters in the Circles to form 'electoral battle units' in support of 'No.' At the same time, the multiplication and growth of *misiones* also caused the Circles to gradually give way to other forms of popular organization.[20]

Thus, as the political climate changed, *chavismo* as a popular movement developed along three dimensions: (1) as a line of popular defense against the opposition; (2) as an intermediary for channeling oil rents to the base; and (3) as a form of popular organizing intent on checking the ambitions and machinations of bureaucrats and politicians. The tensions among the party, the state, and social movements arise not only from the obvious potential for clientelism implied by the second function but also from the familiar problem of diversion of energy from social mobilization to winning elections, which is considerable

146

given that elections have occurred at an average exceeding one per year since 1998. Each election is portrayed by government and opposition alike as the decisive battle for Venezuela's future. The most active and dedicated community leaders find themselves drawn into working for what became, after the *revocatorio*, the 'electoral battle units,' which for a period of time, until the formation of *consejos comunales* (see below) and the Unified Socialist Party of Venezuela (PSUV), became the most important vehicle for generating votes.

Ensuring effectiveness in the partnership between the government bureaucracy and popular organizations requires patience on the part of the employees of the former and a willingness to actively collaborate with and use their know-how to collaborate with local leaders. Several areas of success can be identified here by way of example. *Mesas técnicas de agua* (technical water workshops) have enjoyed a relatively fruitful relationship with well-organized urban communities because of the attitude of employees who work closely with the *Mesas* both to plan the new water and sewer lines and to employ local residents in the actual installation.[21] In the area of health, thousands of neighborhood committees consist of trained community activists who are responsible for identifying families in need of services and educating them in better health practices. Neighborhood soup kitchens run mainly by women activists rely on both community resources and government support to deliver food and support nutritional programs. The women (and some men) involved in these programs have come to see this work as 'political' in a quite expansive sense, including reassessment of gender relations through the work itself (as discussed below).

One of the most successful programs has been the one linking urban land reform to the Comités de Tierras Urbanas (CTUs). Rather than simply handing out property titles for land and ranchos (self-constructed homes) in the barrios, the urban land reform law requires that beforehand residents organize themselves into the CTUs to complete a census, identify areas and buildings that would be designated state or community property, draw territorial borders with adjoining communities, resolve disputes over ownership, and (not least!) produce a history of the community from the original occupation of vacant lands to the present.[22]

By contrast, Misión Mercal, a network of markets offering subsidized, basic commodities (e.g. oil, chicken, rice, beans) to low-income people, has earned a reputation as one of the most corrupt and inefficient programs (though not without benefit to the community). Similarly, although a period of training and education (e.g. through

Misión Rivas) is required before community groups can obtain micro-credits for community projects and cooperatives, there exists neither an effective auditing process on the government side nor a community oversight system. In programs of this nature, and in more traditional large-scale construction projects, there is considerable opportunity for graft and clientelism.[23]

Tensions between government and supporters The clash that results from the pressure from movements to advance revolutionary objectives more rapidly than political leaders find expedient or within the rule of law should be familiar to anyone who has studied radical regimes in Latin America. This tension was evident in the years of Popular Unity under Allende, as activists from the MIR and radical Christian organizers led land invasions and factory occupations that placed the government in the uncomfortable position of enforcing the law by deployment of force against core, popular supporters.[24] This occurs not only when supporters, sometimes agitated by radical organizations on the peripheral left, become impatient with the slow pace of change, but when the government pursues programs that clash with the goals of some popular movement, something less visible in Chile thirty-five years ago but more prominent in Venezuela.

Bolivarian officials often find themselves in confrontation with local movements of core supporters in the working class, the poor and the peasantry. We have already seen that public protests did not abate with the election of Chávez in 1998. One report[25] cites three examples from June 2008 – (1) the occupation of a downtown skyscraper by 100 people demanding affordable housing; (2) the occupation and shutdown of an important Caracas area highway by nearby residents protesting against rationing of drinking water; and (3) the blockade of a hospital entrance in the Caracas area by patients, many in wheelchairs and on crutches, protesting against long waits for operations. Road blockades accounted for 40 percent of protests. Another form of protest takes the form of 'auto-kidnappings,' often by relatives and friends who refuse to leave jails after visits, a protest at deplorable conditions. These activities, especially when carried out by government supporters, should not be regarded necessarily as anti-Chávez. They are more often targeting local officials and bureaucrats – rightly or wrongly, in most cases, exculpating the president. The presidential style of publicly singling out and chastising local officials encourages this tendency.

Given the assertive leadership of Chávez in advancing Latin American unity through petro-diplomacy, the tensions between the popular movements and government play out on the international as well as the national stage. Chávez ran into opposition on the hemispheric scale when Brazilian indigenous and environmental groups criticized his plans (now dormant) to construct a transnational oil pipeline from Venezuela to Argentina, linked to a tributary running from Bolivia to Brazil. Paulo Adario, Amazon program coordinator in Manaus for the environmental group Greenpeace, told the *Washington Post* (12 February 2006), 'This pipeline project caught everyone in the environmental community by surprise. There was absolutely no discussion about this before the presidents sat down together and announced it … It would have enormous consequences not only to the environment, but to the many indigenous groups.' Friends of the Great Savannah (AMINGRANSA) collected and delivered signatures from environmentalists on four continents on a letter protesting that the project would 'increase our environmental and social debt and, therefore, poverty.' The letter also argued, 'Integration of our peoples requires a paradigm shift away from the development model dependent on fossil fuels that has been imposed on our civilization.'

Whatever diplomatic leverage oil exports give Chávez on the international stage, ultimately the worldview of environmentalists may fundamentally differ from that of a petrostate. This tension is manifest in a clash between environmentalists and the Chávez government over mining projects in southeast Venezuela and in the Sierra de Perijá on the western side of Lake Maracaibo. In 2004 the government announced intentions to open in the region three coal mines controlled by a conglomerate of Dutch, US, and Brazilian companies. Not only did the projects directly threaten water resources in an area already badly contaminated by oil production, they clashed with the alternative development priorities of indigenous communities that oppose any new coal exploitation. For a while, Corpozulia, the government-owned megaholding company, and some military officials in the region attempted to link indigenous and environmental activists to Manuel Rosales, the Zulia governor who supported the 2002 coup and was the opposition candidate in the 2006 presidential election. Not until 2007, after the inhabitants of the area demonstrated in Caracas, did the minister of the environment finally announce that by presidential order the project would be suspended. But President Chávez warned shortly afterwards, 'If someday a technology is developed to extract this coal without destroying the forest, well then, that would be a reserve for the future; it is possible.' The coal concessions remain in place, only suspended.[26]

Another area of tension revolves around land reform. The peasant movement complains that the government has not moved fast enough to implement new laws. Land occupations have resulted in assassinations of peasant leaders, stimulating unification of several small organizations of rural producers. The Ezequiel Zamora National Farmers Front claims that 214 rural activists have been murdered in efforts to carry out the provisions of the law, decreed in 2001. Much of the violence has occurred in Zulia and nearby Yaracuy state, and activists blame it on Venezuela ranchers allied with Colombian death squads.[27]

In 2008, a confrontation occurred in mountainous Mérida state when a group of thirty armed, masked men attacked farmers in an ecological cooperative on vacant lands they had occupied in El Vallecito. The cooperativists suspect the action was orchestrated by local landowners who have gained a sympathetic ear, they say, not only from local opposition leaders, but also from some local politicians affiliated with PSUV. Although the National Institute of Lands (INTI) had granted legal ownership of over forty acres of the occupied land to the cooperativists, the Ministry of the Environment continued to treat them as occupiers and to deny permits for their projects.[28]

The peasant movement charges that INTI has been slow to assume public ownership of lands eligible for redistribution. In March 2009, Chávez announced an acceleration of the land reform process, but the national government has sometimes been thwarted by landowner influence over local and state authorities, even in states, such as Portuguesa, which have *chavista* governors. In April 2009 the Portuguesa State Police, which is commanded by the National Guard, evicted and arrested more than sixty peasants and three INTI employees who were working on land parcels in the process of being redistributed. The 'Jungle Police,' as they are locally known, had been created by the government to enforce environmental laws but had fallen under the influence of landowners. The Guard commander in charge told the local press, 'Our idea is to respect the law ... while the land reform law says landed estates are not permitted, the law also establishes sanctions for those who invade private property.' The *chavista* governor publicly denounced the leaders of the land occupation for promoting confrontational land 'invasions' to speed up the process.[29]

Relations between the government and the labor movement may be even more complex and difficult. Much of the labor movement initially remained loyal to the old guard leadership of the Punto Fijo era but became disillusioned with them as a result of their collaboration with the management-organized *paro* in the oil sector in 2002/03. Still, some unions remain under the control or influence of opposition leaders. For its part, the *chavista* labor movement, though now a majority, is deeply divided on a variety of issues, including how confrontational to be with the government. Issues include whether to press for further nationalization through strikes and factory occupations, whether to support or resist government efforts to spur micro-enterprises and cooperatives that compete with more traditional unionized firms, and how much to cooperate with the government's *co-gestión* (co-management) program. Competition among factions can be intense and violent.[30]

Jorge Martín, writing in *In Defense of Marxism*, a Trotskyite organ, described a conflict from a militant point of view involving 300 workers at a Barcelona (Anzoategui, a coastal eastern state) auto parts company (Vivex) in late 2008. The conflict began over worker demands for payments of bonuses but escalated to a demand for nationalization of several occupied factories in the region after President Chávez declared, on 1 December 2008, that workers should take over factories where there were problems with payment of wages and benefits. Martín claimed that the workers distrusted and refused to meet with a regional Ministry of Labor official. The workers argued that management of the plant had failed to live up to an agreement they had signed with the government in 2005 to implement '*Plan Venezuela Movil*,' which provided tax incentives and subsidies in exchange for promises to expand production and employment in Venezuela.[31] The conflict lingered on into 2009, with several worker deaths resulting from clashes with police attempting to implement a judge's eviction order.

Carlos Lanz, a sociologist who has theorized about worker participation and socialism in Venezuela, and who served for a period as chief executive of the state-owned aluminum plant, ALCASA, is sometimes identified by radical sectors as part of the 'bureaucracy' that is slowing the transition to socialism in Venezuela.[32] A supporter of the transitional plan that would require a transitional period of *co-gestión*, Lanz explained in an interview, 'Changing our social relations is causing us to confront the workers and unions often, not just the elites. The union leadership is rather Stalinist and corporatist and so doesn't think much of our aims.'[33]

In the same interview, Lanz says, 'The workers have not been socialized a long time, and many are alienated and want to continue to labor as in the past, resisting the important changes and keeping limited responsibilities.' Rejecting both Keynesianism and traditional Marxist approaches, Lanz notes,

There is a debate ... about the historical subject of the revolution. We prefer to talk about a social and historical revolutionary bloc which includes workers, women, intellectuals, youth, peasants, and others who become involved too. There is not just one line of thought informing the revolution, also – there are five sources of inspiration. First the lessons from indigenous resistance. The Afro-Venezuelan experience, liberation theology, revolutionary Bolivarianism, ... and critical or libertarian Marxism – these sources are guiding us to a new approach.

It is often difficult to determine whether demands for nationalization by workers are meant to force concessions from management or to advance social ownership of the means of production. In either case, they have successfully induced President Chávez to carry out several nationalizations. Nationalized industries are supposed to be co-managed by workers and directors appointed by the state, which is expected to make considerable investment (derived from international oil rents, of course). Over time, workers are to buy out the state share and assume self-management, but the immediate outcome is to shift industrial workers off private payrolls onto government payrolls. In other words, the government now may find itself dealing with labor disputes that were once focused on private owners. Orlando Chirino, leader of a 'classist' tendency independent of government or opposition, argues that nationalization is the result of worker struggles and sacrifice, and he criticizes the government's willingness to compensate former owners.[34] Hence, the Chávez government faces the delicate task of satisfying a small but visible worker movement demanding radicalization of nationalization and worker democracy schemes, while at the same time it attempts to maintain correct relations with Venezuelan and foreign capitalists.

A well-publicized conflict at Ineval, a factory that manufactures valves for the oil industry, illustrates the difficulty of administering the government's program of transition from private ownership to a co-managed industry owned by the state, and then to a self-managed worker enterprise. Workers at INEVAL, which had already been expropriated, were pressing for immediate implementation of self-management, not co-determination. They were also demanding nationalization of several other factories in their region, located in the west. The worker committee claimed that the demand was being sabotaged by the state-owned oil company, PDVSA, because it preferred to import valves. News reports were claiming that workers were failing to produce effectively since the expropriation, forcing customers to turn to imports.[35]

A major problem for the government is relations with key oil workers' unions, especially in Zulia, the second-most productive region, and the traditional heart of the industry. On 14 July 2008, Ramón Ramírez, who serves both as CEO of PDVSA and as oil minister, threatened to not to discuss a new collective bargaining contract (the old one expiring at the end of the year) should the government's slate, one of three given a chance to win, not triumph in elections due later in the year. 'Not a single counter-revolutionary can remain within our company, with our industry,' said Ramírez.[36]

On one level, the conflict is about a familiar problem: how to prevent workers from forming a 'labor aristocracy.' However, the conflict is also about the autonomy of unions, which, like many other movements, are wary of capture by the state, especially after the Punto Fijo experience. Given the cooperation of old guard labor leaders with the 2002 industry shutdown and sabotage, Ramírez's point of view cannot dismissed. Oil production and exports are the lifeblood of an economy in which they typically generate half of government revenues, a quarter of the GDP, and 80 percent of total exports. The sector is too strategic for the government to leave to chance.

Can an industry that generates most of its surplus value not from its own labor and capital from international rents far in excess of the normal rate of surplus value be self-managed by workers? Stalin Borges, a national coordinator for the Bolivarian National Union of Workers (UNT), taking aim at a rival faction within the oil workers, seems to answer in the affirmative.

> [W]hat type of company should PDVSA be from now on? Should it simply be a state company in the framework of the capitalism that prevails in our country, with the managerial structure it has today or should its workers control it? This is a great debate today in the revolutionary process ... [T]he other sector [of the UNT] has an economist attitude without discussing the need for the company to be at the same time controlled and managed with direct and democratic participation of workers. That is the only way to put the company at the service of the country and the revolution, if we want a socialist revolution in Venezuela.[37]

Although ordinary Venezuelans may know little about the Marxist theory of rent, they do understand that the industry is vital to the economy and that what is extracted from the subsoil is part of a national patrimony. In a survey I conducted in 2006 in twelve urban barrios known for militancy and strong support of Chávez, only 4

153

percent of the respondents supported worker self-management of the oil industry. Even in the Maracaibo barrios surveyed, only 6 percent supported direct worker control. Support for worker control in other sectors was higher but still a substantial minority even among residents of these strongly *chavista* neighborhoods. Twenty percent supported worker self-management for a paper factory then involved in a well-publicized conflict. In barrios in Bolívar state less than 30 percent combined of those surveyed supported either *co-gestión* or worker self-management for the aluminum industry located in that region.[38] Given that most Venezuelans work in the informal sector or in very small enterprises, these results should not be surprising.

Government leadership, movement resistance on gender issues It is not always the case that the regime lags behind popular sentiment; at times it gets out front. In contrast to revolutionary regimes that have sacrificed the goals of women's organizations on the altar of religious authority or retreated in the face of patriarchic culture, the Chávez government can be credited with moving ahead with programs that directly benefit women – a Women's Bank, nutrition centers in barrios, extension of benefits for work in the home.

Elisabeth Jay Friedman, while pointing out the shortcomings of the government (such as reticence in acting against violence against women) and acknowledging that Bolivarian activists 'have not been successful at getting the majority of women on board with [their feminist] "agenda,"' credits the Chávez government for 'incorporation of feminists from leftwing parties,' which has facilitated some important accomplishments. Among the latter was the founding of a National Women's Institute (INAMUJER, which became a cabinet-level agency in 2009) that 'has attempted to bring together a "Bolivarian Women's Force" made up of members of the 22,000 *Puntos de Encuentro*, or "encounter points."' The 'encounter points' are social spaces where women come into contact with the relevant *misiones* and other government programs. Together with an increase in women's representation in government posts, this constitutes considerable progress beyond what other left governments have achieved, Friedman concludes.[39] The Chávez government has also created space for visible demonstrations by lesbian, gay, bisexual and transgender activists in support of a proposed Organic Law for Gender Equity and Equality that includes equal rights regardless of sexual orientation and identity. However, the provision faces strong opposition in the *chavista*-controlled National Assembly.[40]

The programs of agencies such as INAMUJER, as with almost any large-scale government program, are largely funded by rents that pass through the government budget. Inevitably, then, there is a top-down character, but does this compromise the ability of activists to carry out their mission's organizations without surrendering their autonomy? Sujatha Fernandes, after eight months of field research in three Caracas barrios, concluded that women's activism in community organizations, nutrition centers, and other programs

> has created forms of popular participation that challenge gender roles, collective private tasks, and create alternatives to male-centered politics. Women's experiences of shared struggle from previous decades, along with their use of democratic methods of popular control, such as local assemblies, help to prevent the state's appropriation of women's labor for its own ends. But these spaces of popular participation exist in dynamic tension with more vertical, populist notions of politics that are characteristic of political sectors of *Chavismo*.[41]

This 'dynamic tension' between popular participation and vertical populism captures the essence of the relationship between the state and movements that are aligned with *chavismo* and/or have benefited from the government programs. It goes right to the heart of perhaps the most important *chavista* project for a transition from liberal democracy to participatory democracy, the creation of a network of *consejos comunales* throughout the country.

The movement to form consejos comunales Like so many other movements in the Chávez era, the movement to form *consejos comunales* does not conform easily to a classification of 'top-down' or 'bottom-up.' As already noted, even before the Chávez era there had emerged a movement to form *asociaciones de vecinos* (neighborhood associations), as well as various barrio assembly movements. In the Chávez years, the *Círculos Bolivarinos*, electoral battle units and urban land committees are among the most important precursors. The *consejos* began to form rapidly in response to legislation initiated by the president in 2006, backed by a generous allotment of the budget. To some degree, then, the movement is top-down. However, the idea and model for the *consejos* were taken from the experience of the municipality of Carora, a city of 100,000 in Lara state, not far from Barquisimeto.

In 2004, Julio Chávez (no relation to Hugo), then a member of the Patria por Todos party, and now a member of PSUV, won the election for mayor of Carora as the candidate of a left coalition. Chávez decided

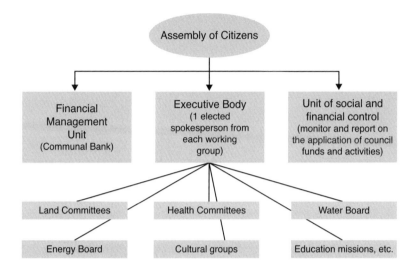

6.2 Structure of the *consejos comunales* (*source*: L. Vidal-Folch, 'Do initiatives such as the "consejos comunales" in Venezuela create a culture of true participatory democracy in the decision making process of the "Bolivarian revolution"?', Undergraduate thesis, Warwick University, 2007, www2.warwick.ac.uk/fac/soc/sociology/rsw/undergrad/cetl/fundingopps/reports/lorenzo_vidal-folch_report.pdf

he would implement provisions in the Constitution of 1999 mandating establishment of participatory institutions. The National Assembly had already in 2004 passed a planning law envisioning cooperation between mayors and governors, on the one hand, and local planning committees on the other. Chávez attempted to implement the law but met resistance from traditionally elected officials – *chavistas* as well as opposition figures. Much as his namesake overcame entrenched resistance on the national level in 1999, Julio did the same by calling a local constituent assembly to write a new municipal constitution. The new municipal constitution not only regularized the process for forming parish councils but established rules of popular participation in carrying out budgeted projects, as well as a system for popular auditing. Chávez then allocated all discretionary spending (about half the municipal budget) to local citizens organized into *consejos comunales* – originally called Local Public Planning Councils.

President Hugo Chávez took note of the mayor's success and included him on advisory commissions charged with designing the legal framework for a national movement to form councils, which was promulgated in April 2006. Significant funding from the government and from the state oil company (PDVSA) created a strong incentive to form councils. For 2007, approximately $7 billion was provided from these two sources. Some of this financing is ad hoc – for example, $140 million allocated to communal banks for micro-financing. By March 2008, 26,143 *consejos* had been registered, and another 10,669 were pending.

Figure 6.2 shows the basic structure of the *consejos*. Each consists of a finance unit charged with managing funds deposited in a communal bank; a unit of 'social and financial control,' which is to audit program expenditures; and a board of *voceros* drawn from different *misiones* and movements working in the area, selected by the assembly of citizens. The latter is also charged with making basic decisions to prioritize applications for funds and to be involved in carrying out projects.

The term *vocero*, 'spokesperson,' is deliberately chosen instead of 'representative' as a signification of the participatory nature of the councils. In 2008 and 2009, the Chávez government began to encourage the formation of area and district communes, a task charged in 2009 to a new Ministry of Communes. This represents a further step toward bypassing the elected officials, particularly mayors and governors, part of an overall design to change the 'geography of the state,' and raises the possibility that Chávez may ultimately seek to replace the latter.

The *consejos comunales*, then, represent more than a mechanism for distributing more of the oil rent to the poor; they are part of an experiment, formed in reaction to the abuses and shortcomings of *puntofijismo*, to create participatory democracy incorporating movements into the authoritative process of allocating rents. There is little consensus about the ultimate outcome of this project. The opposition contends that the goal of Chávez is to push aside elected officials and impose a Cuban-type regime. The government contends that its goal is to decentralize control over fiscal resources.

Consejos have acted synergistically with movements and existing neighborhood organizations in many areas, but the material incentives provided by the central government have a mixed effect. Only by allocating funds can they achieve the goal of democratizing distribution of rents, but the dependence on financing directly from the central government (often from the office of the president or PDVSA, bypassing ministries as well as state and local officials) creates ample opportunity for formation of new networks of clientelism. David Smilde is typical of those sympathetic to the government's goal but wary. He warns, '[T]he Chávez government appears in a strong position to build a hegemonic regime that mobilizes citizen participation but progressively neutralizes its independence and autonomy.'[42]

This concern is magnified by the lack of effective oversight due to lack of experience and training (despite educational missions, such as the new Bolivarian University) at the local level, administrative inefficiency and corruption at governmental levels. 'A large number of Venezuelans do not understand the community councils as transformative, seeing them simply as a means of accessing finance with which to improve their communities,' says George Gabriel, a researcher who participated in organizing a *consejo*.

[W]here money is handed to communities in an *ad hoc* relationship, the situation can rapidly turn clientelistic. The run up to the recent [2008] regional elections seems to provide evidence of such a relation as on the 10th of November, thirteen days before the elections, President Chávez handed over 140 million dollars worth of credit to just over 1,000 communal banks via a fund for micro finance. Though the label 'vote buying' is too crude for this relationship, this is a rapid impact mode of governance, which is therefore easily used for electoral purposes. This further undermines the Bolivarian project by politicizing participation.[43]

A more optimistic assessment of the experiment comes from an unexpected quarter – Centro Gumilla, a Jesuit institution for research and popular education that has often been harshly critical of the Chávez government. The Centro carried out interviews with one *vocero* from each of nearly 1,200 community councils randomly sampled throughout the country. The study attributes modest success to the *consejo* movement because it 'permits resolution of issues that directly affect every resident in those social spaces occupied by popular communities' and because 'communities not only are demanding solutions for service and satisfaction of needs but are proposing and carrying out solutions to the same. These same popular communities are responding to historical needs. From a human rights perspective, people are making real the fulfillment of social rights' (my translation).[44]

Jesús Machado, head of the investigation, comments, 'According to the data obtained, we cannot affirm that the type of participation in the communal councils reinforces patterns of political conduct such as *asistencialismo* [passive presence] or paternalism; on the contrary, the data indicate that there is a progressive process of protagonism and popular responsibility in the construction of collective responses in the search for a better life.'[45] Machado sees the *consejos* as the realization of '*Poder Popular*' insofar as they bring together 'different fragments of oppressed subjectivity' that cannot be easily institutionalized. *Poder Popular* is a 'constituent power,' transformative and changeable according to circumstances. Machado warns, however, of 'dangers that confront these innovative, formative experiences with counter-hegmonic power. In part this has to do with the very origin of popular forms of social and economic associations, born by the initiative of the central power of the state.' He goes on, 'The autonomy of these forms of popular organized systems that constitute the popular movement ought to be encouraged to avoid actual dependency on the actions of a progressive, caesarist leadership, be this derived from collective delegation to, or personal action by, the present leader.'[46]

Party state and popular power

After his sweeping reelection in 2006, and dissatisfied with the performance of the MVR, Chávez called for the formation of PSUV. PSUV is expected, like the MVR, to harvest votes, but it is also supposed to lead to revolutionary transformation of social and political life and avoid becoming the type of party that has generated mistrust among virtually all classes of Venezuelans. Leaders of PSUV announced in June 2009 that it had added one million new members to its ranks, bring the total membership to 6.7 million.

This figure itself raises questions about the character of PSUV. On the one hand, it amounts to approximately a quarter of the entire population. It suggests that the PSUV is indeed a broad movement party supportive of Chávez and his project. However, one must question the motives and commitment of those registered as PSUV members, given that the highest vote total ever achieved by the Bolivarian movement was the 7.3 million votes cast for the reelection of Chávez in 2006. Registrations exceed by 400,000 the total number of '*Sí*' votes cast in support of permitting presidential reelection (and hence the ability of Chávez to stand for reelection in 2012) only three months earlier. Polls have repeatedly shown that Venezuelans who identify themselves as *chavista* constitute approximately 30 to 35 percent of the population; approximately 20 to 25 percent identify with the opposition; and 40 to 50 percent see themselves as '*ni-ni*' (neither-nor). While PSUV organizers boasted 5 million members, the real size of the party is better indicated by the 2.5 million people who turned out in primaries to choose candidates for the National Assembly in April 2010.

Given its size, PSUV would not seem to qualify as a 'vanguard' type of party. Yet it has party organs, including a disciplinary committee, that exercise similar powers to those used by AD and COPEI in the Punto Fijo era. In its first electoral test, in early 2009, PSUV performed well overall in regional elections, accumulating an estimated 60 percent of the vote nationally. However, its candidates in some strategic states and municipalities (Zulia, Maracaibo, metropolitan Caracas, including several popular barrios, and other locations) lost.

Hence, the PSUV would appear to be a highly 'porous' party. This bodes well for a party that seeks to serve as a vehicle for popular movements and to break from the models inherited from the past. PSUV members are drawn from the popular movement in the barrios and show resistance to slavish adherence to the *oficialista* line. However, the PSUV has yet to show a willingness or ability to say 'no' to its charismatic leader – although many of its members must have voted against Chávez in his failed attempt to amend the Constitution via referendum in 2007. AD at one time similarly sought to serve as the vehicle of popular movements.

For Vladimir Acosta, socialism of the twenty-first century requires a more disciplined vanguard, either in the form of a party or movements sufficiently prepared to lead a process of transformation.

Then there is another problem – which I'm simply going to mention – and that is the lack of popular revolutionary organizations. A revolution like this is constantly under threat from the enemy, and here what has been built, which are extremely valuable, are the communal councils, but these are not exactly revolutionary organizations, they are institutional organizations ... What we have to have, as well as these [communal councils], are popular organizations in all parts, at the level of the *barrios*, at the level of whatever space that revolutionary organizations can exist. We had them and we lost them, because the Bolivarian Circles were exactly a practice run of this, and disgracefully they were left behind along the way.[47]

Opposition movements and the state

The opposition, despite its association with *puntofijismo*, is often capable of bringing hundreds of thousands of people into the streets for demonstrations. Hence, in thinking about the evolution of state and civil society in Venezuela, we cannot limit ourselves to a consideration of *chavismo*. In fact, given the inability of the opposition to coalesce into a party comparable to the PSUV, in many ways the opposition remains a movement.

The ability of the opposition in some circumstances to mobilize huge demonstrations poses some difficult dilemmas for the government. The confrontational and often extralegal nature of the opposition places the regime in an awkward situation with regard to law enforcement. Insofar as the opposition can win control of mayoralties and governorships, it heightens the tensions between the traditional apparatus of government and the new networks of *consejos*, which get their resources directly from the central government and PDVSA. Repression, even if justified by violent or illegal tactics by the opposition, has costs that international enemies of the regime are well aware of. Both domestically and internationally, the regime seeks to maintain its legitimacy and commitments to international treaty obligations regarding human rights, rule of law, and representative democracy. Successful provocations eliciting violent repression or jailing of opponents contradict, at least on the surface, one of the most important promises that Chávez made upon assuming office: never to use the security forces against the civilian population, as President Pérez did during the Caracazo. Provoking, if not staging, violent repression of the opposition march of 10 April 2002 was part of the conspiracy by the opposition to win both civilian and military support for the short-lived coup that followed.

The 2007 decision by the government not to renew the broadcast license of RCTV brought about for the first time a significant movement not aligned with either the government or the opposition. RCTV had been deeply involved in promoting the 2002 coup, and the government had a good legal basis for its denial. Still, the action had the effect of mobilizing Venezuelans. Some of them were angered by the loss of popular television shows, but many others saw the move as an attack upon press freedoms. The leadership emerged not from the opposition but from students from the established universities (the Central University, University Andrés Bello, and others).

Quickly, however, the student movement became caught up in the political polarization. The government depicted the students as privileged and out of touch with the popular sectors, labeling them as '*escualidos*,' a term used to discredit the opposition identified with *puntofijismo*. While many of the protesters were from private universities where students were more likely to be the offspring of middle- and upper-class families, many were drawn from the Central University, which has a large population drawn from poorer sectors. On the other hand, the opposition aided the government's cause by attempting, successfully in some cases, to co-opt student leaders. As García-Guadilla documents, the actions by both government and the opposition quickly terminated possibilities for dialogue between students for and against the government's actions.[48] *Chavista* students seized on opposition support as evidence of the students' complicity with a discredited movement of *golpistas* (coup instigators); student leaders protesting the RCTV denial regarded any student who was participating in the *misiones*, particularly if they were accepting a stipend of any sought, as merely *testaferros* (figureheads) for *oficialismo*.

Autonomy – a false ideal?

The social movements that emerged in Venezuela during the declining years of Punto Fijo (1983–98) formed in resistance to neoliberal adjustments and had high on their agenda political reforms to enhance representation and their autonomy. Chávez capitalized upon discontent and followed through by calling a Constituent Assembly to attempt to break with the past – a model adopted recently in some other Latin American countries. In the period from November 2001 to the recall election of August 2004, a period that includes the short-lived coup of April 2002 and the *paro* of 2002/03, popular mobilization had a largely autonomous, if not spontaneous, character, far exceeding whatever support the regime could expect to marshal through patronage.

The period since 2004 is more complex and ambiguous. The massive shift in social expenditures toward the poor, facilitated by both rising oil prices and fiscal policies increasing the state's share of profits from oil exports, took the form of a reward for – or, better said, a 'recognition' of – the popular movement's role in defending the new Bolivarian regime. As the programs were deployed, almost inevitably a degree of clientelism began to emerge. To some extent, this can be attributed to the persistence of practices that have been deeply ingrained since the *trienio* and to the adroitness by which some professional politicians and bureaucrats shed their ties to the old parties and joined the new regime.

Although many government programs reach beyond *chavista* strongholds, even into opposition areas, there is evidence of a correlation between support for the government in elections and expenditures in social programs, one that persists even when we take social class into account.[49] In periods leading up to elections, which are a frequent phenomenon in Bolivarian Venezuela, leaders of social movements tend to put aside temporarily concerns about autonomy to work on behalf of the government.

This volume asks: Do leftist governments view social movements as partners primarily to be co-opted in support of policies, or do they hold them at arm's length as continuing opponents? It also asks whether the government in power reaches out to the social movements and seeks to bring key leaders into posts in the new governments. In the early years of his administration Chávez relied heavily on two sources for filling posts – military allies who were part of the MBR in the armed forces before 1998, and leftist politicians. The latter were especially prominent in the National Assembly, where they were disciplined into a cohesive voting block with a narrow majority by the veteran leftist politico Luis Miquilena. Even since Miquilena's departure in early 2002, grassroots *chavista* leaders often complain that Chávez relies too much on a professional class of politicians whose practices were all too reminiscent of *puntofijismo*. The president seemed to make a similar diagnosis in announcing the disbanding of the MVR and his intention to found the PSUV.

Another question addressed by this volume is: How do leftist governments respond to challenges to their policies? Are the police and military used in the same manner as a rightist government would likely have used them? Despite high levels of political polarization, occurrence of repression has actually been lower in the Chávez years than during the period following the Caracazo and the remaining years of the Carlos Andrés Pérez administration. Far from suspending street protests, Venezuelans continued the high level of activity characteristic of the post-Caracazo period, much of it attempting to call attention to long-standing grievances, to influence the drawing up of a new constitution, or to show support for the new regime.

Despite the appearance of unchecked personal power, Chávez has not had sufficient control over law enforcement and even military units to prevent repression of movements pressing for more radical change. A problem of a different nature is how to deal with the surge in opposition demonstrations that occurred after November 2001, when the government demonstrated its intention to radicalize economic and social policy and assert control over PDVSA. Autonomous popular mobilization in the barrios in defense of the Chávez regime between the short-lived coup of April 2002 and the recall election of August 2004 was met by a campaign of illegal and sometimes violent demonstrations that tested the government's resolve to show restraint in dealing with protests.

To some extent, street mobilizations organized by a disloyal opposition caused little erosion of support for Chávez. However, the protests against the denial of RCTV's license renewal for the first time generated mass opposition that split the *chavista* social base. The year 2009 saw significant protests not only against government programs (e.g. a new Bolivarian curriculum for the schools) but in defense of the 'right to dissent.' The resulting conflict has generated some violence – though arguably less than directed at leaders of land occupations and radical labor movements. Several prominent opposition leaders were jailed or denied the right to run for office pending charges of corruption. The government may have a case, but the prosecutions seem highly selective.

Do the social movements act as independent actors of the government or do they become merely cheerleaders for the implantation of government policies? During national election campaigns, which averaged more than one per year between 1998 and 2008, social movement leaders usually place priority on defense of the regime. In moments of high political polarization, one finds relatively little expressed criticism of Chávez or government programs. However, if one attends community meetings, large- and small-scale, listens to community radio stations, or reads postings on Aporrea.org, a website dedicated to news and political discussion among *chavistas*, one finds no shortage of complaints about political practices reminiscent of *puntofijismo*. Dissatisfaction with government performance has sometimes cost the government, as in the constitutional amendment referendum of December 2007, leading to the loss of some important state and municipal elections in 2009.

Conclusion

The Venezuelan experience of relations between social movements and the state challenges many preconceptions about the need for strict borders between the state and civil society. Autonomy and independence cannot be equated with total separation of roles between social activists and government. An adequate framework for understanding the relationship of social movements to *chavismo* must, then, take into account the paradox that Venezuelans are well aware of the power of their petrostate to co-opt movements and their leaders. It is deeply inscribed in their post-1935 history. Venezuelans are deeply suspicious of party hegemony of any sort. They hope that the PSUV will somehow break the patterns of clientelism and corruption inherited from *puntofijismo*. In the end, achieving that goal will mean democratizing the distribution of rents and 'sowing the oil' in a sustainable project of endogenous development.

Unlike social movements committed, as John Holloway advocates, to 'making revolution without taking power,' most Venezuelan movements over the past twenty years have had to focus their energies on the state.[50] The Venezuelan petrostate is at the center of capital accumulation not because of the productive capacity of its principal industry, but because of the crucial role of the state in mediating the relationship between capital and nature. The state's fiscal resources are not extracted from the domestic economy; it enjoys unusual capacity to conjure up projects of modernization, giving it the appearance, Fernando Coronil observed, of a 'magical state.'[51] The magicians lost their power of illusion when oil prices collapsed. It remains to be seen whether their successors are illusionists or not.

Notes

1 See Bernard Mommer, *Global Oil and the Nation State* (Oxford: Oxford University Press, 2002). The importance of this book is magnified by the fact that its author's neo-Marxist analysis of international oil rents became the foundation for Venezuela's 2001 oil reform, and he later became vice-minister with responsibility for renegotiating major contracts concluded during the neoliberal 'oil opening' of the 1990s.

2 See Steve Ellner, *Los partidos políticos y su disputa por el control del movimiento síndical en Venezuela, 1936–1948* (Caracas: Universidad Andrés Bello, 1980).

3 Women remained an important enough segment of the movement for democracy which remained vibrant after the strike, but as Elizabeth Jay Friedman has shown, the transition to electoral democracy was generally accompanied by an exodus of women from political leadership. See Friedman, *Unfinished Transitions: Women and the Gendered Development of Democracy in Venezuela: 1936–1996* (University Park: Penn State University Press, 2006).

4 See Ocar Battaglini, *Legitimación de Poder y Lucha Política en Venezuela: 1936–1941* (Caracas: FACES, Universidad Central de Venezuela). Also, Daniel Hellinger, 'Venezuela en el siglo XX: la formación de la sociedad civil,' in in Eduardo Cavieres (ed.), *Los projectos y las realidades: América Latina en el siglo XX* (Ediciones Universitarias de Valparaíso, 2005), pp. 159–82; Arturo Sosa A., *El programa nacionalista: Izquierda y modernización (1937–1939)* (Caracas: Editorial Fundación Rómulo Betancourt, 1994), esp. pp. 72–7.

5 Juan Carlos Rey, 'La democracia venezolana y la crisis del sistema del reconciliación populista,' *Revista de Estudios Políticos* (Nueva Época), 74, October–December 1991.

6 Steve Ellner, 'Obstacles to the consolidation of the Venezuelan neighborhood movement: national and local cleavages,' *Journal of Latin American Studies*, 31(1), February 1999, pp. 75–98.

7 See Alejandro Velasco, 'A weapon as powerful as the vote,' Paper delivered at the Congress of the Latin American Studies Association, Rio de Janeiro, 11–14 June 2009.

8 See Daniel Hellinger, 'The Causa R and the *Nuevo Sindicalismo* in Venezuela,' *Latin American Perspectives*, 90(23): 3, 1996, pp. 110–31.

9 Margarita López Maya, *Del*

viernes negro al referendo revocatorio
(Caracas: Alfadil, 2005), pp. 61–84.

10 Daniel Hellinger, 'Political
overview: the breakdown of *Puntofijismo* and the rise of *Chavismo*,' in
Steve Ellner and Daniel Hellinger
(eds), *Venezuelan Politics in the Chávez
Era: Class, Polarization and Conflict*
(Boulder, CO: Lynne Rienner, 2003),
pp. 7–26.

11 Arturo Sosa A., *Del garibaldismo
estudiantil a la izquierda criolla: los
orígenes Marxistas del proyecto de
A.D. (1928–1935)* (Caracas: Ediciones
Centauro), p. 81.

12 Hellinger, 'Political overview.'

13 Data from the Instituto de
Educación Superior, cited by López
Maya, *Del viernes negro*, p. 36.

14 Ibid., pp. 85–106.

15 See Bernard Mommer, 'Subver-
sive oil,' in Ellner and Hellinger, *Venezuelan Politics in the Chávez Era*, p. 131.

16 A good example of this
perspective is Luis J. Oropeza,
*Tutelary Pluralism: A Critical Approach
to Venezuelan Democracy* (Cambridge,
MA: Harvard University Press, 1983).

17 López Maya, *Del viernes negro*;
PROVEA reports are available at www.
derechos.org.ve.

18 Medófilo Medina and Margarita
López Maya, *Venezuela: confrontación
social y polarización política* (Caracas:
Ediciones Aurora, 2003), p. 79.

19 See Maria Pilar García Guadilla
and Ana Mallen, '¿Nuevas caras, nuevas praxis? polarización y politización
del movimiento estudiantil en la
Venezuela Bolivariana,' Paper delivered at the 2009 Congress of the Latin
American Studies Association, Rio de
Janeiro, 11–14 June.

20 By 2006, on a visit to a neighborhood barrio of Catia (a *chavista*
stronghold and, like 23 de enero, a
community with a long history of
organization and resistance), I found
out just how mercurial the poor
people's movements in Venezuela
could be when I naively asked where
the Bolivarian Circle was headquar-
tered, and whether I might meet with
some of its leaders. I was informed
that Catia no longer had such a circle
and that only a few really remained
active.

21 See Margarita López Maya and
Luis Lander, 'El gobierno de Chávez:
democracia participativa y políticas
sociales,' in David Smilde and Daniel
Hellinger, *Participation, Politics and
Culture: Emerging Fragments in
Venezuela's Bolivarian Democracy*
(Durham, NC: Duke University Press,
2010).

22 Maria Pilar García Guadilla,
'Nuevas organizaciones sociales Boli-
varianas y Comités de Tierra Urbana:
¿cooptación o autonomía?', in Smilde
and Hellinger, *Participation, Politics
and Culture*.

23 Leslie Gates, 'The politics
of corruption,' Paper presented
at meeting of the Latin American
Studies Association, Rio de Janeiro,
June 2009.

24 Ian Roxborough, Phil O'Brien,
and Jackie Roddick, *Chile: The State
and Revolution* (London: Macmillan
Press, 1977); see esp. chs 4 and 7.

25 Zachary Lown, 'The conflict
between state-led revolution and
popular militancy in Venezuela,'
Venezuelanalysis.com, 2 September
2009.

26 James Suggett, 'Will the Bolivarian Revolution end coal mining in
Venezuela?', Venezuelanalysis.com,
29 May 2008; Humberto Márquez,
'Venezuela's mega gas pipeline plans
held up,' Venezuelanalysis.com,
3 August 2007.

27 James Suggett, 'Venezuelan
farmer rights organizations united
to oppose assassinations by landed

elite,' Venezuelanalysis.com, 13 March 2009, and 'Murder of small farmer rights organizer sparks protests in Yaracuy, Venezuela,' Venezuelanalysis. com, 20 February 2009.

28 James Suggett, 'Land reform conflict in Venezuela's strategic water source,' Venezuelanalysis.com, 11 August 2008.

29 James Suggett, 'Venezuelan rural activists and National Land Institute workers arrested for occupying estate,' Venezuelanalysis.com, 21 April 2009.

30 See for example, Kiraz Janicke, 'Venezuelan Trade Union Leaders Shot, Workers Call for Armed Self-Defense,' Venezuelanalysis.com, 29 November 2008.

31 Jorge Martin, 'Venezuelan workers take over Vivex factory and demand nationalization,' republished by Venezuelanalysis.com, 4 December 2008.

32 See, for example, Federico Fuentes, 'Venezuela: class struggle heats up over battle for workers' control,' from Green Left Weekly, reproduced in Venezuelanalysis.com, 26 July 2009.

33 Michael Albert, 'Interview on Venezuelan workplaces with Carlos Lanz,' ZNet, reproduced by Venezuelanalysis.com, 7 October 2008.

34 James Suggett, 'Venezuela nationalizes gas plant and steel companies, pledges worker control,' Venezuelanalysis.com, 22 May 2009.

35 'Venezuela's Inveval workers protest against bureaucratic sabotage,' El Militante, reproduced by Venezuelanalysis.com, 9 December 2008.

36 Kiraz Janicke, 'Venezuela: oil minister fuels controversy in union elections,' Venezuelanalysis.com, 19 July 2009.

37 Interview with Stalin Borges

in Marea Socialista, 'Venezuela: after the oil union elections the real battle is for workers' control,' reproduced by Venezuelanalysis.com, 14 October 2009.

38 Daniel Hellinger, 'Defying the Iron Law I: how does el pueblo conceive democracy?', in Smilde and Hellinger, Participation, Politics and Culture.

39 Elisabeth Jay Friedman, 'Gender, sexuality and the Latin American left: testing the transformation,' Third World Quarterly, 30(2), 2009, pp. 421, 431.

40 James Suggett, 'Debate intensifies over Venezuela's proposed same sex civil union law,' Venezuelanalysis. com, 15 July 2009.

41 Sujatha Fernandes, 'Barrio women and popular politics in Chávez's Venezuela,' Latin American Politics and Society, 49(3), 2007, p. 97.

42 David Smilde, 'Three stages in the Chávez government's approach to participation,' Woodrow Wilson Center Update on the Americas, 3, April 2009, p. 6.

43 George Gabriel, 'Financing Venezuela's Communal Councils,' Venezuelanalysis.com, 30 December 2008. Steve Ellner, a US historian who has lived for over three decades in Barcelona, Venezuela, draws a similar conclusion in 'A new model with rough edges,' NACLA Report on the Americas, 42(3), 2008.

44 Jesús E. Machado M., Estudio de los consejos comunales en Venezuela (Caracas: Centro Gumilla, 2008), p. 5.

45 Ibid., p. 6.

46 Ibid., pp. 9–10.

47 Vladimir Acosta, 'Venezuela: a critical evaluation of the Bolivarian process,' Venezuelanalysis.com, 22 June 2009.

48 García-Guadilla and Mallen, '¿Nuevas caras, nuevas praxis?'

49 See David R. Hansen, Kirk A. Hawkins, and Jason Seawright, 'Dependent civil society: the Círculos Boivarianos in Venezuela,' Paper presented at the 25th Congress of the Latin American Studies Association, Las Vegas, NV.

50 John Holloway, *Change the World without Taking Power: The Meaning of Revolution Today* (London: Pluto Press, 2005). Greg Wilpert argues that the Venezuelan experience challenges this notion. See *Changing Venezuela by Taking Power* (London: Verso, 2006).

51 Fernando Coronil, *The Magical State: Nature, Money and Modernity in Venezuela* (Chicago, IL: University of Chicago Press, 1997).

Conclusion: future trends in Latin American politics

GARY PREVOST

The future trend in Latin American politics is not clear. The return of widespread military control is unlikely, but the continued election of progressive governments is not guaranteed. As Latin American democratic politics become more entrenched, the phenomenon of alternating power between parties of the center-left and the center-right may become more common, as has been the case in the United States and Europe. The victory of center-right candidate Sebastián Piñera in Chile in 2010 could well be indicative of this trend. The continued electoral success of the left and center-left may well be dependent on delivering better living conditions for the majority poor who placed them in office. So far the record has been mixed. In Brazil eight years of modest progress on social and economic issues left outgoing president Lula with a high approval rating, and he succeeded in passing on the mantle of power to his chief of staff, Dilma Rousseff, who won a landslide victory in October 2010, vowing to continue the progressive agenda of the Workers' Party with greater representation in the Brazilian legislature. In part the Workers' Party has sustained its power through agreements with Brazilian high finance and agribusiness interests at the expense of the interests of the MST, Brazil's aforementioned landless movement. The Uruguayan socialists also succeeded in gaining an important second term by engaging in programs of limited social reform that do not fundamentally threaten the oligarchic interests that have long dominated the country. The challenge facing the Peronists in Argentina is also significant. Cristina Fernández's term as president, following her popular husband, Nestor, has not gone smoothly, with many confrontations with various elements in society and the loss of the midterm legislative elections. The Peronist strategy was based on the return of Nestor to the presidency in 2011, but his sudden death in October 2010 ended that plan. The less popular Cristina may well triumph because it is not clear that the divided opposition can mount a truly strong and united candidacy. Given the inconsistent history of the Peronist Party in delivering progressive public policies, it is not always clear what a Peronist victory actually means.

The prospects for the progressive forces in Central America are uncertain. The victory in El Salvador of Mauricio Funes of the FMLN, the former rebels, in March 2009 was historic given the long oligarchic rule of the country and its recent domination by the ultra-right National Republican Alliance (ARENA). However, with only a plurality in the legislature Funes has been constrained significantly in terms of enacting significant reforms. Guatemalan president Álvaro Colom has faced even more notable challenges from traditional right-wing forces in enacting significant changes. Without a legislative majority he has not succeeded in enacting significant programs for the country's majority poor. Honduran president Manuel Zelaya, a traditional center-right Liberal Party politician, began moving his country in a progressive direction once in power, but his removal from office by a military coup in June 2009 was a devastating blow to progressive forces in the country. Joint maneuvers by the US government and the Honduran elites prevented Zelaya from returning to power and paved the way for victory by Pepe Lobo, the candidate of the Honduran elites in the November 2009 election. Daniel Ortega's return to the presidency of Nicaragua in 2007 for a five-year term has led to modest social gains for the country's majority poor, helped in part by Venezuelan support in the framework of ALBA. Ortega faces reelection in November 2011, and with the continued hostility of the anti-Sandinista right and their allies in the United States his ability to retain power for the FSLN is uncertain. The prospects for continued control by the left in Venezuela, Ecuador, and Bolivia are not certain, but continuation is definitely possible. Continued electoral success by all three would clearly give a strong anchor to progressive forces in the continent and enhance the prospects for success of their common project, ALBA. Venezuela, because of its size and resources, is the key country. Hugo Chávez has been a clearly dominant and charismatic personality in the progress of the Bolivarian revolution, but his long-term impact on Latin American and Venezuelan history will be based on the success of efforts to create a long-term movement. The current vehicle for this, after earlier false starts, is the United Socialist Party of Venezuela (PSUV). Launched four years ago, the party carried the banner of the Bolivarian revolution in the important 2010 legislative elections and it won a limited victory by retaining majority control but losing to the conservative opposition in some municipal areas that had previously voted for President Chávez. The results have emboldened the opposition, with significant US support, to make a serious run to win the 2012 elections. A PSUV defeat in the 2012 elections would be a major defeat for the Latin

American left and likely a death sentence for ALBA. On the other hand a PSUV victory would represent a significant consolidation of the Chávez project of twenty-first-century socialism. Beyond the success of PSUV organizing the results could well turn on the stability of the value of Venezuela's oil resources, the key lever for the government's ability to maneuver.

The Bolivian progressives are at this point in a reasonably strong position, not facing reelection until the end of 2013 and having carried out important constitutional changes that strengthen their control over the country's resources. However, the lowland-based oligarchy remains committed to gaining back control of the country. Their ability to do that by extralegal means is probably limited, but confrontations with Morales in 2008 did result in a two-term limit in the new Bolivian Constitution that will force the Movement toward Socialism (MAS) and its allies to unite behind a credible successor to Evo in the 2013 elections. Such actions are far from impossible given time to act. A key strength of the Bolivian forces seems to be a strong linkage between the popular organizations and the programs of the government, thereby limiting the maneuvering room of the conservative opposition.

The situation in Ecuador is more complex because the organic connection between the social movements and Correa is weaker. Correa never fully embraced the indigenous movement agenda in the way that Morales did in Bolivia. The indigenous constitute a smaller percentage of Ecuadorean society, just over one third compared to a solid majority in Bolivia. As a result, Correa chose to frame his program of social reform in national terms, seeking to bond with all progressive forces in the country. On one level that has been successful in his two personal victories and the overwhelming vote for the new Constitution. However, it has left him at odds with the indigenous movements while also facing the permanent opposition of the old order with links to the police and military. This potential weakness was demonstrated in September 2010 when elements of the police and a limited number of members of the armed forces created the conditions for a possible coup against the government. Correa survived with significant support from urban backers, but the indigenous leaders did not respond with actions in support of the president.

As the second decade of the twenty-first century begins, the Latin American left embodied in its social movements and progressive governments faces both key opportunities and key challenges. The progressive governments, having chosen the road of reform through the democratic process, must produce tangible results through their government programs in health, education, food security, and jobs. The Brazilian and Venezuelan cases have shown that at least modest progress in creating a form of Latin American social democracy is possible, but their ability to progress farther still primarily turns on volatile, commodity-based economies controlled by the traditional oligarchs, a prospect that by no means guarantees an unbroken pattern of left victories even in the countries where the progressive forces have the upper hand at the moment.

About the contributors

Marc Becker teaches Latin American history at Truman State University. His research focuses on constructions of race, class, and gender within popular movements in the South American Andes. He is the co-editor (with Kim Clark) of *Highland Indians and the State in Modern Ecuador*, and author of *Indians and Leftists in the Making of Ecuador's Modern Indigenous Movements* and *Pachakutik: Indigenous Movements and Electoral Politics in Ecuador*.

Edward Greaves teaches political science at the St Cloud State University, Minnesota. His research focuses on Chilean social movements and their relationships with government authority.

Daniel Hellinger is professor of political science at Webster University, Missouri, where he is academic director of the Masters in International Relations program. He is co-editor of and contributor to *Venezuelan Politics in the Chávez Era* and has published numerous scholarly articles on Latin American politics. He is author of *Venezuela: Tarnished Democracy*, will soon publish a textbook on Latin American politics, *Democracy at Last?*, and is co-editing the forthcoming book *Participation and the Public Sphere in Venezuela*. He was a Fulbright scholar at the Universidad Católica in Valparaíso, Chile. He is past president of the Venezuela Studies Section of the Latin American Studies Association and the Midwest Latin American Studies Association. He serves as president of the advisory board for the Center for Democracy in the Americas, a Washington-based NGO that promotes better understanding between the United States and Latin America.

Waltraud Q. Morales is professor of political science at the University of Central Florida. She received her MA and PhD from the Josef Korbel School of International Studies of the University of Denver, and her BA from the Catholic University of America in Washington, DC. Dr Morales is a generalist in international affairs and comparative politics and a specialist in Latin America (with an emphasis on the Andean region), Third World development, and comparative revolutionary change. She has published articles on Bolivian domestic and foreign policies, women and gender in Latin America and the Third World, the Andean drug war, indigenous peoples in the Andes, sustainable development and human security, Mexican and Haitian political development, Nicaraguan foreign relations, and television coverage of Latin America. She is the author of *A Brief History of Bolivia*, *Bolivia: Land of Struggle*, and *Social Revolution: Theory and Historical Application*; and she has co-authored *Human Rights: A User's Guide* and *Violence and Repression in Latin America*. She has been the recipient of grants from the National Endowment for the Humanities, a Fulbright teaching and research grant to Bolivia in 1990, and a Fulbright Group Study and Travel Grant to Bolivia in 2004.

Index

General Confederation of Labor
(CGT), 31
globalization, 5, 34, 39–40, 49, 53,
55–7
Globo network, 41
Gramsci, Antonio, 107
Greenpeace, 149
Guaraní farmers, 64
Gutiérrez, Lúcio, 9, 13, 17, 117, 119–23,
127

Hydrocarbon Law, 59–60
hydrocarbon nationalization, 58, 60

IFIs, see international financial
institutions
IMF, see International Monetary
Fund
INAMUJER, see National Women's
Institute
Independent Democratic Union
(UDI), 95
Indian land rights, 64
indigenous coca growers, 71
indigenous rights, 52, 70, 95
Institute for Mobilization of
Cooperative Funds (IMFC), 29
Institutional Revolutionary Party
(PRI), 2, 140
Inter-American Development Bank
(IDB), 34
international financial institutions
(IFIs), 3, 27
International Monetary Fund (IMF),
3, 27–8, 34, 142
INTI, see National Institute of Lands
Isiboro Sécure National Park, 71

Jungle Police, 150

Katari, Tupac, 59
Keynesianism, 151
Kirchner, Cristina Fernández de, 9,
12, 16, 27, 29, 31
Kirchner, Néstor, 9, 13, 16, 22, 26–31

La Victoria, 109
labor aristocracy, 153

Lagos, Ricardo, 88, 99, 110, 114
Landless Workers' Movement in
Brazil (Movimiento Sin Tierra,
MST), 1, 7, 13, 18, 31, 24, 36–47,
63–4, 169
Latin American Secretariat of
Popular Housing (SELVIP), 93, 113
Law 1008, 71, 73, 75
Law of Administrative
Decentralization, 1995, 53
Law of Civic Associations and
Indigenous Peoples, 2004, 53–4
Law of National Dialogue, 2001, 53
Law of Popular Participation, 1994,
53
Liberation Theology, 5, 19, 37, 129,
152
Lobo, Pepe, 170
Local Public Planning Councils, 156
lost decade, 4
Lowlander social movements, 62
Lugo, Fernando, 9, 129
Lula (President), see da Silva, Luiz
Inácio, 8–9, 12, 14, 18, 28, 38, 40–6,
129, 133, 169

Mahaud, Jamil, 13
Malvinas, 23
Mar del Plata, 6, 28
martial law, 56, 67
Martín, Jorge, 151, 167
Marxism/Marxist approach/Marxist
theory, 2, 19, 82, 151–3
MAS, see Movement toward
Socialism
MBR, see Movimiento Bolivariano
Revolucionario
Medellín, 5
Menchú, Rigoberta, 5
Menem, Carlos, 9, 12–13, 15–16, 22
MERCOSUR, 29, 41–2
Mesa, Carlos, 13, 58, 71
mestizo, 59, 66, 76
Misión Mercal, 147
Moore, Michael, 56
Morales Ayma, Juan Evo (Evo
Morales), 7, 9, 12–15, 34, 49–52, 55,
57–84, 119, 129, 133–4, 171

Organizations (Organizaciones Territoriales de Base)

About Zed Books

Zed Books is a critical and dynamic publisher, committed to increasing awareness of important international issues and to promoting diversity, alternative voices and progressive social change. We publish on politics, development, gender, the environment and economics for a global audience of students, academics, activists and general readers. Run as a co-operative, Zed Books aims to operate in an ethical and environmentally sustainable way.

Find out more at:

www.zedbooks.co.uk

For up-to-date news, articles, reviews and events information visit:

http://zed-books.blogspot.com

To subscribe to the monthly Zed Books e-newsletter, send an email headed 'subscribe' to:

marketing@zedbooks.net

We can also be found on **Facebook**, **ZNet**, **Twitter** and **Library Thing**.